C000176438

Relationships

On The Hudson
Jung
BOOK SERIES

The New York Center for Jungian Studies presents
conferences and seminars in the U.S. and abroad,
including its Jung On The Hudson seminars held
each summer in the historic Hudson Valley. The
N.Y. Center seminars, book series and continuing
education programs are designed for individuals
from all fields as well as mental health professionals
who are interested in exploring the relevance of
Jung's ideas to their personal lives and/or professional
activities. The Center offers individual, couple and
group counseling, and provides consulting services
and mediation for family businesses and corporations.

For more information, please contact:
The New York Center for Jungian Studies
121 Madison Avenue, New York, NY 10016
Telephone: 212-689-8238 or Fax: 212-889-7634

RELATIONSHIPS

Transforming Archetypes

MARINA VALCARENGHI

NICOLAS-HAYS
YORK BEACH, MAINE

First published in 1997 by
NICOLAS-HAYS, INC.
Box 612
York Beach, ME 03910-0612

Distributed to the trade by
SAMUEL WEISER, INC.
Box 612
York Beach, ME 03910-0612

English translation copyright © 1997 Marina Valcarenghi
All rights reserved. No part of this publication may be reproduced or transmitted in any
form or by any means, electronic or mechanical, including photocopying, recording, or by
any information storage and retrieval system, without permission in writing from Nicolas-
Hays, Inc. Reviewers may quote brief passages. Originally published in Italian as *Una passione per due: La natura degli opposti nella personalità e nella relazione*, copyright © 1994
Tranchida Editori, Milan, Italy.

Library of Congress Cataloging-in-Publication Data

Valcarenghi, Marina.
    [Passione per due. English]
    Relationships : transforming archetypes / Marina
Valcarenghi.
        p.   cm.
    Includes bibliographical references (p.   ) and index.
    ISBN 0-89254-034-6 (pbk. : alk. paper)
    1. Animus (Psychoanalysis). 2. Anima (Psychoanalysis).
3. Theseus (Greek mythology) 4. Ariadne (Greek mythology)
5. Hades (Greek mythology) 6. Persephone (Greek deity) I.
Title.
    BF175.5.A53V3513   1997
    155.2--dc21   96-52506
                                                    CIP

BJ

Typeset in 10 Sabon
Cover and text design by Kathryn Sky-Peck
Cover art is "Lovers," 1974, by Mary Frank, Terracotta, 19 x 62 x 33 inches.
Private collection. Courtesy of D.C. Moore Gallery, New York.

Printed in the United States of America

03 02 01 00 99 98 97
10 9 8 7 6 5 4 3 2 1

*The paper used in this publication meets the minimum requirements of the American
National Standard for Permanence of Paper for Printed Library Materials Z39.48-1984.*

Table of Contents

PART 3
HADES AND PERSEPHONE

Introduction

There is something in ancient mythologies that stops them from becoming lost as cultures change and I think this is due to the typical character of the figures and events narrated: Gilgamesh, Osiris, Athena, or incest, or the theft of fire are not simply protagonists or episodes, they are also qualities, attitudes, and psychic movements that—like a gust of wind or a starry sky—don't change over time.

In the stories the myths recount, we can see a systematic coherence between the characters with their own types, with the entirety of their qualities: in fact, they reveal a profound correspondence between their way of being and the different personality inclinations, behaviors, profound motivations, often unconscious, of all people. There are men who tend to be like Hermes, like there are women who are similar to Demeter or Athena, and while myths tell fascinating stories, they also reveal psychic potentials, existential modalities, the light and darkness of a personality, in whom each of us can recognize ourselves from time to time.

Passionate love, for example, perhaps the most explosive energy that can animate a human being, was a cult for the Ancient

Greeks. It was venerated and even became personified in the form of a goddess: Aphrodite was there to seduce and to be seduced, to make people lose their heads and to lose hers as well in abandon and desire which often goes beyond morals, calculations, convenience and sometimes even surpasses the ridiculous. But all myths which regard Aphrodite respect her typological scheme and her archetypical personality, and thus the coherence is really extraordinary if you think of the whole corpus of myths which has formed over the centuries, through different generations and cultures. Aphrodite is also, for example the lover of Ares, the god of war, and in the different episodes where they both appear the point isn't in a rendezvous between two anthropomorphous gods, but in the indissoluble bond between passion and conflict, between the desire for pleasure and the desire to wound, forever unresolved, inside the human soul.

Passionate love either leads to ecstasy or to ruin. The Ancient Greeks, in dedicating temples and offering sacrifices to Aphrodite, were attempting to placate that terrible, mysterious energy, asking the goddess not to cause too much pain and to protect passion. Thus Aphrodite can die as the historical goddess of the Hellenic civilization, but she has been extraordinarily long-lived as the archetypical symbol of desire, and can be found in Botticelli's paintings, as well as in the dreams of our time.

The mythological figures and stories, removed from their religious correspondences or historical evaluations, thus reveal another possibility for interpretation based on the underlying question "what does it mean?" which is very similar to the question we ask ourselves when trying to deal with dreams. But in the end this is not so surprising, if you think of how myths and legends have been formed by sedimentation, in layers, by the collective imagination, allowing the unconscious structures of the psyche to emerge in a completely spontaneous way.

From this point of view, ancient mythologies are a sort of cistern of the unconscious which has been conserved virtually intact throughout time. If a child invents a story, we can see some of his or her unconscious dynamics in it; in the same way, if a people invent a system of stories, which become a sort of system of faith or of truths and which are passed down with no or few changes for centuries or millenniums, we can try to discover their hidden meaning. The collective unconscious in this system of stories weaves and unravels the basic, constant behaviors of humanity which change form over time, but the quality of the experience doesn't change: the desire for adventure, the thirst for power, the fear of death, the anguish of solitude, the spirit of exploration, the passion of love, and so on. In this sense, Thomas Mann, in a 1936 conference of Freud, wrote that "the interest in mythology is as embedded in psychology as the interest in psychology is embedded in poetic creativity."

Thus, for those who work in our field, it is very interesting to discover what the collective unconscious declared about life forms and their relationships in that period, for those people, and with what meaning their experience has come down to us. It is true, and also obvious, that we are not the same as the Dorians or the Sumerians, but it is also true, and also obvious, that we are exactly the same as them, and the value of our research is linked to this double statement. We must consider questions like: what does this story mean? How are fundamental psychic mechanisms the same or different from those of humanity back then? Why do mythological images with constant symbolic values appear in our patients' dreams? Is it possible to spell out general laws based on this clinical and psychomythological data? And how can we use these theoretical principles in interpreting dreams?

Psychomythology thus has nothing to do with the current way of discussing myths: anyone can say anything about myths, or dreams, and they often do. I think it is very important to root psychomythological research in clinical terrain, systematically comparing the figures in myths with the figures in dreams, active imaginations, free associations and to verify the constant data among these different categories.

In the last few years, however, a certain projective attitude has developed which has damaged research regarding archetypes and mythological symbolism. It consists in identifying the contemporary collective unconscious and the myth being studied, resulting in an uncritical and unilateral acceptance, based on emotion, of the mythological nucleus, which is perceived as a cult object, a revelation of unconscious, eternal, and immutable behaviors. In this way the progressive stratification of the experiences of a people, or of all humanity, are lost as well as the complexity and the differences which the collective unconscious had elaborated over time, as if it had remained substantially unaltered.

This way of working deforms psychomythology into a schematic apparatus, only able to offer a rigid system of translation to apply mechanically in interpreting dreams or the unconscious manifestations of a culture or a civilization. In this way, mythology ends up becoming a sort of psychoanalytic tool, a dictionary which translates a symbol into a single meaning, while in reality mythology sinks into unfathomable complexities, and doesn't offer constant meanings and complicates (rather than simplifies) the interpretation of a symbol.

For example, how many different meanings can a serpent have in a dream? It depends on the color, the form, the size, the position, where it is, what its doing, on the story in which it is inserted, on the emotional reaction it evoked in the dreamer, and on other variables; although it is also true that it is always a serpent. But there are many aprioristic and definitive definitions which one runs into, like: "a serpent is a phallus," "a serpent is a transformation," "a serpent is chthonic energy," "a serpent is transgression," and so on. One does not make much progress this way. A serpent is a serpent. And from there, we'll see. And this "we'll see," for the analyst means taking in that particular image of a serpent and that particular oniric emotion, and all the possible variables representative of that dream, and finally, using her knowledge of mythology, to propose a meaning for that image, that time, in that dream. If the analyst hasn't made a mistake, then the archetype of the serpent expresses its energy and perhaps something happens in the dreamer's psyche.

Thus I believe that mythology is useful for psychoanalysis if it becomes part of the culture of a psychoanalyst, if she takes it inside herself, accepting that those images can't be completely penetrated by the soul, but knowing that they penetrate the soul: mythology is a living organism, in continuous evolution, with an innumerable multiplicity of symbolic meanings which depend on the relationship each time between the images and which, each time, have to be investigated. Only in this way can psychomythology become a real treasure and give meaningful results in terms of interpretation.

Jung, himself, who was the founder of the psychology of archetypes, knew that they could change form and value, and he studied their new manifestations, imagining for example what impact UFOs or certain products of technology (missiles, nuclear reactors, the H bomb . . .) would have on the collective unconscious, creating new archetypical figures, or in certain cases substituting preceding ones (like the car, which replaced the horse).

Jung wrote in 1943, "There are present in every individual, besides his personal memories, the great 'primordial' images, as Jacob Burckhardt once aptly called them, the inherited powers of human imagination as it was from time immemorial. The fact of this inheritance explains the truly amazing phenomenon that certain motifs from myths and legends repeat themselves the world over in indentical forms. It also explains why it is that our mental patients can reproduce exactly the same images and associations that are known to us from the old texts." But, he adds, " I do not by any means assert the inheritance of ideas, but only of the possibility of such ideas, which is something very different."[1]

The two myths studied in this book, Hades and Persephone and Theseus and Ariadne, recount the meeting in love between a man and a woman, the emotions, the conflicts, and the results. But man and woman in symbolic language, that of dreams and myths, mean something else, they mean the complex of opposite psychic movements, typical of the masculine and feminine parts of the personality. Thus, in dreams, like in myths, the meeting between a man and a woman is not only a meeting between two characters, but it is also the union of the two complete parts of opposite energies within a single personality. Thus in the same way that a man and a woman can also meet and join in everyday life, a man and a woman meet and join inside each of us, giving life to a union of opposites. Like in the every day existence between a man and a woman, inside the internal circuit between *animus* and *anima*, the result of the union depends on a complex of variables which are unique every time.

The myths of Hades and Persephone, and Theseus and Ariadne describe thus two possible itineraries in the meeting of *animus* and

---

1. Jung, *Psychology of the Unconscious*, Vol. 7, ¶ 101.

anima, and both of these itineraries pass through the Underworld. Whether it is Hades or the labyrinth, the experience of a psychic death, the renouncement of a part of oneself, seem necessary in order to give life to new energy contained in the union.

In both cases the voyage to the underworld is undertaken because of passion, because they can't help themselves and in both cases life is born from death: "She asked me one day," wrote Denis de Rougemont, "For what destiny was I born? For what destiny? The old song repeated: to desire and to die."

In order to get to the heart of psychomythological research, it seems necessary to examine, in the first part of this book, the form and the qualities of the two complexes of energy which analytical psychology has defined the masculine principle and the feminine principle, or *animus* and *anima*, since they are understood in a very different way today than in the past.

The expressions *masculine principle* and *feminine principle* mean two different and complementary ways of expressing the activity of instinct, feeling, and thought. In neither case am I referring to psychic functions exclusively regarding one sex or the other. In this text, the terms *masculine* and *feminine* have an archetypal meaning which could also be called *penetrating* and *receptive,* and both apply—granted in different forms—to both men and women. Their sexual connotation is attributed to the greater intensity and consciousness with which, in the majority of cases, the masculine and feminine archetypes manifest themselves in men and women.

In this study the terms *feeling* and *thought* do not have the meanings they usually assume in analytical psychology, where together with *sensation* and *intuition*, they form the four fundamental functions that, intertwined in different combinations, define a psychological typology. With *activity of thought* I mean the complex and heterogeneous whole of the way of thinking, of joining thoughts together and of putting them in contact with experience. *Activity of feeling* means the diverse ways of getting in touch with the world of emotions, and of reflecting them on the behavior plan. Finally, the term *activity of instinct* refers to the complex of the drive sphere and the tension of satisfaction which comes from it.

Thus the terms *thought* and *feeling* refer exclusively to their intrinsic and differentiated possibility for manifestation, both in the conscious and in the unconscious in an individual or in a group, apart from their psychological typology. The aim of the first part of my study is in fact to disassemble these actions, which are instinct, feeling, and thought, in order to acknowledge the ambivalence and thus the simultaneous presence, in their manifestation, of a masculine and a feminine component.

We can take on, as the first point of reference, the bipolar image of Eastern culture: *yin and yang* and thus sky and earth, sun and moon; the sun is light, smooth and luminous, the earth dark, wrinkled, furrowed by the abyss; the light of the sun *strikes* in a cutting and direct way, the moonlight blurs the outlines and *collects* all in a tenuous and diffuse way. These are two complementary ways of making contact with experience and the image which is derived from it, a closed circle around the two symbols and their chromatic contrast, affirms the idea of totality and completeness which the union of opposites generates in human imagery.

There is a similar symmetry between the masculine principle and the feminine principle in a psychological setting, and in the following pages we will see how it is reflected on the activity of feeling, thought, and instinct. It is not a question of a symmetry easily recognizable because a culture many thousands of years old has reduced the strength and the wisdom of the feminine principle to a mixture of good and bad feelings, both in a practical and in a *maternage* sense, of hysterical drives and mental insufficiency.

It is also not an easily recognizable symmetry because analytical psychology, in the prevalent theoretical survey, has simplified the problem, anchoring the feminine archetype to nature—that is, to instinct, and natural feelings—and the masculine archetype to culture—and so to thought and spirituality.

In this theoretical framework the terms in question, rather than becoming more simple, are confused between each other, since the masculine and feminine principles do not regard psychic *contents*, but the *form* of the libido: they offer two different ways of getting in touch with the psychic actions (thought, instinct, and feeling) and they are not reduced to a part of them. In other words: feeling, instinct, and thought manifest within the two archetypes, but with different forms, and perhaps also different directions. In my professional experience, and that of the colleagues I work with, I systematically verify how from the unconscious feminine images appear which also refer to forms of thought; symmetrically the unconscious is peopled by masculine figures referable to the life of senses and emotions.

Consequently, I asked myself why, in almost all the analytical psychological texts the masculine and feminine principles are not only opposite and complementary in form and in the direction of energy, but also *cut in half* and divided *on the competence* of the psychic function. The most likely answer is hidden in the folds of the patriarchal cape: psychoanalytical theory in fact, as all Western culture, is the fruit of masculine thinking, which aprioristically acknowledges itself as the only one possible; a division of the conscious (and consequently unconscious) psychic competencies derives from this initial and unconscious distortion between men and women, and thus the development of a mutilating and reductive theory of personality for both sexes, as we will see, in therapeutic practice.

PART 1

Thought, Instinct, and Feeling—
A Way of Discovering the Self

CHAPTER 1

The Activity of Thought

Masculine thought flows in a linear and cutting way and is used to analyze, distinguish, separate, catalog, and define, directing itself to the development of rational, deductive, logical knowledge: by nature, it tends to recognize and face up to situations, because it chooses, plans, and decides; it is more oriented toward building (or destroying) than conserving. Masculine thought, having delimited its object, turns to penetrating it, thus in the end it *possesses* a piece of knowledge; and in doing so, it proceeds with successive separations, in an analytic and systematic fashion, concentrating on a detail which, once explored and defined, becomes the basis for examining another detail, following the principle of cause and effect. Masculine thought is not cold, since it conforms to the subject's personality and not the energy form, but it is lucid and decisive in pursuing a straight line to arrive at the objective.

Feminine thought, on the other hand, does not start with the examination of a detail, but with the contemplation of the whole, and it is not oriented toward *penetrating*, but toward *absorbing* the object of knowledge: thus it is a process which tends to develop toward the inside, at times seeming covered with sand, not existing, like an underground river, until it springs all of a sudden, with its conclusions, after having followed an invisible course.

Verifying one of the many analogies between *psyche* and *soma*, it is possible to see that feminine thought receives within itself, makes things grow, and transforms in the dark, inside, and then expels them; thus we are dealing with a mental process straining not to isolate the different aspects within a context, but rather to examine them within relation to each other, to express a synthesis rather than an analysis, and to elaborate a knowledge that is symbolic and inductive.

Take an apple, for example. Masculine thought is oriented toward the object, proposing an analytic separation: the apple is divided into skin, pulp, core, and seeds; the skin and the pulp are edible, the core can be used to feed animals, the seeds are used for the reproduction of the species, and so on; thus thought proceeds according to a logical order that illuminates and defines the details one by one.

Feminine thought, instead, allows the apple to enter *within itself* where, through induction and analogy, it is put in relation as a whole, in its *appleness*. The result could be, for example: the apple, like a breast, is round and sensual, and, like a breast, with time it withers; the apple, like certain people, is sour on the outside and sweet inside; the apple is desirable and inviting, like something to reach, like an aim, like the apple of discord and the fruit from the tree of knowledge of good and evil, and so on.

These connections can also intertwine, because in the course of time feminine thought collects and, in some way, records and files information that is saved like one would store information in a computer. So, when a new object presents itself, it is inserted in a system and it finds its analogical placement and its specific synthesis.

Let us suppose, for example, that a person communicates the following information to a friend, with a certain period of time between each piece of information, over a year's time: "I'm reading *War and Peace*, but I can't remember the names and relationships between the various characters; My reading of *War and Peace* is going very slowly; I stopped reading *War and Peace* because it requires a less fragmentary reading than that which I can allow myself at the moment: I'll take it up again when I have a vacation." The interlocutor records these declarations and files them. After a few months, during Christmas time, the would-be reader asks his friend: "Guess what I'm reading?" Masculine thought is impotent when it comes to guessing, but feminine thought does not have to guess because it knows: it in fact absorbs the question, which enters into contact with Christmas vacation and with the preceding information, following an internal, illogical and analogical circuit. For this reason, it has often been taken for an almost divinatory or prophetic capacity, but this is an error, because the data useful for the formation of the knowledge was already noted and recorded.

In the same way, feminine thought is frequently, and without reasonable motive, identified with intuition. But intuition is generated like a sudden and autonomous hypothesis about an object, without there having been underlying visible and conscious information, because it is spontaneously formed, and has its origins in the deep unconscious. Receptive thought, instead, seems to take its form like an awareness that has its origin in a series of pieces of information about which the subject is conscious. In receptive thought what *is not seen* is the transformation of these elements of input, which were gathered over time, into a final form that is the result of their elaboration.

Returning to our example, the subject knows that the reading of *War and Peace* presents certain difficulties for her interlocutor; she knows that the reading has been interrupted until a vacation is scheduled and she knows that the vacation involves Christmas celebrations; consequently to the question, "Guess what I'm reading?" translates into consciousness as: "You are reading *War and Peace*." Naturally—as always happens in a psychic sphere—the definitions rest on precarious terrain and it can happen—and does—that intuition and inductive thought reveal themselves to be contiguous and at times intertwined, but their identification is not provable.

Receptive thought and penetrating thought, in virtue of their complementary qualities, need one another in order to create a complete and harmonious mental function, and I have been able to verify how, systematically, in the course of an analysis, the unconscious tries to put these two forms of energy into contact, leading the submerged form toward consciousness.

But before the expressive ambivalence of human thought, psychoanalysis is faced with, at least in the West, a cultural problem. Illogical, inductive, and analogical thought is not considered a form of thought, but in the majority of cases (and also in our field) as a symptom of mental disorder, or even as an undefinable and insignificant *sixth sense*. Thought, *logos*, starting from Greek culture, is then thought in a masculine form, logical, deductive, and rational, and, as such, it is transmitted from generation to generation.

Because one mental form has allowed excessive power over another, every kind of artificial psychic separation is the result. On the one hand, there is an increased shadow related to feminine thought, and on the other we find the delirium of omnipotence related to the masculine mental process. Abandoned to itself and underestimated, feminine thought has, in fact, assumed, over the course of time, completely irrational, chaotic characteristics—magical-religious, often witch-like, and not rarely destructive. But, left alone to guide itself, masculine thought has occupied a space which should have been divided, deforming itself into a tyrant of the human mind, a tyrant so closed within his delirium that he is able to convince himself that the knowable universe was modeled after his form.

The results of the fracture between these two ways of thinking are reflected in everyday life, both individual and collective: just think of a military parade, for example, or a bureaucratic procedure, and we feel overwhelmed by rigid messages, the obsessive and overbearing characteristics of masculine thought in our social life. This mental form is also dominant in our psychic life, since we are taught that this is the only way to work the mind. This lesion, which the dominant culture imposes on the social fabric and on individual psyches, is gravely mutilating both for men and for women, because it deprives women of the right to express a more conscious mental form, forcing them to measure themselves exclusively on more difficult terrain, and because it exonerates men from venturing into the space of symbolic and inductive thought, for their equally fertile unconscious. In light of these facts, we can affirm that the patriarchal culture has not defended itself well by devouring feminine thought, for certain mouthfuls prove, in the long run, to be indigestible.

An ancient Greek myth has already described this oppressive meal and perhaps it would be interesting to remember it here. Metis was a goddess of creation, born perhaps from the depth of the ocean or from the primitive, cosmic, silver egg.

Metis, which etymologically means "wise counsel," was the most wise and intelligent of the immortals, and also the oldest; Zeus wanted to possess her, but he couldn't, for the goddess had the capacity to assume various forms which allowed her to escape his attack every time. But one day the god succeeded in fooling her, and, taking her with both hands, instead of raping her, he swallowed her in one mouthful, because he was too afraid of her intelligence and he feared that she could bear children stronger than a thunderbolt. Metis, however, became pregnant at the same moment that she was devoured and, the right amount of time having passed, from Zeus' migraine Athena was born, the goddess shining in armor, the virgin, the mistress of feminine thought in patriarchal culture, that which remained, and something did remain, of Metis' thought, despite everything.

Repression always produces a symptom, and the eating of Metis, according to the legend, brings on a headache; thus the cranium splits and out comes the father's daughter, more often than not the neglected maternal origin. The owl on her shield brings to mind a nocturnal wisdom, a lunar and mysterious thought that is still alive. By then, however, seething in a self-defensive state, the shield is held up. And meanwhile Metis is still in Zeus' belly.

Psychoanalysis, like other sciences, has established its study on the masculine mental process, repressing its opposite. And yet, due to the particular object of study, psychoanalysis contains within itself the seeds for its own transformation and in time it can change. At present, however, we must acknowledge how the repression of inductive thought maintains or worsens the neurotic troubles of both men and women. When analysts discount the value and the function of feminine thought, or do not recognize its presence in dreams and behavior, it remains mostly unconscious. This in turn induces in some patients a marble rigidity of thought that is extremely discouraging and provokes, in others, a tangle of confused and contorted ideas which periodically invade consciousness with an excess of repressed contents.

On the other hand, the conviction that thought and the spirit belong to the unconscious of the feminine psyche, and that therefore they can be only objects of a progressive integration, is an unprovable hypothesis that has generated some harmful consequences both in theory and in clinical practice. For example, it is harmful to perpetuate the idea that when a woman finally begins to think, she thinks like a man. By not acknowledging the existence of feminine thought and discounting feminine thought in front of a female patient means that masculine thought becomes the only one recognized as it slowly emerges from the unconscious.

Women hesitate to place value upon the usefulness of a form of thought that is more conscious for them. They learn to proceed exclusively following rational thought, and they become *more royal than the king*; that is, more rigid, schematic, and obsessive than men in their same condition, since for men rational thought is conscious and thus more mastered. For women, when masculine thought emerges from the unconscious, it manifests with archaic, excessive characteristics difficult to control. When this happens, the feminine psyche becomes, as we say, *possessed by the animus*, and analysis may even worsen this complex rather than correct it, because it does not allow the masculine and feminine forms of thought to integrate, valuing them both.

C. G. Jung intuited the presence of feminine thought and—without ever having named it—he followed its tracks throughout his works. He was the first to understand the great importance of the illogical and inductive process and its relationship with the symbolic dimension. I am thinking of his studies on alchemy, synchronicity—as the significant opposite of casual connection, and on archetypes—but above all, I am thinking of his passionate and constant interest in the study of *coniunctio oppositorum* and of his conviction of the oneness of the archetype. This area of research, carried forward at least in part by M. L. von Franz, should—I believe—be taken up again, but we need to avoid falling—because of psychic inertia, mental laziness, or sexist pride—into the old trap of masculine inflation. Even Zeus will feel better when Metis is finally out of that cumbersome hiding place. Only when opposites face each other can they unite. From this meeting an energy circuit is activated which unblocks the latent potential, the most significant of which seems to me to be a greater depth in the mental process, as if together one can go where it is not possible to go alone.

A young woman who came to my office was naturally oriented to the meanderings of feminine thought, but the opposite thought was almost completely unconscious: faced with a conflict, or simply a choice, her mind refused to function; decisions were put off and the oscillating motion of her thought, perennially occupied with examining the pros and cons in regard to the infinite possible consequences, paralyzed her existence with big and small problems, to such a degree that other people, coincidence, and life itself made her decisions for her. The logical concatenation of thought and casual connections interrupted each other continuously due to an uncoordinated wandering that lost itself in interminable collateral associations. This woman was intelligent and curious, with various interests, but very rarely were these interests translated into activities or operative choices; even her language betrayed the inflation of feminine thought, and during our sessions it was very tiring to follow her discourse which continually got tangled and lost. One day this woman told me the following dream:

THE WOMAN OF THE VIKINGS: *I was in the North, in the land of the Vikings: they were really them, ancient men, tall and blond; some, on the coast of the sea, were heaping up enormous trunks and others were marking trees. A group of women runs in, a group to protest: they yell, threaten, they intend to impede the cutting of the trees. I go near them and I am on their side. My thoughts are turned toward defending the land, the clean air, the function of shadow, the life of the forest, and so on. Then a young Viking approaches me and says: "If we must eat, we must fish; if we must fish, we must have boats; if we must have boats, we must cut the trees, not the whole forest, but a few trees." I think he is right and I feel indescribably happy and relieved of a weight. At that point a masculine voice behind me tells me that I can never help them because I will never have the strength to use those gigantic swords. In the meantime the youth places one in my arms.*

By association the patient had told me that the North for her was cold, snow, the land of the unconscious, because it was so far from the places she knew and loved; the Vikings were big and strong men, and she wasn't able to imagine Viking women; the youth, who spoke to her and gave her the sword, looked like my son—at that time an adolescent—who she had met a few times. When I finally asked her if the masculine voice outside the scene reminded her of someone, she answered with a shadow of surprise in her voice: "My grandfather, it was an old voice and it seemed like my paternal grandfather."

And thus, in the far off lands of the unconscious, in the cold land of big and strong men, that woman met her logical, deductive thought, clear in path and straight in choice: if I want to eat fish, I must cut the tree. And this mental form can finally be adopted with the joy and relief that always comes with the unblocking of a compulsion. My patient told me that she thought, at first, during the dream, that only the women knew how to think, since they reflected on the consequences of an action; but after, in the words of the young Viking, she understood that behind the actions of those men there was a reasoning, different from hers, but just as legitimate.

The dream also reveals why that woman was blocked in expressing masculine thought: her grandfather was a southern Italian patriarch (the Vikings and the North serve as the antidote) with a very limited opinion of feminine personality. After the premature death of her father, this grandfather took on the responsibility of bringing up my patient and he influenced the development of her identity, inducing her to believe that women were incapable of masculine thought, the only kind of thought that was accepted. "Women don't know how to reason," he used to repeat, "It's pointless to waste time," and the young mother of my patient nodded her head sighing. In this case the conscious acceptance of the familiar model repressed from the start the masculine mental form, leaving the field open for the progressive inflation of the opposite form, which, in time, had degenerated to a tangle of chaotic and confused thoughts. In the dream, the polarization between the image of the Viking—my son (something that therefore comes from the analysis) and the voice of her grandfather at her back (the past which will have to die) cuts the neurotic cord and liberates an energy.

But it was starting exactly with that dream that a complex and delicate phase in our work began, because from that dream two new problems came to light: the first in the conflict, a little by little more conscious, between masculine and feminine thought, which was already traceable in the oneiric context; the second in the primitiveness and in the archaic force of the masculine thought which emerged from the shadow dragging along with it the remains of an old repression; this context, too, was visible in the primitive and wild aspect of the Viking fishermen. On the one hand it was necessary that my patient succeed in liberating her emerging phallic thoughts from neurotic excess and from that too heavy sword; in this way it could untangle the twisted threads of her inductive process. On the other hand, it was also necessary to continue to acknowledge the value and meaning of feminine thought, otherwise it would lose itself in the shadow.

In these cases, it is not a question of developing a prescriptive and ideological attitude on the part of the analyst; rather, it is a question of *not* intervening by discounting what should not be discounted. The unconscious doesn't do it. In the dream we have examined, it doesn't condemn the group of women: the saving of the forest is also a value, like the technique of providing food for oneself is a value. In analysis, the process comes by itself. It happens naturally in that, as we continue to experience the unconscious in the absence of distracting interventions, and interpretations of projections, it will orient itself toward self-therapy. The projective and ideological attitude belongs to the person who *teaches* that the only useful thought is the masculine one in order to finally expel the intricate and paralyzing complex of feminine thought.

Whenever this projective and ideological intervention takes place, the female patient will eventually leave therapy with an inflated masculine thought that is weak, rigid, and competitive, and with feminine thought that has flowed back into the shadow, and this is the starting point for periodic destructive incursions. Perhaps this woman will become able to follow her path, but she will have lost her soft and round way of thinking that was capable of embracing the whole, of working syntheses, relationships, and analogies.

That this mental form is also important in masculine psychology seems evident to me, and I will give an example for usefulness. A man came to my office who judged women as manifestly inferior in thought: a position widely shared by numerous psychoanalysts. Being a refined man, he had no difficulty in acknowledging that intelligence has no gender preference and was astonished that "women didn't know how to think"; it never occurred to him that it could be that he didn't know how to think *like a woman*. He was therefore surprised and amused every time that I, in the course of our work together, "guessed" something about his life, since he attributed my capacity to put wholes in relation to each other and formulate analogic syntheses to a sort of *magical quality*, to an unexplainable inspiration only available to myself.

"I don't know why," he said, "but the majority of women aren't able to follow a logical thread: they digress, they get distracted, they go backward, they get lost in side thoughts. . . so that to reason with a woman for me is usually tiring and dispersive." *They digress, they go backward, they get lost*—these expressions made me think of a labyrinth and the excruciating path following an illogical and analogical thread in order to get to the center.

The symptoms, which that man declared at the beginning of treatment, had nothing to do with the activity of thought and claimed exclusively sexual problems. I had informed my client of the possibility that the defective sexual circuit had its root somewhere else, but my words left him indifferent. He was a passionate man, capable of deep feeling, but his "German" upbringing, as he called it, and a deep affective trauma, had left him frozen. His mind had become a control tower for his emotions, and he was held prisoner; his thoughts were lucid, cold, essential, very effective in his profession, but he was incapable of valuing secondary aspects, the apparently insignificant details in context, of keeping track of two things at the same time. I remember one time he said to me: "Anyway I love my mother; it's logical: she's my mother." How can one be surprised that he was impotent? What exists that is more illogical than coitus?

I asked him one day to try to see things from a different point of view: what if a woman, reasoning with a man, felt caged in by metal armor? And what if a woman declared that men don't know how to think? "If this happened," he answered, "I would say it was her problem." "It's true," I then said to him, "to each his own problem." "No, because we're talking about thought, and my mental form produces thought, hers doesn't." "And so what can a mental form produce?" "In this case I don't know," he concluded, "But in the end, I don't think this has anything to do with me personally." If it didn't have anything to do with him personally, then it had to do with me personally even less. A few months passed after this conversation before my patient brought me this dream.

THE MAN OF THE BALL OF THREAD: *There was something before that I don't remember well, but that concerned you [i.e., the analyst] maybe an appointment of ours that I postponed, I don't know why. Then I have to go someplace outdoors, in the country, where there is going to be a party or something like that; one of those situations I usually succeed in avoiding. I am alone and I am walking on a long path which seems to spiral around the sides of a hill, and all of a sudden I am in a clearing in the woods, in an extraordinarily beautiful place which is the fountain of Vacluse[1]: a source springs from the rocks and, flowing down in a few small cascades, it gathers in a wider basin where there is a watermill; all around a tender green and an almost magic light. Near the source there are some women, some seem to be nuns, but perhaps they are only dressed in antique clothes, others are wearing jeans, they are all different ages and are busy doing I don't know what, and they come and go like a swarm of bees. There are also a few men among them, but I intuit that it is not a party; I approach them because I*

---

1. The fountain of Vacluse is a spring in Provence, which inspired Francesco Petrarca to compose "Clear Fresh Sweet Waters," dedicated to Laura.

---

want to understand what they are doing. But as I am about to enter the group, a hand firmly pushes me away. I try again and the same thing happens: my obstacle is invisible. I meet the gaze of a woman who looks sorry and she shows me from far away a ball of blue thread, as if to make me understand something, and suddenly I know that they are all washing and rolling up thread, even the men, and I can't understand why I can't do it, too. I wake up with an anxiety attack.

In this dream we find a few key images: the spiral path around the hill, the fountain of Petrarch, the source which comes out of the earth, the women of and from different ages, the male minority, the reference to bees, the exclusion, and, naturally, the ball of thread. These images reveal to my patient that the feminine principle does not give life to a boring and carefree party, but to an only apparently chaotic activity, in reality very well organized (the bees), that takes place in an enchanted place, intertwined, in our poetical memory, our love for Laura. The spiral path, the water which comes out of the rocks, the blue ball of thread, represent, in this case, the inductive and subterranean path of feminine thought which avoids shortcuts, but rather slowly follows the path, because it is not only the objective that counts, but also what happens on the way. This activity concerns women from every era and every generation, but it also includes a few men who have understood how to earn their ball of thread. The dreamer, however, feels excluded by the strength of that hand, which is certainly his own, but it also symbolizes the hand of many other men, and of an entire society that has raised its sons to fear the contagion of the feminine archetype.

"Maybe," my patient observes, "the postponed appointment with you at the beginning of the dream equals the exclusion which comes after: I'm not ready yet, I proceed toward something before which I stop myself; and I think it is the fear of losing myself, of not knowing anymore, after, how to find my world again." This is the same fear of losing oneself which was at the root of his sexual symptom. But, in the workings of the psyche, when fear takes the place of disdain, it means that we are on the right track. The sign of the turning point was announced in another dream, about a year later.

THE ROAD OF THE MEETING: *I am on the highway; then the scene changes and I enter a house where a concierge tells me that I can't enter. I don't pay any attention to her and I move toward a very beautiful and elegant staircase which, however, gets narrower a little at a time and, as I slowly ascend, it transforms into a very narrow spiral staircase where I am afraid of getting stuck and also of getting lost, because it goes up, down, it turns, it changes direction and at that point I am not so much following it by choice but because I wouldn't know how to turn back. It is a nightmare. Then all of a sudden I arrive in a big calm room where in the center a woman is sitting in a wicker chair reading: she has very long blonde hair and a blue dress; she lifts her eyes for a moment from her reading and I recognize the gaze of my therapist. She says: "We will begin in a little while." She seems so absorbed that I don't feel like asking her what we are going to begin.*

At this point the ball of thread from the earlier dream has become the staircase that my patient decided to ascend, even if it is scary, because it is certainly not fast, straight, or even familiar like the highway; so it is possible for him to overcome the obstacle of the concierge who prohibits, and at the same time defends, the entry into the world of the anima from occasional or unwanted visitors. The woman dressed in blue and immersed in reading offers a sweet and welcoming image of feminine thought, with the softness of the long blonde hair, and the "warm and attentive" glance that he recognizes from his analyst.

"We will begin in a little while," affirms the woman at the end of the dream, and the man doesn't know what. After having overcome obstacles and labyrinths, perhaps the moment has arrived for him to abandon himself to a different way of being, which cares for, attenuates, completes, and does not substitute what is already consolidated from his upbringing and experience. It was, nonetheless, difficult for that man to loosen his mental defenses and journey in the labyrinth, where it is not possible to choose the path, but only to find it, and this was really, in certain aspects, a nightmare. But, at the end, his "Fort Alamo," as he began to call it, had to give out under the pressure of unknown vital energies. Thus he became less and less boring and predictable, and the rigid, and in general superficial, scheme of his thoughts slowly transformed into a more elastic, relaxed, deeper system.

But above all, "Fort Alamo" having fallen, and with it the fear of losing himself in the feminine, he began to be able to make love. In this case as well, as in innumerable others, the unconscious, indicating the path for the analytical work, had connected the solution to the symptom to the necessity for a different ordering of the whole personality, and for the latter, the recovery of a repressed psychic activity, which in the case in question was the meandering and receptive thought.

I do not know the theoretical value of my *compass* of orientation which isolates three manifestations (thought, feeling, and instinct) in the psychic dynamic of the animus and the anima, but I must verify that, since I have been using it, many dreams seem more understandable and many results more consoling. It is as if the unconscious personality orients itself autonomously toward completeness, toward what Jung defined "the oneness of the archetype," and the only job remaining for the analyst is to recognize and acknowledge the process. Consequently, when meeting with an unknown patient, it is one of the first questions I ask myself about his condition in relation to the three psychic masculine and feminine actions, and, during the preliminary sessions and in anamnesis work, I try to orient myself in this sort of six-pointed star. Then I wait and, with a little patience, the unconscious of the patient begins to send signals, always more precise and pointed, that illuminate the points in shadow and, at the same time, correct the route of the life.

Chapter 2

The Activity of Feeling

In the early 60s I had the occasion to meet a leader of the National Liberation Front of Algeria, the organization which fought against French colonial dominion. Speaking to me about *after*, of how he imagined his country in freedom, he confided in me that he felt conflicted by different feelings which apparently didn't connect within himself.

"On the one hand," he told me, and these are almost his exact words, "I wish to affront my job as a political leader and so I imagine how beautiful and important it will be to face, together with my other comrades, the big problems of our country: illiteracy, the problem of the Cabilia, agricultural reform, the condition of women, and so on, and I feel the enthusiasm and the responsibility that this commitment demands. But on the other hand, I stop myself at imagining freedom, simply imagining being free and owning my land, me and all the others, and inside I feel a solemn emotion, which is the ultimate meaning of our work in these years: I see people in the street, without fear, our flags, joy, pain, the Casbah which rings, and life has a new flavor . . . and I know that this feeling, just as it is, just because it exists, gives me courage and makes me feel different."

I was 20 years old and very moved by those words which described, calmly and passionately, two ways of expressing a feeling of love for one's own country. That man, who I would never see again, was the first to reveal to me something which only much later I would understand and which would become such a part of my work. Neither the masculine nor the feminine archetype belongs exclusively to one sex or the other, and the psychic energy of every man and woman can embrace, in the course of life, both of them, moving toward an image of totality. In the heart of that young man, love for Algeria took on the double form of activity and vibration, it expressed itself in the struggle and in the images, it was strength and abandonment, project and memory.

Masculine feeling orients itself toward feelings to reach an end, and because of this, in a certain sense, it organizes and directs them, activating a penetrative energy, which pushes to act, to assume responsibility, to make plans; in short, to play the game and take risks.

Feminine feeling, on the other hand, tends to remain still, centered on the emotional perception: in this case the energy assumes the form of a center, of an egg, of a nucleus which emanates heat. The psychic disposition is contemplative and its objective seems to consist in witnessing a feeling, and in revealing its deepest meaning, according a behavior scheme oriented more toward being than doing, and which involves relationships between things and people more than the actions of things and people.

Masculine feeling expresses a penetrative energy toward its own object, while its opposite expresses a receptive energy which contemplates its own object and understands it; the former goes toward the nucleus of a situation, the latter lets it permeate.

I believe that an image that leads to the center of the *coniunctio oppositorum* in the sphere of feeling actually exists—it is the image of compassion. Jesus accepts to die on the cross for love and for a faith to which he has dedicated his life: feeling became the motor and the *opus* of an entire existence that has been action, preaching, example, and sacrifice; Jesus organized his emotional energy, directing it toward a goal and pursuing it to the end.

But at the foot of the cross, another feeling is expressed: the compassion of the women, who receive in silence that immense pain, without any scope other than to experience it and become part of it; the meaning becomes to share, beyond formations and objectives: from the women of compassion a large energy emanates which accepts the tragedy and becomes witness to it, so giving it its most profound truth. From this image of the union of opposites—I believe—the symbolic possibility of Resurrection derives.

In classical mythology, Ulysses' tension regarding the return, and Penelope's strength in waiting, seem to me to describe the two energies in action and, on their converging paths, the promise of union. On one side there is a voyage and a series of undertakings against the obstacles which human beings and gods place on the path: on the other there is the waiting, an immobile center which contains feeling and keeps hope burning; the weaving is the symbol, since it is a virtual object, which absorbs energy from an only apparent action, continually undone by a contrary action: the weaving does not exist, but the energy that prolongs the waiting does. Ulysses and Penelope express complementary and convergent feelings which join together in that eternal image passed down by Homer.

> The royal pair mingled in love again
> and afterward lay revelling in stories:
> hers of the seige of her beauty stood at home

from arrogant suitors, crowding on her sight,
and how they fed their courtship on his cattle,
oxen and fat sheep, and drank up rivers
of wine out of the vats.

Odysseus told
of what hard blows he had dealt out to others
and of what blows he had taken away—all that story.
She could not close her eyes till all was told.[1]

In personal analysis, I have been able to verify how the unconscious, in the majority of cases, intervenes as a corrective function, compensating for the energy of deeply repressed feeling. Regarding this, and in my own experience, at the beginning of my career as a psychoanalyst I dreamed about the desert.

MARY'S DESERT: *I was alone in a landscape of sand and rocks; in front of me, at a certain distance, I saw a woman wrapped in a black cloak. Now we approach each other and I see her brow is furrowed and her face is illuminated by a very clear gaze. "But you are Mary," I say to her, and she answers: "I am Mary because I have chosen to be Mary."*

When I began to work, strong with masculine feeling aimed at treating and transforming the suffering of others (and my own), that dream came to remind me how, before everything else, that pain should be received, accepted, and shared, *for what it is*. Everyone, within the limits of the possible, makes choices, and the unconscious asked me to remain loyal to mine, to accept eclipsing Me in

---

1. Homer, *The Odyssey*, Book 23. Robert Fitzgerald, trans. (New York: Anchor Press, 1963).

front of You, embracing the furrows, putting on the mourning veil in front of the cross of another, and ultimately risking every feeling for what it is, without asking myself immediately and only where it would take me.

Another dream about the necessity and importance of receptive feeling, in particular for those who practice our profession, was told to me one day by a colleague.

THE CENTER OF LOVE: *I am in front of a door which has drawn on its surface a series of concentric circles, like a bullseye, and I have a lance in my hands with which I will try to hit the center. The door, however, slowly begins to open, moving the target: if I want to throw, I must do it in a hurry, before it becomes impossible due to lack of visibility. Meanwhile, in the same room, some children are playing, running around me and I become agitated because they are using up my time and concentration. Then I see among them a handicapped child, held up with infinite love by two of his playmates, and I understand that theirs is a total love. Then all of a sudden I know that the center for me now is that handicapped child and love as experience of others.*

In front of a very masculine personality, the unconscious shifted the shot and oriented the libido to the construction of an image of completeness; to *hit the center* it was necessary to set aside the emotional tension toward a goal (the center), in order to let him abandon himself to a feeling contained within itself (the child). It is not a question of either treating or curing, but simply to accept that child as he is. What image of feminine feeling is more intense and what metaphor is more precise for a such large part of our work? Hit the center means, above all, love the sick child which hides in each of us and inside each person that destiny accompanies into our offices.

With the same compensatory character, oriented toward the same image of completeness, the unconscious also intervenes by encouraging the development of masculine feeling, as it is possible to observe in the following example.

A woman, who had dedicated her life to her family, came to my office when she was about 50 in very compromising psychic conditions. Her symptoms were *borderline* and her first dreams oriented me toward discovering in childhood a serious problem in bonding with her mother and, thus, later, the projection of that unsuccessful symbiosis on her husband and children. A little at a time a reciprocal projection between husband and wife came to light: my patient had invested her companion with her animus, and her husband had done likewise with his anima: in this way the woman's masculine and the man's feminine had remained, for the most part and for a long time, unconscious, provoking deep damage, and not only within the marital relationship.

The masculine feeling of my patient was perhaps the most damaged by neuroses and was at that point completely repressed. She tried to express her civil passion in political action, taking initiatives and behaving in an autonomous and active way, but afterward she allowed her husband to occupy that territory and to reaffirm his leadership, and she readapted herself to the familiar, reassuring role of squire.

My client's emotional heritage was, at this point, spent alternatively between caring for and destroying the familial framework: when she felt strong, she wove the daily web of relations; when she felt tired and weak, she became a threatening and self-destructive victim. In the course of time, the dependent and passive aspect, which had been made worse by maternal coldness, was slowly dismantled by transference and then by the emergence from the unconscious of masculine images which opened her to the desire for action.

At a certain point, contact with masculine forms of feeling and emerging self-confidence pushed her outside the domestic walls toward new interests. She moved toward a world in which her unsatisfied need for love no longer was put aside in order to do something sensible, something good for others, and thus in the end, good for herself. In this context even the overbearing shadow of feminine feeling was progressively attenuated. The family remained at the center of her emotional life, but she no longer asked her husband to replace her mother in a total relationship, nor, at the same time, did she allow territorial invasions of her social and professional initiative. The progressive autonomy of her adult children and their imminent abandonment of the family home were no longer, as before, sources of anguish, but rather of that particular melancholy which stresses important passages in the phases of life.

The complaining and exhausting victim, who had to make the family pay for her frustrations, became a woman who had taken on her history and didn't have time to lose. Toward the end of her analysis, marked by the acceptance of her masculine feeling, my patient brought me a dream, whose final image was the following:

THE JEWELS OF THE ASCENT: *Together with others I am walking on a mountain path toward the summit. In my hands I have many jewels, but they aren't mine; I let them drop behind me one by one, as if to mark the path, so that the others, who will come after, can pick them up.*

That ascent, together with other people, describes the human force that enlarges the horizons of each person and allows one to feel part of everything, of a plan which involves collectively taking away the space from self-centering and fear. By leaving the house and learning to ascend the mountain with other people, by deciding to make effort in order to reach a goal, this woman married her unconscious masculine feeling and simultaneously came into contact with herself. What are the jewels in this dream? Are they not the deepest values that animate her personality? And she drops them for those who will come? The joy of living, love for somebody or something, curiosity, courage, the meaning of existence—these are the jewels that sometimes appear in our hands and which, like a treasure that be left to those who follow.

Through the union of the double energy of feeling, this woman liberated herself from the verbal and vindictive attitude of a woman who feels that life owes her something and, as in the dream, she became very wealthy and absolutely poor at the same time. Even in this case, as Jung intuited and repeated many times in his writings, the union of two opposites is the origin of the image of Oneself.

The last example relative to the dynamic of feeling is about a young man who conserved both forms of affective energy in the shadow. When he first came to my office he was 28 years old, and claimed to have a sexual symptomatology. He was the son of the central Italian bourgeoisie which feeds the bureaucracy and bases its identity on "a secure job, a place in the Government," and on a secure social status. He was—as he himself acknowledged—a *dodger* who "didn't do hardly anything" in a government controlled establishment just outside Milan, where he had been transferred.

The culture in which he had always been immersed was based on a few indisputable commandments: "Mind your own business," "Don't get mixed up in things that don't concern you," "Don't say what you think," "Serve the ones in power and in return ask for protection." These kinds of assumptions exclude any evolution in the activity of feeling, which remains stuck in an embryonic and archaic form, that includes the feeling that the family is against everything and everyone outside the family itself.

This patient of mine was an intelligent and sensitive young man, and perhaps just because of that, so as not to suffer beyond his endurance in the affective desert in which he had grown up, he had rejected in his unconscious the whole emotional complex, both in the masculine component as well as in the feminine one. Thus he was not able to feel or receive feelings, nor could he feel an emotional tension oriented in any direction: he was completely cold; he wasn't even able to feel anything when his grandmother died, who according to him, was the only person who had ever loved him.

Working with this patient, the solution to his psychosomatic sexual symptom was relatively simple, but it was much more difficult to liberate his feelings from the fetters of his upbringing. He couldn't imagine that he could work or study following personal inclinations and respecting personal values. The words "to take great interest in something" were incomprehensible to him, but so was "to cry" and "to risk."

He didn't like to be touched, and, when this happened unexpectedly, even the simple contact of a hand on his arm, made him start, and the contact provoked rash reactions. He didn't want to be touched, either internally or externally.

This problem was intertwined with a negative maternal complex (a probably psychotic mother who had spent time in psychiatric hospitals) and a dependence relationship with a weak father who was withdrawn in his frustrations. In any case, the dreams of this young man continued to bring up the feeling complex with very intense images of pain, joy, and personal involvement.

About two years passed without any significant transformation, when one day he said, almost incidentally, that he had gone to the dance recital of the daughter of a colleague of his. To my question *why* he responded that the child was nice and she had invited him; besides—he continued—children in general were nice and kind to him. I encouraged him to talk and I saw him almost become animated when he told me how interesting it was to play with children and how fun it was to listen to them; he also told me he felt an unbearable sensation when he thought of suffering or abused or abandoned children. In fact, he immediately tried to drive away these thoughts. That day I had the impression that children were able to spark contact between himself and his feelings, which seemed to assume, at first, a warm and receiving feminine form, a nucleus of receptive energy, which allowed him to *feel good* in the company of children and *feel bad* when thinking of their pain.

The years that followed were hard, but thrilling, work, during which I was witness to the end of diffidence and the birth of the desire to feel: a little at a time my patient felt more able to bear pain, joy, and pleasure; then there were other more complex emotional situations, together with the violence of terrible memories. And, at the end, even masculine feeling appeared in the conscious: it began with a great interest in cycling, and he spoke to me at length about the long riding trips he made. He made friends and had flirtations, he discovered the warmth and the limits, he was enthusiastic and disappointed, and in time he discovered new interests and realized he was happy and curious; he had a beautiful smile which lit up his face. He always said that "sooner or later he would do something with children," but his words ended there.

A couple of years after his little friend's dance recital, my patient was able to finish analysis: he was in love, he was comfortable with his sexuality, he had recuperated important memories, he devoted himself to social discrimination, and I felt him slowly becoming deeply involved and interested in his life. I knew his personality was still at a formative stage, but the moment for him to risk by himself had come.

For about a year every now and then I received a postcard or a call from him, then for a few months nothing. One morning I found a letter of his postmarked from a small city very far from Milan; except for personal parts, the following is the contents:

Hi, How are you? It's sort of sad how, since analysis ended, we don't see each other or hear from each other anymore. First you become almost like a mother and then . . . poof, nothing more.

However this is to tell you that I've changed address, telephone number, career, region, and even hair style. Now I live in XXX, at a center for the mentally ill. Mornings I go to school in XXX: a 3 year program to become a social worker; afternoons and evenings I spend with the crazy and the less crazy at the center. For the time being I am not getting paid. I quit my old "secure" job; I haven't told my parents yet, they think I am on a leave of absence. Nonetheless they are very sad and they treat me like I am a lunatic. It's enough to say that they haven't tried to lecture me. Neither they nor my other relatives have asked me anything about what I am doing exactly. They think I'm crazy.

Naturally this isn't pleasant, but I'm happy here; I'm enjoying school a lot, and I like the center. The problem if anything is that I've only been here a short time (5 months) and so, considering how "immersifying" it is to live at the center, I haven't got a personal life on the outside. Sometimes it would help me get rid of tension, the attention continues. It will come!

Maybe I will go to work with children, even before finishing school, for now I go every so often as a volunteer.

I won't make this too long. I hope you are well. I would really like to hear from you, whatever you think. So long. Kisses.

Refound feeling allowed this young man to discover his path, or at least, a stretch of it. He wanted to work with children, he was preparing himself to do it, and in the meantime he was living and working with "crazy people," progressively bringing closure to the complex issue of his mother's madness and perhaps his own. To do so he had to disturb the family mentality and the supreme value of tribal egoism, which he has submitted to and shared, accepting to transgress the laws of the Father, shattering the myth of security, quitting and working "for no pay."

The melancholy of solitude, and the acknowledgment of a recognized and accepted diversity represent, in that letter, the inevitable counterbalance to the enthusiasm and the the joy of living for what one is.

Feeling, at this point brought back to the surface, has perhaps become the mainstay of his personality and he can direct himself toward his objective: the love, the care, the sense of responsibility toward children who suffer.

In analytical psychology, the only energy of feeling acknowledged is the feminine one, which prevalently inhabits the unconscious of men and the consciousness of women; I have never heard of a masculine feeling with a penetrative orientation characteristic of the masculine conscious. I have never heard of this in the theoretical sphere, but I have systematically met with it in the conscious and the unconscious of my patients, my friends, men or women as they were, and my own self. This partiality which denys a specific masculine feeling produces just as serious consequences as the partiality which (as we saw in the preceding chapter) denys a specific feminine thought.

In this case, the result that one obtains is, in fact, the maintaining (or the sending) of phallic feeling into the shadow, and forcing the personality to measure itself exclusively on the terrain of receptive feeling. To maintain phallic feeling in the shadow is not to acknowledge its existence, meaning, or value for the emotional energy, which, in a human being, directs behavior toward a goal and marries the passion to a sense of responsibility, courage, risk, and moral laws.

Fatherhood, civil commitment, attachment to one's job, the desire for consciousness, the struggle for freedom, are just a few of the ways of being in which humanity expresses masculine feeling. Not to acknowledge it for what it is, to attribute to it an autonomous meaning and value, and to attempt to enclose it in a notion of vague spirituality, or in an all-understanding sphere of thought, deprives that energy of its warmth and of its emotional strength.

Further, if phallic feeling remains in the shadow, the personality slowly becomes coerced into expressing feelings exclusively in the receptive form, and this distortion damages men more seriously, obviously, from the moment that it forces them to measure themselves on terrain more unconscious and less *natural* for them. I have seen, over time, many analysts wreak havoc with their patients' feelings. Men, in particular, when they finish this type of analysis, aren't even able to recognize their specific form of erotic energy and they compensate for it with an inflation of feminine feeling.

They are men who are softened by a trifle, who are easily moved, who discover themselves to be available, soft, and welcoming like an old cushion, and who, because of this, believe they have "recuperated their emotivity," while they are experiencing either a partial or an unpresentable superabundance of it. They have only elaborated one form of the energy of feeling, and they express it with the urgency of someone trying to make up for lost time. Meanwhile they have lost sight of the other form of that same energy, so fundamental for their equilibrium, along the way. In my opinion, there does not exist a man less erotic than one who doesn't know his masculine feeling.

The shadow zone which surrounds masculine feeling is usually occupied by vanity, sectarianism, and violence, because when emotion goes straight, and does not see anything other than its goal, it necessarily assumes a unilateral, arbitrary, and even egocentric character. Men (and women) dominated by masculine feeling become overbearing and cruel because they ride the wave of their emotions without caring about what is happening around them, without being able to embrace the complexity of an emotional situation.

In opposing symmetry, it is possible to observe a cone of the shadow projected by feminine feeling. This obscures the inability to take sides and to risk. There is a need to always justify and a difficulty in assuming moral responsibility for a choice, and most importantly, a habit of affective dependence or even living according to others is formed.

The bloody and archaic aspect of this type of masculine shadow, and the passive and morally irresponsible tendency of this type of feminine shadow are simultaneously traceable, in my opinion, in the tradition of *crimes of honor* or restorative weddings in southern Italy. Following an ancient custom—only recently fallen into disuse—if a girl was raped, just for the fact that she was no longer a virgin, she covered herself and her entire family in dishonor. At this point there were two ways to reinstate the group socially: the first was to wash away the dishonor with blood by killing the girl or the rapist, or both. The second was to proceed with a restorative wedding. This tradition was so rooted in the penal laws, that up to a few years ago, the penalties provided for the so-called *crimes of honor* were ridiculously low, and there was no prosecution for rape if the victim accepted to marry the rapist. The weight of this tradition was so strong that the first girl who, in 1964, refused to marry the man who had raped her, denouncing him to the authorities, began a judicial case. The ambiguity of this social behavior—and of the norm which sanctioned it—crime exists, but marriage extinguishes it.

The shadow of masculine feeling manifests itself, in this case, in the capacity to kill a daughter or a sister in the name of a supreme value (in this case honor) without keeping in mind the value of life, or of the complexity of the web of affective and familial emotions. But in the same context, the shadow of feminine feeling is traceable, in the passive acceptance of the restorative wedding which humiliates the body, desire, and dignity. The life of a woman, in this case, depends on the clan and on the familial sentiment of honor. It is consumed in dependence and in the resigned justification of orders given to save family honor.

In both cases it is possible to recognize what seems to be a constant of the shadow of feeling, and that is its adjustment to the collective feeling, as if a subject, deprived of the possibility to define himself or herself through a personal feeling, falls prey to archaic residuals in which individual identity tends to be overwhelmed.

If, for example, as in this case, self-respect and the aversion toward the rapist are repressed personal feelings, due to complex cultural mechanisms, then the only possible feeling that remains is the one dictated by the clan, the one shared and sanctioned, the feeling of honor that is bound to virginity and marriage.

On the other hand, if a man can't express his feeling of pain and protection toward his raped daughter, then it reflows into a behavior collectively approved of, which in this case is revenge, and in this way he projects the suffering onto the loss of honor, that is, on something that can be restored.

From time immemorial, thought has been considered the origin of knowledge. From Rousseau on, instinct, as well, has found its place at the source of Western culture. From this point of view, however, the condition of the psychic activity of feeling seems to me to be controversial.

Are hate, love, fear, sadness, respect, distrust, and all the other emotional states of the human soul directed toward knowledge, or do they obstruct the path? Or, finally, do they not have any pertinence to knowledge?

Like instinct and thought, feeling places a subject in relation to an object, but the form of the relation, in this case, is an emotional nucleus; the object is not thought of or perceived by the senses, but felt through the emotional impact generated in the subject.

Over time, every human being gets used to feeling certain feelings in correspondence to certain contexts and, in the absence of consistent neurotic blocks, the flowing of emotion seems capable, by itself, even without self-reflection, of guiding the subject toward consciousness.

The faith in feeling as a source of knowledge is naturally more evident where the weight of thought is less determined: for example in Eastern civilization and the early infancy of every human being.

A 2-year-old child, for example, placed in front of an unknown adult, observes for a long while in silence, and then, on the basis of the emotional circuit that has been generated, decides his attitude, which oscillates from total availability to complete rejection. The child *knows*, because he feels it emotionally, what he can expect from that situation and that meeting.

During a long stay in Afghanistan in the early 70s, I found myself in the desert between Kandahar and Erat, in nomad territory. Having sighted a camp, I approached and asked to speak with the leader. While waiting to know if I could be received, I began to fraternize with some children who were playing in front of the tents; nomad children were very proud and, different from the permanent

inhabitants of the oases, they would not have, at that time, accepted money. I showed them my knitting (completely unknown to
them) and how to knit; they showed me a white goat, named Marco
Polo, and they were very proud of it. Meanwhile they observed me.

At a certain point they were brusquely called into the tent of
the head-villager and when they came out I was received. It was not
difficult to understand what had happened, and the meaning of that
infantile consultation was subsequently explained. I will never forget the look of the old man when I was able to distinguish him in
the dimness of the tent, and, remembering many other looks
throughout my life, I must conclude that if the language of instinct
is in the body, and that of thought is in words, feeling must be in the
way of looking.

CHAPTER 3

The Activity of Instinct

I f we examine instinctual energy in its archetypical manifestations and in biological and sexual symbolism, we must acknowledge how it expresses a fundamental ambivalence in masculine and feminine character. In sexual relations, the separation between the two forms of instinct is analogous to the different genders: desire in one case is to receive and in the other to penetrate; but in the spheres which refer to the symbolization (or to the sublimatio⌐ in Freudian terms) of the *libido*, a space exists in which a man can also be receptive and a woman penetrating, thus reaching a completeness and a complexity which seem to belong to the psychic form of every human being.

The aggressive drive, for example, which is an aspect of the penetrative instinct, is evident in the behavior of both men and women, even if, in the latter, it has often been so disturbed or repressed by the upbringing that at this point it almost only manifests itself in the shadow.

On the other hand, the receptive aspect of instinct, even if socially devalued in masculine behavior, is traceable in the desire to protect, nourish, and nurture that children manifest, for example, toward small animals, or in the desire of the adult man to abandon himself every now and then to something that has to do with nature.

If we examine feminine instinct more deeply, we verify how it, in turn, presents an ambivalence: the sexual sphere and the maternal sphere, interdependent between themselves and yet different; the biological images referring to this ambivalence are evidently the vagina and the uterus, where satisfaction depends in one case on feeling penetrated, and in the other on waiting for the fulfillment of birth, in warmth and protection. The analogy of feminine instinct with the earth is, from this point of view, tremendous: the earth is opened in order to receive a seed which, in the mystery of obscurity, transforms and grows until it strains against the turf to be born to life; the frequency and constancy of these chthonic images in dreams seems to confirm an irreducible fact of feminine psychology in this symbolic analogy.

But, over time, patriarchal culture has dedicated itself to separating the two poles of receptive instinct, repressing sexual desire and consequently inflating the maternal dimension. It is customary to attribute this schism, and the consequent repression, to the threat that the collective patriarchal conscious perceived in feminine sexuality. Feminine sexuality is the bearer of a bursting energy capable of overwhelming the reasoning of *logos,* and the basis of rational knowledge; it was feared that culture would succumb to nature. This explanation has never convinced me: it is possible that the strength and the diversity of feminine instinct projected threatening shadows on the emerging masculine culture, besides it is reasonable to hypothesize that women, as well, were frightened of the violence of their libido. Both fears are evident even now in the dreams of men and women when they refer to the emotional reaction of feminine instinct in front of the shadow.

But this verification does not resolve the problem because it seems to approach it from the end rather than from the beginning. Feminine sexuality, in fact, becomes *shadow exactly because* it is repressed and it is not repressed because it is *shadow.* A characteristic of the shadow is to receive aspects of the Ego sunk into the unconscious because of incompatibility with values of the conscious. Thus it is the conscious, personal or collective, which judges the feminine sexual charge as unacceptable and represses it *before* it becomes shadow, and makes sure it becomes shadow.

If we avoid examining this aspect of the problem, we will never get to the end, and a series of questions, not completely secondary in respect to feminine psychology, will remain without an answer. Why has women's sexuality been pushed back into the shadow? Why has it been separated from maternal instinct? Why, in our culture, has it assumed the semblance of the devil, identifying itself with evil? This state of things has lasted for thousands of years and we cannot get away with affirming that the cause of the panic and of the following expulsive judgment is a shadow which is not the origin, but rather the consequence of repression. What then has the collective conscious judged to be morally and esthetically unacceptable? What aspect of feminine instinct has proven itself to be incompatible with the ego? Let's begin with a few observations.

First of all, a very elementary psychological mechanism (traceable in infantile and primitive mentality) pushes to attribute evil and threatening intentions to the *other* when the *other* is perceived to be stronger. A second psychological mechanism orients toward aversion that which attracts, but at the same time on which one risks to depend: one ends up hating whoever generates a need because it creates slavery, even if slavery is a desire. Yet another psychic mechanism is the one summarized in the saying "Divide and rule": if there are two enemies, the foremost aim is to separate them and then make a pact with the less dangerous one, while trying to neutralize the second.

Now, starting from a phase of evolution, feminine instinctuality in its wholeness must have generated all three of these reactions in the collective masculine conscious, because the extraordinary energy which it expressed in sexuality and maternity had been seen over time to be overwhelming and dangerous. In second place, the world of men must have felt, in an endemic way over the course of evolution, the necessity to defend itself from a desire bordering on need, from a drive potentially castrating, because it is unconsciously linked to the maternal relationship.

And, finally, receptive instinct is, as we have seen, ambivalent—in its sexual and maternal polarity—while phallic instinct is univocal, because the sphere of paternity pertains to feeling: the long months of pregnancy, the birth and the suckling, from an instinctual point of view, enclose the woman in a solitude which the masculine psyche has always experienced as an exclusion.

Reviewing, then, starting from a very far back past, a man felt at risk before feminine instinct because his instinct was weaker, but also because desire could make him lose his head, and finally because, on the other hand, there wasn't only the lover, but the mother as well. And thus it was necessary to divide this terrible feminine strength—which is the invisible power of the earth—and in part repress it, in order to face it.

In light of these considerations, we can see how the patriarchal conscious, in the course of evolution, came to consider the feminine instinct incompatible with its own development. They feared the strength (and not the shadow) of instinct, they feared being dependent on it, and they feared the anguish of being excluded. Thus there seems to exist a hidden symmetry to penis envy and not keeping it in mind contributes most likely to the conservation of these two complexes.

In ancient commentaries on the Bible, an episode of extraordinary symbolic density describes this historical and psychological process. Lilith, in fact, not Eve, was the first woman in the Book who *forgot* it.[1] But in the comments of the ancient Rabbis on Genesis, she reappears as the image rejected by the desire and fear of Adam. In the same Bible, the censorship regarding this first woman is indirectly traceable; as the Beresit Rabbi wrote: "*From the beginning*[2] he created her; but when the man saw her full of saliva and blood he went away; he created her again, as it is written: *this time*. This woman and that woman from the first time."[3] *This woman* is Eve and *that woman from the first time* is Lilith, who wasn't made from one of Adam's ribs because she was probably born *together with* man, such that when Adam finally sees Eve he can exclaim, after due consideration, "Now this, at last—bones from my bones, flesh from my flesh!"[4]

Other ancient rabbinical comments also recall the duplicity of the first feminine image: another version, similar in content,[5] recounts that Lilith asked Adam to invert the sex position and that, faced with his refusal to lie beneath her, she went away forever.

In both cases the man's fear seems to be prey to an overwhelming energy: the saliva and the blood, archetypal images of the

---

1. In the Bible there is no trace of Lilith, but she is spoken of in great detail in ancient comments which refer to biblical episodes regarding her. See also Robert Graves and Raphael Patai: *Hebrew Myths: The Book of Genesis* (New York: Doubleday, 1989).
2. The italics are mine. See footnote 4.
3. T. Federici, Commento alla Genesi di Beresit Rabba
(Milan: Utet, 1978), p. 142. Translation mine. Tr.
4. Genesis 2:22-25. The New English Bible (New York: Cambridge University Press, 1971).
5. Robert Graves and Raphael Patai, *Hebrew Myths: The Book of Genesis*.

libido, are at the origin of the repulsion since the libido is not
shared, or at least not with the same intensity.

On the other hand, to accept lying beneath the body of a
woman, it is necessary to not be afraid of it, and thus to be able to
allow it: yet again it is fear which generates scorn for the feminine
principle and lets sexist pride loose, and not only regarding sexuality.

Lilith goes away toward the Red Sea, whose waters, according
to Jewish tradition, attract demons, serpents, and evil spirits;
repressed into the *shadow,* she has become a creature of the shadows, but, as I said above, Adam was afraid of her *before* and not
after; on the contrary, it was precisely the terror of man that sent
female instinct into the shadow.

And I am convinced that regarding this last problem the whole
of patriarchal civilization, starting with psychoanalysis, must examine its conscience very seriously, not only to end a tragedy which has
lasted for thousands of years, but also to work out the guilt feeling,
still unconscious, for having so seriously injured and obscured *half
of the sky.*

The God of the Jews reprimands Lilith for her desire for the
man,[6] but he does not reprimand Adam respecting feminine
instinct, and Lilith stays where she is. Coupling with demons on the
shore of the Red Sea, the first woman bears 100 devils per day,
which Javeh kills every time; but she herself is pitiless toward her
own children, and at night she stalks the earth strangling babies in
their cribs and invading masculine dreams, firing up men's desire
and enticing them into mortal embraces.

Sexual instinct, precisely because it has been repressed, has
fallen into the shadow where its energy, with equal intensity,
changes signs and becomes destructive; maternal instinct invariably

6. Robert Graves and Raphael Patai: *Hebrew Myths: The Book of Genesis.*

follows the same destiny and transforms itself into the death drive. Since then, on an individual level, Lilith has lived in the shadow of power, and in aversion to the masculine world which poisons many women's lives. On a collective level, she can be found in phenomena like witchcraft, secret rituals, and the Sabbat, which, in different forms, endemically express in feminine culture of the West.

The psychic constellation is, from this point of view, very different in the East, and in particular in India, where there have never been witches because feminine instinct, in its double form, has always been an object of respect. In the *Niruttara Tantra*, for example, it is written:

> When Kali nirguna [attributeless Kali] becomes saguna [manifest], she is engaged in viparîta-rati [sexual union with the female partner in the superior position] while Siva is the passive one. It is she who has brought the universe into existence . . . If Siva is united with Sakti he is able to exert his powers as a lord; if not, the go is not able to stir.[7]

What was not possible for Lilith was possible for Kali, because the fear and the attraction the Indian goddess inspires become objects of conscious reflection through a series of rites, a few of which provide for the contemplation of a nude woman. The value of this ancient cult has been commented on by Mircea Eliade:

> Every naked woman incarnates *prakriti* [an emanation of Kali, ed.] Hence she is to be looked upon with the same adoration and the same detachment that one exercises in pondering the unfathomable secret of nature, its limitless capacitiy to create. The ritual nudity of the

7. Ajit Mookerjee, *Kali: The Feminine Force* (Rochester, VT: Inner Traditions/ Destiny Books, 1988), p. 36.

yogini has an intrinsic mystical value: if, in the presence
of the naked woman, one does not in one's inmost being
feel the same terrifying emotion that one feels before the
revelation of the cosmic mystery, there is no rite, there is
only a secular act, with all the familiar consequences.[8]

This same nude woman, driven away from our dominant culture by
the stigmata of sin, reemerges again after a long time from the collective repression and appears in dreams asking for citizenship. But
how many are willing to give status and dignity to this inevitably
wild and embittered energy? How many recognize the pain that
inhabits the shadow and the promise of redemption that it hides?

Lilith seems to be an evil witch, like a fury, like something
destructive and overbearing, and she is surrounded by such pain, it
is true, but Lilith has also endured a few thousand years of isolation. Adam and Javeh have been her prison keepers; for thousands
of years women have been frigid or guilty of their desire; they have
been subdued, passive, inert, and consequently also spiteful, shifty,
and meddlesome, but always at men's heels, in their shadow. Who
can indemnify the inconsistency of identity, the prohibition of personal affirmation, the torment of a missing, or an unhappy or a
guilty sexuality, and the awful and so unnatural grip of the *natural
role?* Who can compensate for that infinite suffering? One at least
must have the patience to endure excesses, violence, and the dangers
which the liberation of feminine instinct requires in the course of the
analytical process. A psychic content that appears from the shadow—as it is noted—is always encumbered with negative energy
which accumulates in the unconscious, and this happens even more
when what has been repressed—for such a long time and on a collective level—is a psychic complex among the most inconstrictable.

8. Ajit Mookerjee, *Kali: The Feminine Force*, p. 80.

But one works on the shadow and, if one works on it, with time it transforms. Too often, instead, we see reactions of panic and flight before Lilith who returns from the sea: sometimes analysts themselves carry forward with diligence the work begun by Adam and his God. Lilith causes horror—furious and desirous, desperate and excessive. Women in analysis who bring murderous images cause horror; some want to sleep with everybody, or never want to fall in love again with anybody, who make light of the desperation of a man, and thus in a great hurry tries to bridle Lilith in the snare of the moral code or in the wrinkles of an adaptive process. I believe instead, because I verify it, that, if we are able to wait beyond the blood-thirsty witch, the great pain which generated her appears, and the witch can be received, and finally feel *inside* rather than *outside* the game. But only when this pain has been expressed, accepted, and shared can the energy of death transform itself into life energy, at least most of the time and in the majority of cases.

A young woman received a very mental upbringing which, together with the collective repression of the feminine instinct, had made her disorganized and insecure in her sex life. One day she told this dream to her analyst:

THE BLOOD WOMAN: *I go to the butcher's and, when I am in front of him, I lift up my shirt, remaining completely nude from the waist up. I ask him to touch my shoulders, my back, and my breasts with his hands dirty with blood, so that I am smeared all over.*

In this dream, so archaic and contemporary at the same time, the only man remaining who is not afraid of blood is the butcher, and thus one goes to him; the request is first of all to be touched by his hands in a high tension erotic contact, and then to be covered with blood. The desire, still unconscious, of the dreamer is to let herself go with the energy of the libido, which the blood symbolizes, under the hands of a man who is not afraid of it, but on the contrary helps her rekindle the Lilith in her, for the moment only from the waist up. The analyst is naturally also the butcher, the man who deals in blood and who restores it to her, who touches and reawakens her, activating a transference which compensates for a rigid and blocked father. In this way the image of Lilith re-forms which, with time and patience, can be integrated by the ego, transforming that fragile and cerebral girl into a warm and strong woman.

Men also dream about Lilith, for example, in the image of a toothed vagina, or a spider web, or a cave from which one is not able to exit; she also appears as the woman who does what she pleases with a man, thanks to the power of her seduction and the strength of her desire. And, often, men are afraid and they run away, but in life I believe that a man truly becomes a man only when he has succeeded in truly dealing with the instinct of a woman. A man brought me this dream one day:

THE MAN AND THE DANCER: *I am with a friend at the theater. On the stage a young woman appears who seems to be my analyst as I imagine her when she was younger. She performs a ritual dance, alone, and her movements are very sensual. She comes down from the stage and approaches us; she stops in front of my friend; she leans against his body and has him penetrate her. She moves in such an exciting way, that he quickly has an orgasm. Then the woman turns to me with an inviting smile and I say to her: "I don't like things done in this manner."*

Which transference is this dream talking about? Which energy reawakens the desire and the fear of that man? The woman, while she moves on the stage in a performance, belongs to no one and everyone, and one watches her with pleasure, but when she comes down from the stage, the game becomes dangerous, because the woman becomes the mistress of the man's orgasm and so he tells her: "I don't like things done in this manner." In other words, it is the ancient fear of Adam that appears again to reject Lilith, to nail her to her place, and, not different from the first man, that patient of mine who was afraid of being overwhelmed by an instinctual feminine energy which he projected onto the analyst. He was so afraid that he imagined that the sexual encounter burned out very quickly and was directly with another person. On the other hand, luckily, the fear in that case was not able to neutralize the desire, and the dancer was dreamed to be young and beautiful. Thus the fear and desire to yield to feminine instinct was the meaning of the transference.

The panic which blocks men in front of feminine instinct is one of the possible causes for pathologies like premature ejaculation, impotence, and sexual violence. In the case of premature ejaculation or erection problems, the symptomatic answer is depressive, for the man is not able to withstand the tension and thus collapses. In the case of violence, though, the symptomatic response is aggressive and serves to inhibit and unpotentiate feminine desire: terror returns the woman to her place, beneath the man. These pathologies naturally can have diverse and complex origins. Here I limit myself to observe an aspect which they have in common, an aspect which perhaps can contribute to explaining their concomitant increase in the last twenty years, just when Lilith has reemerged from the darkness with the women's liberation movement.

In the Bible the second woman is Eve, who is born from the body of the man, like Athena; it seems that patriarchal mythology felt the need to have woman be born from man, at least once, so that he could consider her a daughter and thus subordinate in some way. So here is Eve: she is not covered in saliva and blood, she does not demand equality, and does not inspire so much fear. Yet the serpent—the devil—slithers behind her and so in some way is a fragment of Lilith, the chthonic energy which gives life if accepted and brings death if denied. Thus not even Eve is *innocent* in the end, and besides, without that energy, stronger than repression, masculine culture would not have been able to imagine the *felix culpa* which gave origin to the history of humanity.

In Greek-Mycinean culture, another very different root of Mediterranean civilization, the attitude toward feminine instinct was profoundly different: the Greeks too were afraid of it, but as one fears something that has been willed by a God, and that human knowledge does not have the right to annihilate.

Aphrodite, the archetype of sexual desire, was the most powerful among the goddesses and the most beautiful, propitious to men and fatal to women who realize where desire can push them to go. Behind the luminous face of Aphrodite hides the dark images of the shadow—the object of fear and veneration—like Hecate, for example, or Pandora, the former more similar to Lilith and the latter to Eve.

Hecate was a chthonic and lunar goddess, pre-Olympian, the heritage of the original matriarchal culture; she was so important that Zeus recognized her right to take part in the decisions that regarded the earth, the sky, and the sea. Her image was always disquieting: an animal-like head was supported by a caudate body, and her lower extremities were supplied with terrible claws. Sometimes she took on the form of a dog or a wolf, and abandoned herself to primordial embraces from which monstrous creatures were born. At night she roamed the earth, accompanied by the barking of dogs and the shadows of the dead, disseminating panic and death. Exactly the opposite to Aphrodite, Hecate was hostile to men and sympathetic to women who performed magic rites and occult practices in her name on the margin of the official religion. Like Lilith, Hecate is the power of feminine instinct in the shadow, but her name has not been erased from sacred texts, and in the cities and villages of ancient Greece, her three-headed image was found in front of the doors of houses and at crossroads where three roads met: she was, after all, a goddess, and as such, a cult object.

Pandora, instead, is a woman, the first feminine creature in Greek cosmogony, and she is a very beautiful creature, the perfidious gift that Zeus thought up to punish a humanity up until then exclusively masculine. Hephestus molded her, the winds breathed life into her, and the goddesses of Olympus covered her in perfumed veils. She was almost more a goddess than a woman, perhaps she was a transitional creature between the two layers, for she was the archetypical image of feminine seduction. Like Eve, Pandora was made after man and for man, but, like Eve, she breaks the rules and becomes a protagonist because she is the unknowing keeper of the box which contains all evil and, disobeying, she opens it. So humanity, which until that moment experienced only good things, and thus did not know it, experiences things and the shadow of things, and in this manner is exposed to knowledge and morals. The sexual metaphor of this myth is too evident to require a symbolic translation.

It is not difficult to recognize in Pandora an extraordinary analogy to Eve: both are given to man, both are tempted and transgress, both give origin to the knowledge of good and evil and this to the life of the spirit; both finally, conquered by the same desire that the box and the serpent represent, go beyond the life of instinct toward the painful complexity of the human condition. But the two characters are different on one point: Pandora is not punished, nor does she feel shame, nor is she chased away because, as everything, it was willed by a far away Fate, above humanity and above the gods, and which must be accepted by both.

In psychoanalysis it is a widely held opinion, and I have already made references in this chapter, that men have felt a danger in the development of the knowledge of female sexuality and the power of its seduction, as if desire and pleasure could reabsorb masculine humanity in the shadows of the maternal unconscious.[9] On the other hand, we cannot ignore how, in both Jewish and Greek myth, the transgressive drive that starts humanity going toward knowledge and history comes from feminine instinct.

And so: what can this mean? Why should men have ever felt the evolution of knowledge threatened by an energy which set itself up as responsible for the start of the process? Perhaps it is true that the female libido excites men to the point of risking swallowing them into the darkness of regression, but perhaps the opposite is also true: desire lights up a personality and pushes it to overcome limits and boundaries, to risk, and to challenge divinity; but all this is nothing more than the premise of every new piece of knowledge. And so one could conclude from this that knowledge does not have its origin in thought, but in instinct, since it seems to be, first of all,

---

9. Regarding this, Erich Neumann's position is particularly univocal as he wrote: "The terrible mother, the all-inclusive symbol of this devouring aspect of the unconscious, is therefore the Great Mother of all monsters. All dangerous affects and impulses, all the evils which come up from the unconscious and overwhelm the ego with their dynamism, are her progeny. This is precisely what is meant when Goya uses, as a motto for his *Caprichos*, 'the dream of reason breeds monsters,' or when, in Greek mythology, Hecate, the primeval and all-powerful goddess, appears as the mother of the man-eating Empusae and of the lamias who devour the flesh of boys. She is the archenemy of the hero whom, as horsemen or knight, tames the horse of unconscious instinct, or, as Michael, destroys the dragon. He is the bringer of light, form, and order out of the monstrous pullulating chaos of Mother nature." *The Origins & History of Consciousness*, R. F. Hull, trans. Bollingen Series, Vol. 42 (Princeton: Princeton University Press, 1958), p. 162.

an object of a drive which, only after a certain point, becomes conscious of itself.

This form of energy seems to be particularly active in the female gender: the blood and saliva that cover Lilith also describe a particular libido charge which lets desire go toward transgression, and, thus, toward knowledge. Perhaps this is the force which has always scared men, not only and not so much for its regressive temptations, as for the opposite, for its transgressive potentials: the knowledge becomes mental, but its origin is in the drive to go into the forbidden space, to eat that apple or to open that box. It is possible that knowledge, and thus consciousness, had their beginnings, as myths remind us, in a transgressive and brazen curiosity, in the force of a desire which surpassed fear. If this is so, then at the origin of human consciousness there is ecstatic knowledge and awareness of the self, of life and death, of the infinite that sexual abandonment allows a glimpse of.

From this point of view the importance of orgiastic and blood cults from antiquity should be reconsidered. For example, the Dionysian rites, the Eleusinian mysteries, the bull sacrifices, and the cult of Isis are attributed exclusively with the value of a symbolic representation of the principle of natural fertility and the creative force of blood, based on a cycle of eternal return and regeneration. But this meaning subtends another one more hidden and more profound. The abandonment to ecstatic imagination and to the most intense and extreme physical sensations includes the possibility of experiencing something new which then allows for the posssibility of thought about that experience.

We still see today, in ancient images, the priestesses of Dionysis, when they run, with the head tilted back, in total abandon, crowned with laurel and a branch of thyrsus in their hands. The Maenads, as they were called ("the mad women")—during the nocturnal rituals in honor of the god—gave themselves over to the violence of their desire, and, in this state of frenetic possession, did not recognize anyone or anything. But exactly because of this they engaged contact with a knowledge which at the beginning is always secret. Were not these women the ancestors of witches? And do they not resemble Lilith as well? And was not Dionysis a god before he became a devil? This archetypical context in the Greek world was an object of fear, but also of respect, and because of that, it became ritualized. The Greeks tried to contain the risks within the boundaries of a cult, and placed it at the feet of a god, since surely a god must have wanted it.

Moreover, in India where blood rites still survive, the faithful ascribe a sacred area of spirituality and knowledge to the vagina of the goddess, where subtle forces act; in traditional iconography the goddess Sakti is often depicted sitting, with her legs spread and her vagina exposed to the cult, or else standing, while the worshippers, underneath the arch formed by her two spread legs, drink in the *sublime essence*. In these cult forms the vagina becomes the symbolic place for an instinctuality which, when fulfilled, produces regeneration and thus knowledge. Ajit Mookerjee writes:

> In Saktism the menstrual taboo is broken down and the menstrual fluid is regarded as sacred and becomes an object of veneration. . . . In the *chakra-pūjā* (group ritual worship) of "left-hand" tantrikas menstrual fluid may be taken as a ritual drink along with wine, and a speical homage is paid to the yoni, touching it with one's lips and anointing it with sandalwood paste, as the participant offers libation from a yoni-shaped ritual vessel. A menstruating woman is placed in a special category during ritual practice. Her energy at this time is said to be

different in quality, and the rhythm that occurs in her body appears to be related in a mysterious way to the processes of nature. At menstruation, when the body passes its blood-food, a woman often feels an ingathering of her energy and feelings to a deeper center below the threshold of consciousness.[10]

But if it was just a question of celebrating natural fertility and the lunar cycle which governs it, I do not believe that these cults would have passed through centuries and millennia, surpassing the Middle Ages and coming down to our day in the East. Nor could one truly understand why the theme of blood is so frequent in the dreams of women in relation to the theme of knowledge. It seems that physical regeneration subtends a deeper and more hidden meaning: sexual libido, blood, and genital organs seem, already in instinct, to come before the mediation of thought, meaning also something else.

Jung wrote that, in the absence of ulterior scientific information, it was necessary to acknowledge that instinct had the capacity to produce symbols. And instinct, in fact, already seems to charge its own manifestations with symbolic meaning and value, and thus knowledge.

The cult of the goddess Sakti, as in antique European rites, and not differently from the dreams of our time, ascribes the light of profound knowledge perceived in an analogical and symbolic way through the truth of matter to the sphere of instinct.

The successive repression of feminine sexuality in the West, and thus its fall into the shadow, has not erased the existence of dri-

---

10. Ajit Mookerjee, *Kali: The Feminine Force*, p. 32–33. Also see Ann Belford Ulanov, *The Feminine in Jungian Psychology and in Christian Theology*, cited in Mookerjee's book.

ves, but it has bound them to guilt, rendering them perverse or repressed. Repression induces frigidity or the absence of desire, perversion moves the libido from its natural direction; in both cases I have always had to verify how unfathomable the depth of the offense is.

Frigidity and the absence of desire—when they depend on the repression of instinct—are part of an hysterical symptom and mark the psychic impossibility of withstanding sexual tension to the end. Thus the necessity to break the circuit of the libido, isolating the brain which constitutes the switchboard. So when desire and pleasure reach an imaginary warning limit, beyond which guilt lies in wait along with the unbearable fear of losing control, an automatic lifesaver goes off and pleasure is blocked, neutralizing the underlying pain as well. In certain cases, psychosomatic symptoms appear which are able to inhibit the sexual relationship: cysts, vaginitis, allergic itches, and the absence of secretions all undertake to impede an impossible game. Over time I have verified how, among the different forms of feminine frigidity, the type described above is particularly tenacious, as if for too long it has been sunk in a guilt feeling rooted in the collective unconscious, and for which, at this point, individual consciousness has lost the trace.

The perversion of the repressed instinct shifts the *libido* from its natural direction, toward the pleasure of overbearing and meddling, toward the anxiety of social conquest, toward an activity always more convulsive and compulsory, or finally toward the extremely insidious identification of sexuality with love. This is when the devil appears in dreams—the poisonous spider, the toothed vagina which attracts in order to castrate, the cave full of mice and beetles—images which, in feminine dreams, denounce the anxiety for power which compensates the desperation of a lost instinct.

Many women today are meddlesome, poisonous, and violent because they have forgotten their instinct: they are the faded descendants, the lost daughters of Aphrodite; but on the other hand, when the goddess of love smiles again in a woman, behind her Hecate appears, and this scares many, not infrequently even analysts.

Sometimes culture acts to compensate. Once a patient of mine dreamed that she woke up from something that bothered her and stung her, and she realized she had a big and rigid form between her legs. In the actual social context, more often than one might expect, culture acts as a chastity belt which a woman imposes on herself to protect herself from a guilty and doomed instinct.

The last and perhaps the most subtle form of perversion is the one which solders love and sexuality in an indissoluble bond, as if desire and pleasure could obtain social dignity, and thus be disconnected from guilt feelings, only in the presence of an *elevated* feeling. This mutilating and artificial connection forces many women, even now, to persuade themselves that they are in love every time that they feel like making love, contrary to men who often believe they only want to make love, even when they are in love! "I'm not interested in sex without love," "I'm not able to make love if I'm not in love," "Sexuality just for itself is squalid." These are the phrases that I still hear repeated daily in my office by women of different ages, like the echo of a thousand years' oppression.

It was not always like this: in the Greek and pre-Greek cultures of the Mediterranean *sacred prostitution* was a rite which girls underwent before marriage. For a brief period they became sacred prostitutes, and in the temple of the goddess they coupled with strangers. They did not know these men and would never see them again. Their relationship was at the same time mercenary and disinterested—mercenary because the men gave an offering to the temple in exchange for the meeting, disinterested because nothing but instinct united two human beings for a moment. They shared an initiative experience which was at the same time a religious rite. The girls approached sexuality acknowledging instinct; they acknowledged it as a sacred value for itself, outside the complicated game of the love relationship and eventual marriage.

This ancient custom, which returns in the dreams of women, seems to be a moving testimony of the spiritual value that our progenitors attributed to feminine instinct, in a rite that was simultaneously both exorcism and sacrifice.

In this way, when the image of a sacred prostitute appears in the dream of a woman, leaving her disconcerted and without either possible references or associations, I have the impression that the unconscious is trying to correct a sexophobic education by recalling to the surface from great depths the image of an instinctual contact—reality in the far past and today translated into a symbol by the unconscious—outside of any other kind of relationship. The following are a few examples of this type of feminine dream.

THE WOMAN AND THE FIRST THING TO DO: *There is a man with whom I know I must make love: with him I must lose my virginity. I know that this is something I must do "first." My boyfriend is waiting in the other room and he knows what is happening, perhaps he can even see me because the door is open. I and the unknown man lie down on the floor, in the space between the double bed and the wall. He is tall, robust, with long soft hair, fine and blond. He is lying on the floor and I am on top of him. Then I get up and I sit on the edge of the bed to put on my panties: everything has already been done.*

THE STRANGE PROSTITUTE: *I am in a place outdoors, surrounded by very ancient walls, perhaps excavations from an archaeological dig; I am with my companion. As if in a film, I see some men approach a very young girl and I know they are going to make love to her, one after the other, as if she were a prostitute, even if she is not a prostitute. She won't receive money for this, but no scorn either. At this point I realize that I am that woman and I want to take her away from there, from that violence by unknown men. But then I realize that there is a desire in her, I see it from how she smiles and from how she moves her body, inviting a man. At this point I wait for what must happen to happen.*

WHAT HAD TO HAPPEN: *I am making love with a man that I don't know and who, afterward, will leave me forever. Nonetheless, this situation seems natural to me, as it also seems natural that it is happening in my house, in my bedroom. I feel a great transport for this man whose features are already forgotten. I know that my husband will not be jealous, but rather that he will be happy for this relation, because it is not a question of betrayal, but something that had to happen.*

In all three of these dreams, the man is always unknown, the boyfriend and the husband are not jealous, and the sexual relationship is just that, devoid of any sort of future. It is this last fact, in particular, which moves the interpretation away from being a figure of the animus. That man is going to leave, after, and the relationship has meaning exactly because he is going away; thus he will not be integrated into the personality, he will remain an unknown, and he only represents the occasion to discover something: one's own *virginity* and the autonomy of desire.

One could, however, object that the appearance of a lover, unknown and destined to disappear, could describe the conflictual context of the dreamer before her unknown animus, more than the condition of being a sacred prostitute. In a few cases this is an acceptable objection, but there are dreams—like the ones above—where the context is devoid of an objective whatsoever, and also any feelings, the ritualized form, the faded masculine image, and the force of a desire just for itself orient the interpretation of the dream toward the affirmation of contact between the woman and her instinct, in full autonomy from the whole of the relations linked to feeling and thought.

Another subject which seems of great importance is the inextricable, underground connection between the sexual instinct and the maternal instinct, which seem to me like the intertwining of two tree trunks which sink into common roots. In the absence of neurotic blocks, which generate anomalies in interdependence, the desire to open oneself and be filled then becomes the desire to swell to give life: these two drives express themselves autonomously, certainly, but they are not artificially separable; in other words, sexual instinct and maternal instinct seem disconnected from one another in their manifestations, but united by an unconscious interdependence. In the absence of psychic pathologies linked to instinct, we can verify systematically how the more sexually active a woman is, the more maternal she is. If this direct proportion is not so frequent, and if many problems with one or the other, or both, parts of feminine instinct are the object of our daily work, this is due to a culture that, intervening on the common roots of the instinctual complex and amputating one to enhance the other, has made both gravely ill. One has ended up in the shadow and the other has become inflated.

The elephantiasis of the *maternal sense* which oppresses Western society, in particular in the Mediterranean basin, is a consequence of that schism. The entire instinctual complex has been shifted onto maternity, forcing sexual identity to go in only one direction. And as far as feminine psychology is concerned, this perversion is at the origin of at least three widely diffused phenomena.

The first has to do with the hostility toward men that many women experience as compensation for an unconscious sexuality. It is a question of a prejudiced hostility, aprioristic, overtly aggressive, and spiteful today. Years ago it was more underhanded and indirect, but just as tenacious.

The second phenomenon is the need to transfer a sexual libido by then submerged onto sons. Naturally, here I am not referring to the Oedipal situation which follows its own autonomous path in the evolution of the personality; I am referring to a so-called optional attitude—on the mother's part—which creates a dependency relationship with the son, with strong neurotic tones. The son becomes, in the eyes of these women, the man that they could not really love, and, at the same time, also the masculine energy that it was not possible to express themselves. Becoming the object of a possessive feeling and full of expectations, the son tends to adapt himself and to feel that the anxiety, the over-protectiveness and the satisfaction are expressions of love. For these women, the male that they love must be the son, according to the psychological scheme of the Great Mother, because he *belongs* to the mother, he is smaller than her and must remain so. These women are deeply convinced that there is a substantial inferiority in the male gender, and they place themselves as protective dominators in a relationship scheme that often assumes the form mother/son even when the other person is their companion.

The third phenomenon, finally, which originates from the repression of sexuality, is the concentration of negative maternal energy. I recalled earlier the desperate revenge of Lilith who kills her own and others' children, and who poisons the dreams of men with desire. A need for power derives from the forced renunciation and the mother of life becomes the mother of death. This compensatory tension expresses itself, for example, in the anxiety to keep daily and family reality under one's own incessant control, in a perennially anxious attitude, in emotional blackmail for sacrificial love, in the insidious overbearing of small daily gestures, in the discounting of autonomous initiatives of the husband and children and in a need to seduce that is never innocent.

The personalities afflicted with these neurotic behaviors are defined as *phallic* by some, and I have never understood why, since they are that way exactly because they are devoid of penetrative energy. They are well-stocked, instead, with castrating intentions: it is the desire for castration, not for phallicization, that generates hatred and overbearingness. In fact, even the oneiric images which I mentioned earlier, in reference to the *shadow* of feminine instinct (the spider web, the toothed vagina, the insidious cave, and so on) are vaginal images, not phallic ones, charged with a vindictive and castrating tension purely feminine in character.

LET'S DISCUSS the masculine instinct now to see how it relates to the feminine. From time immemorial, and in the most different religions, the phallus, as the representation of the biological and psychic strength in the masculine instinct, has been considered a sacred image. It serves as a reminder that the desire to open, explore, and possess is an instinct, as it is an instinct to move toward the unknown, to go elsewhere to discover and conquer unknown territories.

As with the feminine instinctual complex, the masculine one as well, when tested against the facts, seems to go way beyond the sex drive and to contain *within itself* a large part of what Freud considered to be sublimation. In 1918 Jung wrote a few pages regarding this which are very interesting and in my opinion are still extra-ordinarily current.

> I am convinced that a truly scientific attitude in psychol-ogy must likewise lead to the conclusion tht the dynam-ic processes of the psyche cannot be reduced to this or that concrete instinct—we should merely find ourselves back at the stage of the phlogiston theory. We shall be obliged to take the instincts as constituent parts of the psyche, and then abstract our principle of explanation from their mutual relationship. I have therefore pointed out that we would do well to posit a hypothetical quan-tity, an "energy," as a psychological explanatory princi-ple, and to call it "libido" in the classical sense of the word, without harbouring any prejudice with regard to its substantiality. . . . [I]f we reject the exclusively sexual theory of the unconscious and put in its place an energic view of the psyche, we must say that the unconscious contains everything psychic that has not reached the threshold of consciousness, or whose energy-charge is not sufficient to maintain it in consciousness, or that will reach consciousness only in the future.[11]

In the course of time studies in different disciplines (ethnology, anthropology, psychoanalysis) have brought to light the complexity of the phallic instinct and the variety of directions that it can go in every time.

To explore or conquer an object or a territory, to build dens, to organize a group, are all behaviors traceable to the animal world

11. C. G. Jung, *The Collected Works*, Vol. 10, *Civilization in Transition*, R. F. C. Hull, trans. Gerhard Adler, et al, eds. Bollingen Series No. 20 (Princeton: Princeton University Press, 1970), § 6, 7, 8.

and which, with difficulty, seem referable exclusively to the survival instinct, or which, at the least, constitute a complication of it that connects to creative manifestation.

The pre-Judaic, Christian, and Eastern traditions intuited what psychoanalysis has discovered through the unconscious, and that is: the phallus and the vagina symbolically place humanity in relation to the creative energy, since it is through their union that human beings participate in a process of creation apparently without end. Such energy, perceived as unknowable and boundless, has always constituted a formidable link of transmission between human beings and the spirit.

But there is more: the sexual relationship is the experience that perhaps more than any other pushes beyond the boundaries of the Ego, opening the human being to the perception of infinity. Orgasm, madness, death, and a few moments of creative intensity constitute, in fact, the *climax* of an ecstatic condition. Because of this I believe that these border-situations are often found intertwined in the archetypes of instinct: in Lilith, for example, and in Hecate, and then in Dionysis, in Hermes and in Pan.

And, finally, arousal, orgasm, and fecundation are events partly or completely detached from the control of the conscious personality: in the past this relative autonomy provoked the respect of the mystery; today we know that sexuality, like the creative disposition, is unforeseeable and capricious because it is in contact with psychic layers that are very deep and completely unconscious, where fantasies, desires, experiences, and fears lie, and whose condensed form mysteriously emerges, reawakening the drive. It is possible to affirm that instinct places human beings in contact with the spirit, but also with the unconscious.

This relative autonomy of the phallic instinct—and also its possible symbolic manifestations—is the evidence that our culture is not able to accept. Dominated by a consumeristic and efficient attitude, Western society demands regularity and constant production even in sexual activity and in the creative dynamic.

Over the years many men have come to my office complaining about the caprices of orgasm, of erections, and even of desire. Numerous human beings have also confided the unforeseeable discontinuity of their creative tension. In both cases embarrassing *dèfaillances* and lost chances were reported, but above all I heard a lot of anxiety because the common conviction is that it is a personal problem, and not a normal or characteristic behavior of the instinctual dynamic. It is possible that this relative autonomy of instinct is recognized with difficulty at present because the ego, always more insecure in the present social context, expresses an undifferentiated anxiety for control over all the aspects of reality which surround it.

Different from the feminine sexual instinct, the phallic instinct has not suffered repression, but has been deprived of value and autonomy for a long time. In fact, in the West there is an important libertine tradition, a culture of conquest and pleasure where the woman is both prey and instrument every time, but this tradition is permeated with guilt feelings, and consequently it tends to transform itself from pleasure into compulsion, giving life to a behavior interwoven with self-punishing anguish: Don Juan, after all, could not have lived but here.

The separation of instinct from the awareness of its value and the moral discredit which derives from it are at the root of the *underground* character of everything that regards sex in the West. The awareness of the intrinsic value of instinct and its bond with the sacred was, instead, deeply rooted in pre-Christian cultures, and the analogies between that far off awareness and contemporary psychoanalytic studies are traceable when comparing the phallic images of those cultures and the forms of the unconscious in the dreams of our patients.

On the basis of my experience, I tend to consider that a significant part of masculine analysis (and, in regard to the animus, of feminine analysis, as well) is concentrated on allowing the lost value of the phallic instinct reappear, with all its energetic potential aimed toward pleasure, knowledge, and creation. In this way the phallic instinct loses its servant/master characteristics in the Ego to become an important, even if unpredictable, ally.

As far as I have been able to verify, instinct from early infancy unites men in a particular solidarity which is also, but not only, homosexual tension. The games between boys, for example, which examine the penis, are always secret games, but certainly not irrelevant in masculine formation. In analysis, this underground initiation always ends up returning to light with strong symbolic density. One day a little boy contemplated perplexedly his small erect penis, while those of his friends around him lay in repose; so a companion observed: "Yours has a bone." I believe that experiences of this type are more important and significant than they seem: they certainly have to do with pleasure and with the affirmation of male body identity, but also with a need to share a mystery in ritual games, to not feel alone in front of a worrisome fact: little boys know that *he* is the only visible part of the body which moves by itself, obeying commands not connected to the will.

This type of initiative brotherhood, which continues in different forms as adults as well, recalls the custom of the men of Ancient Greece who threw a stone when they passed a particular point at a crossroads; in this way a pile of stones formed, which every day grew larger and took on the form of a phallus. These piles of stones were called *erma,* and Hermes (etymologically, "the one of the pile of stones") is also a god of masculine instinct. The big stone phallus represented a divine image, and it epitomized the meaning of a common undertaking: the sexual and spiritual creativity of each man joined with that of every other, giving form and continuity to the biological and psychological history of male humanity.

Hermes, on the other hand, is the god who, more than any other, stresses the complexity of masculine instinct, and, as such, he appears in the dreams of men today. He seems to be the closest thing to the definition Jung gave for *maleness:* "Masculinity means knowing what one wants and doing what is necessary to achieve it."[12]

So let us see how the instinct of Hermes acts in this direction. As soon as he was born, the baby god opened a tortoise, emptied it and made a lyre with which he sung the praises of his parents: thus the instinct in man is to open in order to transform, to know in order to build, to submit, but also to make something beautiful and sweet, something which vibrates and excites.

A man, very much imprisoned in his mental system, brought me this dream one day:

THE TORTOISE MAN: *I am with my son [who was 1 at the time] and we see a tortoise on the ground. He picks it up, opens it, dividing it into two parts, and he shows it to me calmly saying: See daddy, inside there's poopoo, but you shouldn't be surprised or displeased because it's something absolutely natural.*

Matter is part of instinct and it is indispensable for him. That child, that new baby Hermes, reminded my patient of the humoral naturalness of drives, and encouraged him to accept it because, besides everything else, it is only the desire to open the tortoise, to look at

12. C. G. Jung, "Women in Europe," in *The Collected Works*, Vol. 10. § 260.

its contents, and to consider it natural, which then allows one to also play the lyre. By beginning to love Hermes in his child, my patient began to follow the path.

The second undertaking in Hermes' life, still in diapers, was the theft of Apollo's oxen because—as it has been sent down in the Homeric hymn—"he desired to eat meat." Here the instinct is to desire and to take, but also to steal in order to possess, and, naturally, to kill in order to eat. Cattle-stealing was one of the first forms of theft, because it was one of the first forms of possession: in this sense it has become *the theft* assuming an archetypical tonality. As E. Monick writes:

> The sexual importance of possession is analogically extended to property and wealth of all kinds, since, in Jung's "first step," earth and the earth's produce belong to the feminine realm. An antidote for castration on this level is ownership, a sense of substance which comes of possession.[13]

There are, in my opinion, two interesting details in the episode of the theft of the oxen, which involve the testing instinct. Hermes resists the temptation to keep them all for himself and sacrifices part of the animals to the gods, and later, before Zeus, he spontaneously restores part of the cattle. It seems a paradox: masculine instinct is to take, but within instinct mediation also takes place as a means of resolution. This is why the images of Hermes and the piles of stones are found at crossroads, in fields, and on roads as markers of limits between directions, territories, and properties. He, in fact, lives on the edge, and he represents it, because he acknowledges and respects it.

---

13. E. Monick, *Phallos: Sacred Image of the Masculine* (Toronto: Inner City Books, 1987), p. 80.

Hermes is sly, versatile, and even servile when he is in the shadow, and he knows how to adapt himself because it is instinct which finds a way, for example, to survive in prison, or on a deserted island, or in a multinational atmosphere, such as a large international business. But he is also elusive and wandering, because he loves unknown spaces and the mystery of night, where he goes to snoop and to deal; perhaps due to this herders and merchants felt particularly close to him, but so did prostitutes, outcasts, vulgar and low-life people, the *borderline* and the different-from-the-rest feel Hermes inside, since he reigns over the unexplainable, the dark drives, the base material, perversions—over the whole psychic *underground*—magmatic and unfathomable.

Since he knows the abyss, Hermes has winged feet and can be the messenger and mediator between heaven and hell, passing by the earth. It is exactly because of this that he can guide the dead to their eternal rest, because he testifies to the sacred value of instinct and confirms the desire for death which hides behind every desire for life.

In the character of Hermes it is possible to find confirmation for what I alluded to in the preceding pages, the relationship between instinct, the anima, and the unconscious, since in his complexity he already contains both the flesh and the spirit, both matter and energy.

A son of Hermes is born with a beard, horns, and hooves, and the god takes him in his arms and carries him to Olympus; at the gods' table the baby amuses the banqueters who call him Pan, that is *everything*, since as the Homeric hymn says, "he cheered the spirit of everyone." Wilder and more unrestrained than his father, Pan reigns over the borderline dividing human beings from animals. The *human beast* is a wild animal, sometimes noisy, other times solitary, who follows nymphs and rapes them, who masturbates spying on young girls, and who, at the mercy of the drive, is afraid of losing himself, and this fear sometimes becomes panic and sometimes madness. This psychic complex is at times repugnant, often amoral, always unreasonable, but it is part of nature. Sexual violence, war, terrorism, persecutions show to what extent the shadow of phallic instinct can extend; but there are also other situations where the dominion of this type of shadow over the conscience renders men headless: they are diffuse and socially approved behaviors like, for example, the concept of masculine superiority, or arrogance about who controls science or power.

Thus it is good that a man commits himself and his intelligence to keeping these moments of psychological priapism under control, but a man must remember, at the same time, that he is an animal, learning to recognize when and how to let it go. The Judeo-Christian religion has intervened on masculine instinct, separating physical drive from spiritual virility: hostility to matter, placed in rigid opposition to spirit, kills Pan, the small god-animal, and sends him to hell, where he becomes the devil—a pan/devil, precisely. A tradition, referred to by Plutarch,[14] recalls the news of Pan's disappearance, the only god in Ancient Greece for whom we have a death certificate; and a Christian legend places this event on the day of the crucifixion of Jesus. They send the spirit to heaven and the body to hell, the Church celebrates and concludes the discounting of instinct.

The *sexual liberation*, which in the West was one of the objectives of the protest movement of the 60s and 70s, but which was very rapidly hegemonized by the industrial culture, brought the physical body back to light, but more as an object to consume rather than the center of instinct, more as a legal subject than a legislator, so that the body today, in the majority of cases, continues to

14. Plutarch, *Morales,* C. W. King, trans. (London: George Bell & Sons, 1882), p. 93.

be the source of sin in the unconscious, while in conscious life it is loved as a *status symbol*. The "hedonistic-permissive" culture, superimposed over the sexophobic tradition, has produced a disconcerting result, because the body, which is both a cult object and an object of shame, continues to be a source of discomfort.

Sexual problems are always more frequent in our patients, but I have also had to verify how the instinctual desire to explore, know, venture, and risk in whatever direction has progressively become weaker. I believe that E. Monick is absolutely right when he writes:

> It will be many years before the phallos fully emerges from its catacomb entombment. It will be many years before the devil is seen as a psychological factor in each person—and, according to Jung, in the deity itself—rather than as specific to phallos, to sexuality, and the flesh.[15]

Besides, dreams are oriented in that direction, and I systematically verify how, in the presence of sexual pathologies, the oneiric images orient a man so he can become aware of the relationship that exists between his symptom and the repression of the *maleness,* the instinctual complex. Therapeutic intervention does not intervene on the symptom (besides, how does one intervene on a symptom?), but on the progressive recuperation of the entire instinctual complex, synthesizable perhaps, in light of the preceding pages, with the capacity to grab, explore, possess, destroy, and build both in the physical life and in that of energy and spirit.

For our second meeting, one man brought me the following dream. In our preliminary session I had not been able to understand his motivations.

---

15. E. Monick, *Phallus*, p. 42.

71

THE BARBER AND THE AIRPLANE: *I go to the barber's, but it is closed; I look for another, but it seems that there is not even one barber open in the whole city. The scene changes and I am in a plane; I am about to leave, the plane rolls down the runway, always getting faster, the motors turn faster, but the airplane doesn't lift off, and there's nothing to do about it. I wake up sweating and very agitated.*

In association, my patient said that the barber's seemed the only place when one does not see women, a place only for men. At this point I had the well-grounded suspicion that his unconscious had revealed to me what his conscious had refused to tell me the first time. The true motive that had pushed him to me, his impotence, was translated symbolically in the unsuccessful take off of the plane. But that image—and the underlying problem—follows a loss of contact with the masculine world, aimed at caring for the body, where one speaks about men's business—the barber shop. When one no longer finds a masculine point of reference, a place where beards and mustaches have value and meaning, then instinct may go and hide; if the *erma*, the social phallus at crossroads, is no longer constructed, then individual sexuality can become blocked and compulsive. If it is no longer possible to attribute sense and meaning to the character of masculine instinct which is, at the same time, wild and curious, ingenious and moody, then sexuality— which is part of it—no longer has meaning and value, because it seems somehow detached from its complex. It is probable that the psychological unease which derives from it is translated into a symptom.

In its sexual manifestation, the phallic instinct concerns—as is obvious—only men, but, in its symbolic form it concerns women as well, and constitutes a feature of the animus in the feminine psyche.

As far as my own experience is concerned, the phallic instinct is, in the majority of cases, the first part of the animus that appears in the feminine conscious. It is usually indicated by a contaminated shadow aggressiveness, which is subconsciously experienced as overbearing, intolerant, and envious. It has to do with drives which women begin to acknowledge as a painful conflict between their natural phallic instinctiveness and their oppressive upbringing. I remember, when I was a child (and this may be a collective memory), that I heard adults affirm that "little boys are nicer than little girls," because, while boys are impetuous and rough, they are spontaneous; while girls, apparently affable, reveal themselves to be meddlesome gossips. What more despairing charge could be made about the damage produced by a repression of natural aggressiveness?

When I was a journalist, I happened to take a survey of a sample of children in grade school in order to verify whether or not traditional sex roles were internalized in preschool life. One of the questions I had prepared was: "You are with your little brother or your (male) friend (little sister or female friend, if the subject was male) and there are only two pieces of a cake which you really like, but one is big and the other is small: who will eat the big one?"

It was the beginning of the 70s and there was not one boy who did not respond "Me" or one girl who did not respond "Him." The following question was "Why?" Here the boys' answers were clear: "Because I want it," "Because I like it," "Because if not, I'll beat her up," and so on. The responses of the girls were evasive, distracted, interrupted by giggles, and they expressed an underground unease, a feeling of guilt aimed toward themselves: "I don't know," "Nothing," "Because he got there first." Until the real answer came strong as a gunshot from a little girl from southern Italy who, looking at me with serious dark eyes, said: "Because he wants it *more*."

The behaviors that the repression of the phallic instinct generate in women's lives often contrast with the reason and mentality of the subject: many women, for example, are not paid adequately for their work, or they dare not speak in public, or they don't allow themselves to have ambitions, or they easily renounce affirming their point of view. In the majority of cases, the women detest this behavior and despite themselves, they feel constrained. When women begin to realize that they can *want* something and *get* it, or *affront* a problem, or *conquer* a position, and *grab* their cake, then it means that Hermes and Pan have awakened, and that *maleness*, about which Jung spoke, in its symbolic dimension, is finally constellated.

A young woman, who came to my office, was discovering how difficult it was for a woman in the university setting to have the floor in a meeting, to succeed in making herself heard, to speak loudly without being shrill, or make her position heard. Through university politics, which deeply interested her, she discovered that she did not have enough aggressive energy, and she was not able to express it, but at the same time she was terrified of losing her own femininity. In vain I urged her to reason about the absurdity of her fear (which is diffuse in the collective conscious and not only the feminine one) suggesting the hypothesis that she could become a more intense and vivacious woman if she learned to defend and conquer positions. One day she told me this dream.

THE SECRET IN THE CAVE: *I am walking in the mountains with a group of women friends; we want to reach the top where they told us there is a little church and, I hope, a restaurant as well. We get to the top and I am dead tired; I see only a cave, no church and no restaurant. I go into the cave alone and I see a trunk column of porphyry in the middle. I feel a strong and incomprehensible emotion, which is discovery, and at the same time, fear and joy and other things, too, and I feel like crying.*

That young woman and her friends wanted to find what hides at the summit. The arrival point of the trip is not the reassuring presence of a church, not the comfort of a restaurant, but the unexpected and numinous discovery of a strong and hard phallic energy, which we have never thought of as ours, which does exist and does belong to us, but it was closed in the darkness of the unconscious; from there comes the sense of responsibility in managing it, which generates fear, but also the awareness of a potential as yet unexpressed, which brings out joy and surprise, and finally the contact with an initial *coniunctio oppositorum* (the cave and the column) which moves intense and inexpressible emotions.

Another woman came to my office, a woman who was rigorous and masculine in thought, squared and reasonable, but very weak in instinctual manifestations, both masculine and feminine. After having remembered a serious traumatic experience that accompanied her throughout her childhood, one day this patient brought me this dream:

PAN'S MOTHER: *"I had had a baby boy and I was holding him in my arms; I felt great love for him already, and I was happy. I discovered however—or someone old me—that my baby's feet weren't normal, but they had a single nail; I knew, with time, that they would become goat's hooves.*

We can recognize the appearance of Pan in this dream, for the animal-like nature reemerges from the low depths in which her upbringing had confined him, where he had become only *shadow.* Desire, caprice, the vein of madness, and the sudden reawakening of

the senses could now reappear in the conscious, making that
woman more erotic, soft, more natural, but also more courageous.
A short while later, and all of a sudden, she decided to learn how to
ride a horse, a sport which had always fascinated and terrified her.
She felt that the horse, for her, was the animal, the instinctual force
that gallops, that can unseat consciousness, a huge beast, but one
also warm and tender, sensitive to command, only if one is able to
make it go. Between insecurity and fear that woman continued her
athletic apprenticeship first walking, then trotting, then galloping—
which was a conscious metaphor for her approach to instinct.

CHAPTER 4

The Shadow of Instinct in Analytic Psychology

The projection of the whole complex of instincts onto the feminine psyche is an unresolved question regarding instinctual dynamics. This distortion, which constitutes a hinge of patriarchal culture, has been transferred, in different forms, into the foundation of post-Jungian analytical psychology, even slowing down the development of theory and clinical practice.

In Western tradition, feminine sexuality is deformed into lust, and women are burdened with this dead weight; the masculine sexual instinct is, in turn, darkened by brutality, and this weight is also placed on women. Abandoning themselves to instinct, women surrender to their own intrinsic weakness, while men give in to the demonic temptation that women incarnate. In the traditional opinion of the church, and in the prevailing culture, sexual instinct is feminine, because nature is feminine and spirit is masculine. It is thought that men would be in constant spiritual mystical practice, if women did not drag them down to satisfy the senses.

An ancient rabbi once made a comment on Genesis: "The man obliges the woman not to go out, because every woman who goes

out falls in the end. This is the supremacy of man over woman."[1]
The ancient rabbis spoke clearly, but they did not say with whom
the woman falls when she goes out; presumably with a man, but
men do not fall, unless by chance they are overwhelmed. The fault,
as is noted, falls on Eve; in fact another rabbi remembered the following: "Why do women walk in front of the dead at funerals? He
answered: Since they brought death into the world, they precede the
coffin."[2] From the era of the ancient rabbis to Pope John Paul II,
masculine imagery, from this point of view, has remained substantially unaltered, and it makes its regular appearance in dreams and
in active imagination, even if there is no longer an analogous social
behavior which corresponds to it. Today women live, at least for-
mally, almost in equality with men, their anima and their spirituality are, at least on a conscious level, almost always beyond question,
and almost nobody thinks that women bring men to perdition,
stealing from them a precious destiny of mystical practice.

We need to understand how cultural values enter into conflict
with the imagery of the unconscious, where women remain torn
between the two archetypal images of virgin-mother and demon-
siren. It is worth going to the heart of the problem in search of possible causes for these values.

The first point regards—in my opinion—the masculine ego
and the persona. At a certain point in its development, patriarchal
culture most likely judged irreconcilable the unpredictable, disconcerting, and at times, violent, presence of the masculine sex drive
with the evolution of the persona. But since this energy persisted
with its uncivil manifestations, and it seemed impossible for men to

1. A. Ravenna and T. Federici, *Commento alla Genesi di Beresit Rabba* (Milan, Utet, 1978), p. 162. Translation mine. Tr.
2. A. Ravenna and T. Federici, *Commento alla Genesi di Beresit Rabba*, p. 16.

keep it under control, a scapegoat solution was adopted, which transferred the responsibility for masculine instinct to women.

This psychological process is traceable in the religious traditions of the Mediterranean. It is also evident in the records of the witch trials. In these texts, of great interest for psychoanalysis, is the projective attribution onto the accused of a violent and demonic orgiastic experience parallel to the masculine imagery of the accusers. In these trials the men—Dominican priests—in the majority of cases constructed the hypothesis of the crime, proposing and suggesting the erotic scenario that thus first of all was in their heads; and the twofold, unpleasant task to confirm that *reality* was up to the accused, accepting the projection, and then paying the price. In those days, the devil was, in masculine imagery and in the unconscious, the sexual shadow which was repressed and projected onto women. The devil arrives, but it is the woman who calls him.

A pale trace of this far-off past is still heard in rape trials around the world. As it is said, the devil arrives, but it is the woman who calls him: the violent shadow of masculine sexuality often induces the magistrates to feel that the victim is *a little* guilty because, if she has suffered violence, it is because deep down, in some way, she went looking for it. It is not uncommon for judge or jury to concede extenuating circumstances to the accused.

But there is another, more profound reason which has induced the collective masculine unconscious to get rid of the responsibility of its own sexual instinct. It derives from the fear that men have always felt for women, and from the most hidden origin of this fear. It is not only a question of the fear of feminine sexual energy, nor of the power to give life, and it is not even the fear of emotional dependence and its castrating consequences. It is something different; it is a fear which has its origin in an intolerable diversity, a diversity which men bear with difficulty because they, too, are born from a woman, and they have been one with her body and psyche. For the male, the separation from the mother is both a detachment, and an acknowledgment of an irreversible diversity, for where there was once total union is an eventual separation, which may be subconsciously experienced as a betrayal, and this is the root of great pain. Fear then serves to deter the risk that a similar relationship could reproduce itself and once again end in pain, and, as a consequence, every time love and desire for a woman push a man back on the trail of another love, another desire, and another detachment.

Today, when a man fears a woman, the woman reawakens in the man an unconscious resentment which can be, in extreme cases, the source of violence against women in general. For men, it may be necessary to separate the mother from the woman, and the woman becomes the one who wants to abandon the man because he wanted to (or wants to) lose himself in the mother. Since the mother induced the first trauma of separation, because she is a woman and therefore different, all women who afterward inspire love also reawaken that fear, because they recreate, in the mind of the man, that first physical fusion and also that first abandonment.

Because of this I believe that, while the fear a woman experiences in meeting a man is a fear of the unknown, but the fear of a man toward a woman is, above all, the anguish of loss.

These seem to me to be the principal motives which induce the masculine psyche, beyond any reasonableness, to project the phallic instinct and its shadow onto the feminine personality. The first fear relates to the ego and *persona,* and it is more controllable by the collective conscious; the second takes root in the unconscious, from where it exercises a large and uncontested power that affects the life of women. This unconscious fear is also profoundly damaging to the masculine personality, for the man, precisely because he is unaware, risks remaining partially a prisoner to this anguish and pain all of his life.

And it is precisely the phallic instinct which, paradoxically, in this case can be the liberator: if a man desires, seduces, conquers, possesses and *makes a woman his* (even if it is not the same woman actually responsible for that long past betrayal) the accounts, as much as is possible in human affairs, equal out. In order for this to happen, it is necessary for a man to feel allied with his instinct. When the value and meaning of masculine sexuality are located in the shadow, and when this shadow is projected onto a woman, a man feels powerless because he cannot take back what long before seemed to him the same as him, and to which he belonged completely. It is at that point that the anguish of castration rises, due to a sense of impotence before the abyss subconsciously experienced in the separation from the mother.

If one is not able to conquer and possess the object of fear, then one must demoralize it; and modern men are still subscribing to the devaluing of the phallic instinct performed by our Judeo-Christian culture. Because of this, men still need to demoralize women, in order to separate her symbolically from the mother. This—it seems to me—is the ultimate meaning of the projection of guilt on women which has so profoundly mutilated both the masculine and feminine identities for so long.

Now, however, it seems that psychoanalysis has also followed the trail of the Judeo-Christian tradition as far as handling the thorny problem of the relationship between nature and culture within the psyche. In particular, in the theory and practice of analytical psychology, the masculine projection described earlier still exists, even if psychoanalysis has liberated instinct from sin and restored to it the archetypal complexity which is its own particular characteristic.

In the majority of cases, in fact, as I wrote in the first pages of this book, analytical psychology inscribes the anima of a man in the sphere of instinct and natural sentiment, never of thought. Feminine thought is not considered, it remains unconscious in men, making its appearance only in dreams or in occasional irruptions in masculine life. In the same way analytic psychology tends to place the animus within the limits of rational thought, a logical-organizational capacity, calling it one of spiritual tension. Very rarely have I heard the *animus* spoken about as a phallic instinct, or as a masculine feeling that resides in the unconscious of a woman.

In this way, however, neither the autonomy of masculine instinct (which results as mother dependent), nor feminine thought (which remains linked to the father) exist. On the basis of this artificial and unprovable separation of the two archetypes, the routine, prevalent in the last two generations with psychologists has been constructed and has found its theoretical placement in the philosophy of Erich Neumann. In *The Origins and History of Consciousness* Neumann writes, for example:

> Hippolytus himself is at a stage of critical resistance to the Great Mother, already conscious of himself as a young man struggling for autonomy and independence. This is evident from his repudiation of the Great Mother's advances and of her phallic orgiastic sexuality. His "chastity," however, means far more than a rejection of sex; it signifies the coming to consciousness of the "higher" masculinity as opposed to the "lower" phallic variety. On the subjective level, it is the conscious realization of the "solar" masculinity which Bachofen con-

trasts with "chthonic" masculinity. This higher masculinity is correlated with light, the sun, the eye, and
consciousness.[3]

And successively:

> Mythologically the phallic-chthonic deities are compan-
> ions of the Great Mother, not representatives of the
> specifically masculine. Psychologically this means that
> phallic masculinity is still conditioned by the body and
> thus is under the rule of the Great Mother, whose instru-
> ment it remains.[4]

In these lines, and in the context of the entire work, Neumann
affirms how the separation from the mother necessarily involves the
detachment from the world of drives, because the mother is seen as
the only repository of the dark and heavy world of matter, of the
body, and thus of the instincts and their biological and psychic
movements. To write that "phallic virility is still conditioned by the
body and thus subject to the domination of the Great Mother"
means to affirm that the male does not have, from a psychic point
of view, an autonomous body and his own center of instincts and
that, in order to liberate himself from the mother, he must liberate
himself of his own body or, better yet, he must acknowledge that he
does not have one; only in this way can he direct, undisturbed, his
superior virility toward the luminous goal of consciousness. It is in
this theoretical context, and in its taking root in upbringing and in

---

3. Erich Neumann, *The Origins & History of Consciousness*, R. F. Hull, trans.
Bollingen Series No. 42 (Princeton: Princeton University Press, 1954), p. 92.
4. Erich Neumann, *The Origins & History of Consciousness*, p. 309.

the collective conscious, that the drama of a symbolic emasculation has its origins, in my opinion.

This, in fact, is what happens in the psyche when a man is not able to feel the value and the knowable potential of his instinct and desire, and thus is not capable of entering into deep contact with either nature or sex with his body. He can experience sex relations, but he does not desire it, and he cannot get himself a woman and seriously possess her, because he has left his body in deposit with his mother, sacrificing his phallus for her. At this price a man can move toward the evolution of consciousness and knowledge, developing a superior virility devoid of the body and his instincts. This self-castration, which ideologically forces masculine nature to forget its animal origin in order to liberate itself from the maternal world, is, instead, a bloody rite which celebrates definitive dependence. Since no man is devoid of a body and drives, nor free from desires, it follows that he can only deprive all this of meaning, relegating the drive complex to the shadow and projecting it onto the feminine world.

In this way there are substantially three results that one obtains from the psychological point of view: the first, as I have said, consists of the definitive dependence on the maternal and female world in the drive sphere, with the consequent tendency to inflate instinctual manifestations on the part of women and of latency regarding the same on the part of men.

The second results in the repression of instinct: in these cases, as regularly happens with the contents of the shadow, natural force periodically reappears in an archaic and violent way, with bursting energy that derives from repression. Rape and sexual sadism are the extreme manifestations of it, but in the day-to-day life of many men, we can see the unconscious suffering from the forced exile from the body. I am thinking of rough attitudes, of the compulsion for sexual promiscuity, of the anxiety about *performance*, of the need to drink to lose inhibitions, of the separation of sex from the rest of life, of the embarrassment and the rigidity of a body by this time reduced to a foreign body.

The third result produced by this unconscious self-castration is the vertical and uncontrollable development of *solar virility*, sublimated, at this point without any solid roots in the material body. The *solar phallus* is separated from the *chthonic phallus* (using Neumann's terminology) and no longer has weight, it becomes a mental fact. Without doubt, humanity owes to this separation an immense patrimony of knowledge and progress, but at what price for everyone? Chemical weapons, Nazism, atomic bombs, the degradation of the planet, the hole in the ozone are only a few of the latest results of a mentally rigorous civilization which has projected the entire instinctual complex onto the feminine world, devaluing both of them.

On the basis of this division of *psychic competencies* between men and women, the masculine and feminine principles are not only opposite and complementary in the form and direction of their energy, they are also *cut in half* and divided between function, according to a mutilating and reductive theory of personality. In my opinion, we need to abandon this theoretical postulation, which is still prevalent today, in order to change the direction of our research, respecting the data that clinical experience constantly reproposes. We need to recognize the completeness and complexity of the masculine and feminine principles, and how they function in the sphere of instinct, feeling, and thought, in dreams, and in the behavior and problems of patients.

Looking anew at the masculine and feminine principle will bring us closer to the theoretical sphere in which Jung placed himself, especially during his last years, when he insisted on the hypothesis of *unus mundus* and on the univocal and psychoid nature of the archetype. Jung put the intuition of the oneness of the archetype, which could contain, in itself, a complex of possible manifestations of matter and energy, and it could be brought back to the most general formula of *unus mundus*, at the center of his research.

In this context, the ambivalence of the masculine and feminine principles explored in these pages should be referred to only as a phase or transition in the cognitive process. It can be used to recognize the unconscious emersion of that part of a whole which is still submerged. According to Jung, it can be useful to recognize that the archetype is one, and that we are directing our research toward the progressive recognition of that oneness.

This also seems to be the orientation of the unconscious which, through what we call the principle of compensation, tends to structure a progressive completeness in the personality, orienting itself to compensate every time for whatever culture artificially represses. On this subject Jung wrote in 1946:

> The psychoid nature of the archetype contains very much more than can be included in a psychological explanation. It points to a sphere of the *unus mundus*, the unitary world, towards which the psychologist and the atomic physicist are converging along separate paths, producing independently of one another certain analogous auxiliary concepts. Although the first step in the cognitive process is to discriminate and divide, at the second step it will unite what has been divided, and an explanation will be satisfactory only when it achieves a synthesis.[5]

5. C. G. Jung, *The Collected Works*, Vol. 10, §852.

Physics, with Einstein's equation, demonstrates that matter and energy are not two opposite realities, but two aspects of the same reality, the one being the transformation of the other in a fixed relationship; not differently from how analytical psychology proceeds in its research, recognizing the union of opposites—and thus the unity of the archetype and its character both psychic and physical at the same time—in a point of synthesis which Jung places in a *second phase* of research, only, however, for our consciousness. And again on this subject Jung wrote:

> In themselves, spirit and matter are neutral, or rather, "utriusque crepax,"—that is, capable of what man calls good or evil. Although as names they are exceedingly relative, underlying them are very real opposites that are part of the energetic structure of the physical and of the psychic world, and without them no existence of any kind could be established. There is no position without its negation. In spite or just because of their extreme opposition, neither one can exist without the other. . . . Matter therefore would contain the seed of spirit and spirit the seed of matter. . . . The "psychization" of matter puts the absolute immateriality of spirit in question, since this would then have to be accorded a kind of substantiality.[6]

From this point of view atomic physics and analytic psychology truly seem to follow converging trajectories: perhaps the universe is a psychophysical entity and energy and matter are two manifestations of a single constituent. In this perspective, the individuated process evidently cannot direct itself to the separation of matter

---

6. C. G. Jung, *The Collected Works*, Vol. 9.1, §197.

toward the spirit in an ascensional process pregnant with a finalistic ideology. It seems to actually express itself in a progressive extension of consciousness toward the synthesis of opposites—matter and energy, body and spirit—both different and entirely present in men and in women.

PART 2

Theseus and Ariadne

CHAPTER 5

The Origins of an Encounter

Theseus and Ariadne were born far away from one another: Theseus in the masculine world of organized thought and moral feeling, and Ariadne in the dark meanderings of the feminine spirit and inductive thought; in one case, the solid, continental terrain and the emerging culture of Athens and in the other, the changeable island and the ancient civilization of Crete, made it so that they both grew up without meeting. The two States had been enemies for a long time, since the son of the king of Crete, Androgeus, died in unclear circumstances in Athenian territory: perhaps he had fought unluckily against the terrible bull of Marathon, or else he may have been killed on the way to Thebes where he was headed for the funeral games in honor of Laius. In Crete they did not know, but at any rate, the responsibility for that death fell on Athens.

Minos, the king of the island, was at Paros for sacrifices in honor of the Charites, the joyous moon goddesses: that cult was noisy and happy as one would expect for goddesses named Pasithea, Cale, and Europhrosyne, but at the news of his son's death, the king took off his crown and ordered the flutes to be silent, and since then, on that island, the rite has been celebrated in silence.

That mourning demanded vengeance and the vengeance was a terrible tribute: every nine years the Athenians had to send seven young man and seven young women to Crete to be sacrificed. Like in the myth, also in life the compensation that we often demand for a long past pain is much more costly than the pain itself. Since then eighteen years had passed and Minos was sailing toward Athens to demand for the third time his tribute in human lives.

Coming gently out of the Attic plane, wavy with olives and wheat, protected from behind by mountains and situated in front of the sea and Asia Minor, Athens could have become a big city if only it could win back its independence. This is what the people of Athens thought, but Aegeus, who had founded and wisely governed the city, was too old to lease a fleet against Crete.

Theseus, his son, was a brave young man, and the fame of his undertakings had already spread over the entire region; he loved that city, although he was not born there, and he could not bear to once again have to bend before Minos. As the day approached, the youth became more and more thoughtful and closed within himself, not being able to free his mind from the thought of the horrible end that the victims would meet: torn apart by the Minotaur, a monster half-man and half-beast, who lived hidden in the center of a strange palace. Theseus didn't yet know whether he would be chosen by Minos, but he felt in any case that the problem had something to do with him. Up to that day he had fought against enemies he had met on the road; he had fought for himself, in the light of day, against other men or animals, like every man must do; but now the enemy was a monster enveloped in darkness, and the battle to be undertaken was, above all, for the others and perhaps also for something invisible, yet concrete, like the desire for freedom and justice. This time it was certainly different: Theseus was young and these unfamiliar feelings enlarged his heart, filling it with energy; and at other times they painfully oppressed him, filling him with fear. His thoughts collided with each other and he was faced again and again with the same alternative: either to submit or to rebel, to face the shame or to struggle for freedom; in the first case, destiny was clear, in the second, unknown and uncertain. Perhaps it was at the end of this internal struggle that one day Theseus finally asked his father to let him go with the victims, to try to kill the Minotaur; but every time that a son asks his father for permission to risk his own life for the sake of a value, he is not asking for permission but for a blessing, and Aegeus, who had so desired to have his only son, was a man who knew this.

Finally Minos arrived: he was welcomed with honor, as a victorious enemy, and he made his selection; thus Theseus was chosen, whether by choice or by destiny, to be one of the victims: the king of Crete had immediately noticed the young prince; he was luminous with his extraordinary red hair and his light eyes, and his body emanated a particular force, but there was something anxious and undecipherable about him, the tension of someone who has a mission which encloses him in solitude; he certainly would have become someone, that youth, so it was better to have him perish in the jaws of the Minotaur rather than let him become a dangerous enemy.

One morning Theseus left for Delphi, heading toward Thebes, where the oracle of Apollo spoke to men; the god, over time, had announced important events, such as the founding of Thebes and its fall, the founding of Athens and the birth of Theseus from a sterile father. The youth wanted to know under what auspices his undertaking would begin, and at the temple the priestess told him in the voice of the god: "Go to Crete and let the goddess of love lead you." Thus if this were fate, there was nothing else to do but to meet it.

On a windy morning Minos decided to depart, and Theseus said farewell to his father. The old king placed his hands on his son's head and entrusted him to the gods: "If you return," he said, "promise me that, if you are alive, the ship will hoist white sails, and if they have killed you, black ones. Every day from Cape Sounion I will watch the horizon and I will know before anyone else." And so the Cretan ship departed, headed south, with its sails unfurled and its cargo of pain and hope, carrying Theseus toward Ariadne.

> One of the great island in the world
> in midsea, in the winedark sea, is Krete:
> spacious and rich and populous, with ninety
> cities and a mingling of tongues.[1]

With these words Homer recalls the solitary island in the middle of the Mediterranean where about 5,000 years before, the first European culture blossomed. Dorians, Cretans, Cidoni, and Pelasgi lived together peacefully on the island and each people spoke its own language; without town walls or fortifications; the cities were divided by only mountainous terrain and wheat fields. The Cretans had become sailors to break their isolation, and they had learned to trade goods and make acquaintance with people from the near East, North Africa, and Sicily; they cultivated the land and, with the same commitment, the joy of living, art, technical skill, and religion.

The remains of the Cretan culture which have come down to us show images of sensual, elegant women, and smiling, unarmed men: there are scenes of music, dance, games, sometimes a hunt, but never war and the frequent motifs of leaves, flowers, and fruit are

---

1. Homer, *The Odyssey*, Robert Fitzgerald, trans. (New York: Anchor Press, 1963), Book XIX, v 172–175.

testimony to the deep bond with nature perceived as beauty, nourishment, and harmony. Together with art and the joy of life, the Cretans cultivated knowledge and technical knowledge in particular: not only were their houses frescoed, but they also had running water and windows, and the disk of Phesto brings down to us writing, still undeciphered, which the Cretans knew about 3500 years ago. On a round gold plate, incised on both faces, a hieroglyphic script follows a spiral path from the external edge toward the center and from left to right. The result is a small labyrinth of great enigmatic beauty, a religious symbol even before it is an art object and a means of communication.

The relationship with the divine constituted the fulcrum of Cretan civilization and it oriented itself in the identification with nature in the image of the Great Mother goddess and her symbols: the double-edged ax, the bull, the labyrinth which we find on the frescoed walls in the monuments and in the caves of the island. On Crete the cult of the Great Mother refers to the time when the need was felt to name and venerate the mysterious power that presides over life, and this force, in the personal and in the collective unconscious, always takes on a maternal semblance as in the equation: nature=earth=womb=mother, which contains a symbolic and psychic density of archetypical character.

But, I believe, it would be a grave error to confuse the image of the Great Mother with the feminine principle, as the Great Mother, being the goddess of all origins, still contains *within herself* opposites, and thus both the feminine and masculine principle. Such a union presents an archaic character, still undifferentiated, and thus *uroboric,* and it has nothing to do with the *coniunctio oppositorum* which, from the point of view of psychological evolution, constitutes an objective to aim toward starting from the differentiation: the first is a fusion of opposites without the consciousness of their diversity, the second a union of polarities constellated by the conscious.

For these reasons a civilization based on the archetype of the Great Mother cannot be but *double, opposite,* and *undifferentiated* in its manifestations; she is both things at the same time, in both the aspects in light and in shadow. She is wise and mad, harmonious and perverse, tranquil and sanguine, tolerant and vindictive. On Crete they did not build defensive perimeters or armed fleets, but they carried out human sacrifices and a woman could fall in love with a bull; the great goddess of the island was a welcoming and protective mother, and also the queen of serpents and savage demons[2] and the lunar sorceress who practiced witchcraft. The contradictory, unorganized, and chaotic aspects from a cultural phase linked to the maternal archetype are charged with energy, because they are in a certain sense still in contact with the primordial chaos and the power of the unconscious. We systematically verify, in examining a personality, how much energy the unconscious contains, even in its delirious explosions, and we can only imagine the extraordinary concentration of unconscious energy previous to the enucliation of a culture of origins, to the first awareness of themselves as individuals belonging to a group. What happens in the infancy of humanity does not seem substantially different from what happens in the infancy of a human being, since a baby expresses undifferentiated and unrecognized opposites, behaving in unpredictable and contradictory ways. A child is also close to a preconscious situation, and is pervaded by immense energy. And in fact, human infancy and the infancy of humanity have the unilateral and totalizing maternal image as a common reference. Crete, in the

2. These demons were called *curets* or *coribants*, and still earlier, in the Middle East, *dactyls*.

Minoan era, seems to have experienced the ambivalence and energy of this infantile state of psychological evolution in the anima of its inhabitants.

Ariadne, the daughter of Minos, grew up in this vibrant atmosphere where shadow and light, death and life, wisdom and madness alternated and united like clouds in the sea. Her mother, Pasiphae (which means "light") was perhaps a moon goddess, definitely knew the art of magic, and, in order to escape from the torments of jealousy, cast a spell on her husband, so that as soon as he touched a woman, his/her body would be covered with scorpions, spiders, and cockroaches. But Pasiphae, so intolerant when it came to her husband, was not able to resist her desire when the moment came and every time Ariadne heard people talking about this story, her face clouded over and she withdrew into herself, because here a secret began and it was her duty to keep it so to the end. The story went like this:

One day Minos, fearing that he would attract the jealousy of the gods because of the prosperity on the island, asked Poseidon how he could stay in divine favor. "You must sacrifice to me the first thing that you see come out of the sea" the voice of the god replied to the old king kneeling on the beach. The temptations of omnipotence that lie in wait for people who lead prosperous lives were not unknown to Minos, but he was weak when it came to pleasure and so, when he saw a splendid white bull come out of the sea, he felt deeply tormented: did he really have to obey the voice of the god and find the courage to renounce, or could he follow his desire and take possession of that marvel? Minos ended up sacrificing another bull to Poseidon and keeping the white one for himself, without imagining the consequence of that disobedience.

The god hurled a curse against Minos: "Your wife will like that bull much more than you!" Thus as soon as Pasiphae saw the bull, she felt herself invaded by a violent and monstrous desire which she tried to fight in vain, it was as if a devil had taken possession of her senses, making her a prisoner. As time passed, the desire to be penetrated by the white bull and feel his strength became more and more violent and wouldn't leave the queen in peace, taking away her rest and tranquillity, sense and dignity.

Finally one day she decided to call upon Daedalus, the genius architect who had built the palace for Ariadne's dances, and she confided her secret to him, asking him for help; in everything that the queen said to him with a grieved voice, Daedalus was only interested in one thing—technique. He wanted to find a way to make that embrace technically possible, and in order to do this it was necessary to fool the bull. The rest didn't count much: Daedalus was Athenian and the passionate blood of those island dwellers had always bothered him a little. Soon his mind devised a trick similar to the one which later on, not far from there, Ulysses would imitate for a different purpose: he built a pretty, light colored cow out of reeds, and he put her in the middle of a field; then he made Pasiphae enter it, so that when the grazing bull saw her, what had to happen happened.

The union between human beings and animals is part of our most ancient history, like incest, and similar to incest, it is feared as a guilty regression, like a push backward which annuls consciousness in the abyss of animal life. So the fruit of this meeting couldn't be but monstrous: the son of Pasiphae and the bull was the Minotaur, the tragic hybrid with a human body and a bull's head. Minos, not being able to bear the sight of the incarnation of his guilt, had him shut up in the palace that Daedalus had built for Ariadne's dances, from where the Minotaur would never be able to escape. In fact it was a particular palace for a particular dance: a long procession uncoiled in a line where each dancer was tied to the person both in front and behind with a thread or by a ribbon of clothing, and it went both forward and backward, with an oscillating movement, while forming a spiral figure, which wound up toward the center and then unwound toward the outside, similar to how one makes a ball of wool. Thus for this dance Daedalus had built a meandering palace where the long procession could follow its hesitating and winding path: a spiral-shaped corridor which finally opened into a central room; to exit, it was necessary to follow the same path again without getting lost in secondary, deadend corridors. Thus it was originally a palace for initiation dances, which could make one's head spin and lose one's way; it resembled the meanderings of the brain, a snake that uncoils, the shape of a shell. Perhaps Daedalus was inspired by the monumental Egyptian palaces for Mendes and Prammeticus, or by the even earlier one near Lake Meri, which Herodotus speaks about, and which housed all the tombs of kings.

And Daedalus' palace had also become a tomb: from a place for sacred dances to an obscure hiding place for the shame of Crete. Something was getting entangled in the civilization of Crete, and Ariadne only knew that one day it would be up to her to untangle it.

THE VOYAGE TO CRETE

During the long hours at sea, Theseus thought of his brief life and he remembered his mother: she was called Aethra and she was a princess from Troezen, in the Peleponese; he had lived with her for sixteen years, which already seemed so far away and which he now recalled; he remembered her caresses, which at times had bothered him, her sweet and subtle voice, the softness of her body, and the games they played by the sea; a severe and straight wrinkle between her eyebrows made a strange contrast with her childlike smile; she knew a lot of things and she didn't talk about many things, she was changeable and unknowable like the moon, and like the moon she was luminous.

Then one spring morning Aethra asked Theseus to accompany her into the fields behind the house and she stopped by a big stone: "Try to lift this," she said to him, and the youth, tightening his muscles and holding his breath, was able to move the stone, discovering underneath a finely worked sword; with great surprise he took it in his hands and questioned his mother with his eyes. So Aethra told him this story:

"At the time I was a young girl living with my father. One evening Aegeus, king of Athens and Medea's husband, passed through the city on his way back from Delphi, where he had asked the god if he would ever have the son he so desired. My father invited him to our house and asked him what Apollo has replied: 'Don't open your goatskin until you have returned to Athens,' Aegeus recounted, and he confided to us that he didn't understand the meaning of the oracle, and felt confused. My father intuited that the divine words advised Aegeus not to make love until he returned because now, and for one time only, a child would be conceived. Perhaps my father feared the development of Athenian power and he didn't want children born to the hero founder of that city; so he tricked the old king, offering him an aphrodisiac drink and then accompanying him into my room. You were born after nine months. But that night another event happened: I dreamed of Athena, the goddess who protects the Athenians, who ordered me to go immediately to the island of Sphaeria, which is nearby, and which you know by the name it has had since then, *Iera, the Sacred*. I obeyed her command and I left Aegeus sleeping in my bed.

The sea at night is black, it is scary, and I was a young girl inexperienced with oars, but how can one disobey a goddess? I reached the island trembling, and immediately Poseidon, in all his majestic beauty, came out of the sea. He very sweetly approached me and united himself with me under the light of the moon. So, son, you have two fathers, and the strengths of a man and a god, so different, are mixed within you. The next morning Aegeus woke up with me next to him and he asked me to accompany him here, to this stone, which he lifted and where he hid the sword. Then he gave me his sandals, the ones you are wearing now, and which this morning I asked you to put on. Then he said to me: "If a child is born from our union, and if it is a son, when he turns 16 bring him here to this stone; he will draw out the sword and my sandals will be the right size. Then send him, alone, to Athens."

Aethra stopped talking and her face was serious like the secret which she had been keeping for so long. Theseus was also thoughtful: he had often imagined his father and he desired to meet him, but he loved his mother, Troezen, and the life he had always known. Finally one day he decided to leave for Athens and now, on the deck of Minos' ship, he thought of his mother with deep love, and of their parting, so tender and painful.

"If this child is male," this is what Aegeus had said, and if the child had been female, then she would never have known her father; and he wanted him to be strong enough to lift a huge stone and big enough to wear his own sandals. And so Theseus would be a big and strong youth because the oracle, Poseidon, Aegeus, and the circumstances of his fate had so decided.

There were many enemies and difficulties which obstructed Theseus' path to Athens, but he overcame them all and finally one day—exactly the 8th of the month which is sacred to Poseidon—he reached his paternal city, alone, with his young appearance and wearing his hair long, as was the custom in the Peleponese. Some laborers on a scaffold made fun of him: "Since when do marriageable girls walk alone in the street?" Theseus' reply was to take a cart which was nearby and overturn it with one strike of his hand.

Medea, Aegeus' wife, was a witch, and she knew that the youth who was approaching the royal palace would one day be the leader of the city, and she said to the old king that the youth, so strong, whose gestures on the way Athens were known to everybody, would overthrow him, and she persuaded him to receive and poison him. The moment for the banquet came, and Theseus took the poisoned cup from his father's hand, offering him at the same time the sword for recognition; the king saw the ivory hilt, and lowered his gaze to the sandals, and with one blow of his hand struck his son's chalice.

It had been sad to leave his mother—he now reflected watching the seagulls around the sails—it had been moving to meet Aegeus, and painful to have to leave him as well, but he had not met his other father, Poseidon.

In that moment the youth—seeing Minos humiliate one of his female Athenian companions with heavy caresses—was roused from his thoughts and confronted the king to respect the prisoners; an altercation followed in which Minos bragged about his divine origin and invoked Zeus by asking him for a lightening bolt in the calm sky as proof of his protection; immediately a bolt shot through the limpid air with tremendous noise. So Theseus looked Minos in the eye and said; "I, too, am the son of a god; Poseidon is my father." The king's face darkened: and if it were true? He had committed sacrilege against the god of the sea many years before, refusing the sacrifice of the white bull. And if Poseidon had wanted to procreate a man capable of ruining Crete? Minos was afraid, but he decided he must know and, throwing a ring into the sea, he provoked Theseus to find it "if Poseidon had truly generated you."

The youth dove in, abandoning himself to the waves, and was received in the splendid palace of the god who crowned him with a crown and gave him back the ring; Poseidon had also recognized him, and when Theseus returned to the ship with the jewel, he read the dismay in Minos' eyes.

That which differentiates a victim from a rebel is not always evident; they are often on the same boat, in the same division, in the same prison: Theseus had made the difference visible on Minos' ship, reaffirming his dignity as a free man even in slavery.

The young prince now felt completely alone: his family was far away and he had taken leave of the past, but he knew—without knowing the reason—that this detachment was part of the oracle's invitation which continuously returned to his mind: "Go to Crete and follow the goddess of love." A page of his life was being turned; a little easygoing, a little thoughtful, he was waiting for the next page.

THE MEETING OF THESEUS AND ARIADNE

Ariadne was weaving on the beach when Minos' ship entered into the port, and she immediately approached the prow of the ship to greet her father. There was a restless crowd around, curious about the voyage, and especially curious about the new victims for the Minotaur. Shouts and yells filled the air.

Then Theseus got off the ship and his eyes met Ariadne's. Something very familiar struck both of them, as if they had always known each other, and finally found each other after a long time, even though there was nothing more unknown to Ariadne than that serious face, half-hidden by the long red curls, and Theseus knew he had never even imagined anything as sweet as that blond girl. They were separated, pushed ahead by the crowd and left to their thoughts: Ariadne felt she could not accept the death of that young man, because from that moment the law of love was stronger than family ties. That evening the two met at the banquet in honor of the Athenian victims, and later, alone in the perfumed garden, they were absolutely happy, despite everything that was happening. Was this love, Theseus asked himself, the desire and the fear of losing himself in her? Was this love, Ariadne asked herself, the desire and the fear of abandoning herself to him?

"I will help you get out of the labyrinth," said the young girl after a long silence. Theseus was astounded: "How do you know that I intend to fight the Minotaur?" "I know," Ariadne smiled giving him a ball of wool and a crown which gave off a vivid light, "You must know that the labyrinth is a winding place, a little like the intestine of an animal: it is easy to enter, but it is difficult to reach the center where, in a big circular room, the Minotaur lives; and it is almost impossible to come out, because there are many dead ends which make you lose direction. Keep this ball of wool," Ariadne continued, "and when you enter the labyrinth, tie one end tightly to the top of the architrave of the door and then let it unwind slowly as you make your way through the labyrinth. After you have killed the Minotaur, you need only follow the thread to find the way out again. Be very careful not to break the thread, and, as you go, do not move quickly; the crown on your brow will illuminate your path as you proceed."

Theseus hid the two treasures, and, after a brief silence, declared: "After, you will come to Athens with me." "And will I be your bride?" "You will be my bride." "Do you promise?" "No promise is easier." It was very difficult for both of them to separate that night, and all of a sudden the meaning of the oracle became clear to Theseus: to follow the goddess of love was to follow

Ariadne, with her, and only with her, could he triumph.

At dawn the youth carried out sacrifices in honor of Aphrodite and then he made his way toward the palace of the Minotaur before the city awakened and someone might see him. He had the ball of wool, the crown, and his father's sword with him. Upon reaching the entrance, Theseus tied the end of the thread to the architrave and began to go in; the darkness became thicker and thicker, and the path more intricate; the thread unwound sweetly and silently: a deception to overcome a deception. Every now and then a hesitation, a pause which allowed his eyes to get used to the darkness, which the light from the crown barely lit up, to slow down the beating of his heart. Fear gripped him: in any moment, from any turning the Minotaur could attack him and yet he felt strong, because he felt the presence of Ariadne, it was as if she were there, next to him.

As he slowly proceeded he heard the monster's panting breath grow louder and louder; then, all of a sudden he found himself in a vast, circular space: the center of the labyrinth. And here he was, the Minotaur, in a corner, with a stone in his hand, his legs apart, and an amazed and furious expression on his face. He let out a desperate moan when he saw Theseus to scare him because he was afraid; there was a tremendous struggle: the strength of the man-animal was overwhelming and he used a stone to cause wide wounds on the body of the youth. Theseus tried to protect himself by striking out left and right and waiting for the most propitious moment to strike; he wasn't afraid any more, now he was perfectly calm. All of a sudden a small space opened between them, the Minotaur's arms were open and Theseus buried the sword in the Minotaur's heart.

The Athenian prince knelt down and thanked the gods, then he loaded the Minotaur's body on his back, so that everyone could see that he had been killed, and so he could be buried honorably. Following the thread, Theseus made his way back to the light.

There were no wars, but there was the grief of Crete, and the suffering of Ariadne at the sight of her brother's body. In her heart, the woman said these words to him: "This had to be destiny, that you died so that a man could live, and in order to make me follow their commands, the gods made me fall in love. And now I am desperate before your innocent death, and I am happy because I love Theseus. How powerful the gods are, and how indecipherable are their designs!"

Theseus departed to return to Athens together with his companions, and he brought Ariadne with him. During the voyage they stopped at Delos, in the Cyclades, where they carried out sacrifices in honor of Aphrodite. All the young Athenians together, under the guidance of Ariadne, learned the dance of the labyrinth here.

In the serene Delian night, the young people were asleep, before the dawn put them back to sea, and Theseus had a dream: Dionysis appears and asks him to renounce Ariadne because he has decided to make her his bride. The youth, awakening, disbelieving and full of anguish, sees his companion sleeping beside him; he calls her sweetly, he caresses her hair, but no one can awaken her: Artemis has killed her and only Dionysis can restore her to life. Theseus realizes that he must give in and depart alone; once again he contemplates her long fair hair and her eyes which will no longer open unto his. He tries to burn their color into his memory, the soft curve of her side and her luminous smile, then he moves away from her and hoists sail to Athens.

During the long days at sea, Theseus thinks about his destiny which always places farewells before him. Would his life be dedicated only to overcoming trials, killing monsters, and liberating cities? Always alone? He felt very sad and confused, and it was the first time he felt this way, for he had fallen in love for the first time.

In the view of Cape Souinon, Theseus, immersed in his thoughts, forgets to hoist the white sail, and Aegeus sees the funeral boat approach the shore. So, not being able to bear the death of his son, he throws himself into the sea which had taken Theseus away. Athens was free and Theseus was king.

CHAPTER 6

From the Bull to the Minotaur

Examining this myth from a sociological point of view, it is not difficult to recognize in the story of Theseus and Ariadne one of many episodes with which the collective conscious translated the passage from maternal culture to paternal, referable in this case to the migrations of the Indo-European people who, passing through the Balkans around 2000 B.C., penetrated Greece and brought a nomadic, pastoral, and bellicose culture to replace the preceding Minoan one, and before that the Anatolian one, which were sedentary and agricultural.

This is certainly not the place, nor my competence, to address the historicity of a matriarchal phase that was discussed by Bachofen.[1] I will limit myself to recalling that—prescinding from the sexual collocation of the political and social *arche* —on a religious and cultural level, the dominant matriarchy, with its complex archetype of functions, seems to have guided the psychology and behavior of both men and women through the initial path of human

---

1. See J. J. Bachofen, *Myth, Religion and Mother Right*, Ralph Manheim, trans. Bollingen Series No. 84 (Princeton: Princeton University Press, 1967).

109

civilization. It is a fact that all cultures refer to the Great Mother—earth—nature—moon—water—the supreme power of granting good and bad, life and death, uniting creative and receptive energy, and following hidden patterns of evolution. And as Erich Neumann affirms, the maternal psychological stage seems to refer to the first phase of human civilization, not unlike the first cycle of every individual's life.[2] Athens, then the bringer of the new masculine *logos*, defeats Crete, the center of maternal *eros*, following in the myth the trail of a tradition historically given.

But orienting the reading toward a psychological study, to understand what the intertwining of Athens and Crete, of Theseus and Ariadne means for the human soul, it is necessary to investigate the symbolic terms of the story, the internal significance of the characters' behavior, the archetypal value of their existence. The first episode in the succession, because it chronologically precedes Theseus' and Ariadne's decisions, is about the complex of the bull and the Minotaur.

In ancient cultures, animals (and later on anthropomorphic gods), represent one or more particular *qualities*, based on their analogic characteristics and the resemblance between the animal's physical and character traits and a particular quality complex. The animal became a cult object in that *it was* that way of being, and it let loose that particular power.

From this point of view, the bull incarnates one of the most ancient religious images[3] venerated in all of the cultural areas of the

---

2. Erich Neumann, *The Great Mother: An Analysis of the Archetype,* Ralph Manheim, trans. Bollingen Series No. 47 (Princeton: Princeton University Press, 1964); *The Origins & History of Consciousness,* R. F. Hull, trans. Bollingen Series No. 42 (Princeton: Princeton University Press, 1954).

3. One of the most ancient images which has come down to us is a copper bull of extraordinary beauty from the Sumerian civilization (3000 B.C.), now at the British Museum in London.

Great Mother,[4] to whom a profound archetypal solidarity is linked. The psychological complex referred to the bull is legible from its body and in its character: the stocky figure, heavy and dark, makes one think of the compactness and the solidity of the earth, while the sexual strength and vigor transmit the idea of fertility, and its destructive energy is expressed in the drives analogous to the violence of many natural phenomena. The horns are similar to waxing and waning moon crescents, and recall the lunar cycle: the life-death-rebirth rhythm—which is governed by the moon—the mystery of time, and the alternation of the seasons in human life. The horns of the bull form, in their design, a natural crown, a symbol of majesty which has to do with nature, and which draws its origins *from within* the being; not rarely were the great Middle Eastern divinities represented with a bull's head or with curved horns on their heads, as if to declare their sovereignty over nature, and, at the same time, the mysterious origin of their power.

The character and physical aspects of the bull join its image to the strength of nature, and thus, in the psychic sphere, to the instinct complex in which it is possible to recognize two fundamental ambivalences. The first refers to the double masculine and feminine character, in that it is partially linked to the lunar cycle and to the earth, and thus to the female belly, and partly to sexual potency and masculine fertility. This ambivalence refers to the uroboric bisexuality of instinct; that is, to the phase of evolution in which the gods and nature, and thus the psyche which imagined and knew them, contained the instinctual complex of the masculine and feminine principles, without yet having awareness of their intrinsic diversity.

The second ambivalence refers to sexual vigor and destructive violence or, in other words, to life and death, to *eros* and *thanatos,*

4. Erich Neumann, *The Great Mother.*

and it reproduces the duplicity of nature and blood; duplicity, yet not a contradiction, because nature, like instinct, is the carrier of life *in that* it is the carrier of death. Because of this, the bull is associated both with funeral and fertility rites from the earliest times.

The archetypical solidarity between the Great Mother and the bull is brought back to a common ambivalence in the instinctive dynamic: the Great Mother existed before the separation between feminine and masculine, and she is at the origin of both; she refers to historical and psychological time when humanity was still unconscious of itself and immersed in the original fusion between nature and the mother. The great goddess is also an image linked to natural power that gives life and death, a power that involves a mysterious and hidden cycle that transforms energy and matter. The Great Mother contains in herself the instinctive ambivalence of the bull: the masculine and feminine principle, fertility and destruction, life and death and through this ambivalence she expresses her sovereignty.

According to Greek tradition, Cretan civilization, the first important European culture that blossomed around 2000 B.C., had its beginning and its end in a bull. A Hellenic myth recounts that one day Zeus fell in love with Europa, a young woman who lived in Libya. In order to possess her, he transformed himself into a marvelous white bull and he went to curl up at the feet of the young woman in a meadow full of flowers. Europa caressed him sweetly and, since he was as calm as a lamb, without fear she climbed onto his back; but at that point the bull suddenly got up and started to gallop, carrying the terrified girl on a long journey; from Libya they passed into Egypt, and then into the Middle East and then into Anatolia, and finally they crossed the Bosphorus and arrived in Crete, where they stopped and united and generated three children. One of these children was Minos who, as we saw, became the king

and founder of Crete. The first European civilization was born, and
its roots, as the myth recalls, sunk into the matriarchal culture of
the African and Middle Eastern countries. Speaking about the union
of a god, or a sacred animal, with a woman in the matriarchal civ-
ilizations, Erich Neumann writes:

> In her character of Great Mother, the feminine a "vir-
> gin": a creative principle, independent of the personal
> man. For many good reasons, the basic matriarchal view
> saw no relation between the sexual act and the bearing
> of children. Pregnancy and sexuality were dissociated
> both in the inner and outer experience of woman. This
> may be readily understood when we consider that these
> early societies were characterized by a promiscuous sex
> life that began far before sexual maturity . . . the woman
> always conceived by an extrahuman transpersonal
> power. The myths and fairy tales of all times and peoples
> teach us that she was impregnated by contact with numi-
> nous animals, e.g., bird and serpent, bull and ram, but
> also by the eating of fruit, by the wind, the moon, ances-
> tral spirits, demons, gods, etc. And the totem was an
> impersonal fecundating spirit of this sort.[5]

Cretan civilization thus develops on matriarchal terrain, starting
from the fecundation of a totemic bull: his muzzle and horns can
still be seen incised on the stones of the island, and it is a recurring
theme in the frescoes and on the vases which refer to cultural practices and Taurocatapsia.[6]

---

5. Erich Neumann, *The Great Mother*, pp. 269–270.
6. *Taurocatapsia* was a rite, perhaps a funeral game, in which youths of both sexes
would hurl themselves in audacious acrobatics, jumping on the back of a bull, and
turning around in the air while holding onto the horns of the animal.

The bull was the animal sacred to Crete because it was the origin and the basis of its culture, or, in other words, people felt a *psychological* belonging in the complex of qualities incarnated by the bull and more abstractly referable to the great maternal divinity: the religious practice (*re-ligio* means connection) linked the life of both individual and group to the numinous force of the totem, working a communion between the individual, the collective ego, and the sacred animal's qualities. The ancient inhabitants of Crete affirmed their deep adhesion to the mysterious dynamics of natural life in this manner, recognizing the ambivalence in nature, in the totem, and within the individual personality. This is psychic context which analytical psychology would define as *identification*.

From this point of view I believe that the totem animal in primitive cultures corresponds to the symbolic animal in the individual unconscious. Today it is recognizable in dreams. In a world like ours, which has deserted instinct, depriving it of its sacredness, meaning, and cognitive value, the bull bursts into dreams (especially dreams of women) generating chaos, fear, and unexpected feelings but, when it can be symbolically embraced and elaborated, it liberates a new energy that unblocks the personality, restoring to it the natural instincts and its cognitive potentials.

A few years ago I was seeing a young woman whose particularly sexophobic upbringing had separated her from her instinct: she was frigid, Amenorrheic, and she felt a radical repulsion for feminine shapes; in particular she couldn't tolerate having breasts, which she tried to flatten in every way. The rejection of her body had become the rejection of pleasure and satisfaction, but also of the calmness and awareness that comes with the acceptance of instinct. One day she brought me this dream:

Communion with the Bull: *There is a bull who is going around the city, perhaps he is furious; the police are looking for him in order to catch and kill him, but they haven't found the bull yet. I hurry home and I cross the Cathedral Square, which as always is full of people. At a certain point I hear someone yell, the crowd breaks up, a space opens up and I see the bull: he is in the middle of the parvis facing the cathedral; I step back, I hope to slowly go up the steps and hide in the church, I think that he will not go in there. I stop because I see a woman dressed in white, perhaps she is my analyst, who moves toward the bull: now they are still, one in front of the other and the woman puts her arms around his neck. I hear people say that hugging the bull brings luck to women. Other women do it, they form a line, like for communion; now the bull seems calm and I get in line as well.*

The church is the place where animals have no space and thus where my patient searches for safety from the violent eruption of her instinctive patrimony. But a woman, who is perhaps myself, and this is an image referring to analysis, shows her that she need not run way, it is possible to *meet* it, and that instinct calms down if it is accepted. The bull is all the more threatening as the forces of order of a rigid and conventional upbringing try to suppress it.

The virgin in front of the bull—the woman in white in the dream—belongs to the collective imagery of far off times and, following an underground thread of memory, reemerges from the unconscious to describe an image of sacrifice. In it the bull, who is both nature and instinct, nourishes himself on the precious blood of an uncontaminated youthfulness to potentiate natural fertility. In this sense, the sacrifice of the young girl to the bull is inscribed in fertility rites common to the Mediterranean area. In my patient's dream, she does not experience the maternal culture of origin, and the ego is no longer sacrificed to a divine Nature, but neither is instinct killed or repressed, for it finds integration within the personality in the inviting embrace of the women. The dreamer feels that this agreement is sacred because it takes the form of a rite in which the women individually establish a pact with the instinct complex. In another case, one of my patient's dreams concluded with this image:

THE BULL AND THE VINEYARD: *I am in a country house which I have never seen, modest but very nice; in front, in a vineyard, a bull calmly grazes, and seeing this scene I feel strangely invaded by a sense of peace and tranquillity.*

In this case it is possible to see the image of Dionysis within the vines, the god who opens the senses and attenuates inhibitions: the archetypal *Dionysis-Bull* manifests itself in this dream. This is the great concentration of instinctive energy at the origin of ecstatic religions and irrational aspects of knowledge. This image is well-integrated in the personality of the dreamer, since the bull grazes *calmly* among the vines; thus fear vanishes, and a sensation of peace begins which derives from an acceptance of the instinctual complex within conscious life (the house and the cultivated terrain) and from its tranquilizing effects.

A dream dominated by the image of a bull was told to me one day by a man:

THE BULL AND THE CAPARISON: *I see a bull covered to its knees by a caparison; a growling and mean dog forced him to do a sort of ritual dance along the meanderings of a labyrinth drawn on the ground. The bull seemed to be a prisoner of the dog and the hood.*

In this dream the entire instinctual complex—in its masculine and feminine ambivalence—seems prisoner to a labyrinth from which it cannot exit due to a growling guard dog and a hood, or harness, which represent a moral code and a principle of order perceived, in the unconscious of the dreamer, as inhuman oppression. If the bull could see its guardian, he would liberate himself with one kick, but the repression, and that is the caparison which covers him, impedes him from being seen, from seeing, and thus from affirming his rights.

In a culture like ours, in which the sacredness and the cognitive value of instinct—both feminine and masculine—have been forgotten, it is understandable that the image of the bull, with all of its archetypal power, returns from the unconscious to affirm its rights within the personality.

Respecting a symmetry of opposites, it—if for the same reason that Poseidon asks Minos to sacrifice a white bull—constituted the mythical origin of Cretan civilization and represented its cultural basis. At a certain point in the personal and collective evolution, it is exactly the supremacy of instinct that must be sacrificed to leave space for the development of other psychic competencies. It is also necessary to abandon the projective attitude and renounce *identification* with the archetypical image. But it is not yet possible to sacrifice something with which one still identifies: you cannot kill a bull if that bull *is* Crete, if it *is* the symbolic image of the Great Mother with which the anima of an entire people identifies itself. When, notwithstanding, following a trauma or an act of violence, this type of situation if verified, the consequences on a psychic level are incalculable, and remain so as time passes. Just think, for example, of the price that German civilization paid for the sacrifice of Wotan when he was still identified with the anima of that people; to repress that god meant to push him into the shadow, making him unconscious, and thus uncontainable and dangerous for everyone, as successive history has dramatically shown and continues to show.

Thus the difficulty—in the life of groups and individuals—seems to be in being able to embrace the moment of transformation, and thus the sacrifice of a part of oneself. There is a time when it is possible to kill something so that something new can be born, and it is a brief period in which one no longer identifies with the past and in which it has not yet had a chance to destroy the promise of the future. Too soon and too late are periods just as dangerous. When the moment arrives, things change in any case, and to step back in the face of the many deaths that the many new lives demand is sacrilege and brings us to ruin, both in the myth as well as in human existence.

Thus, one day Poseidon asks Minos to kill the white bull who came out of the sea, so that Crete could continue to have the favor of the gods; and it is exactly this order that the king is not willing to carry out because he wanted to continue to believe that that white bull, so similar to the one which had impregnated Europa, was the symbol of the guardian deity of the island and, by extension, of the island itself. But why did Poseidon ask in that moment for that sacrifice to guarantee the prosperity of the island? And what force disarmed Minos? To kill the bull meant to bring an end to the predominant influence of instinct in order to open a space for the complexes of feeling and thought which until then were latent or subordinate. The god asked to kill the old Crete so that a new Crete could be born, and, since a transformation without sacrifice is not possible, the bull had to die.

That was the moment to change because Minos' internal voice, through the god, requested this profound upheaval that was both psychological and social; but a principle of psychic inertia opposed this calling by activating an internal conflict which it would win. The old king, capable of making laws and judging men, was not able to make a revolution; it is possible, and at times useful and necessary, to transgress human laws, but not one's own internal law: this loyalty to oneself is sometimes costly, but in the end betrayal is much more so. The weakness of the Cretan king is thus the origin of the decadence of Minoan culture, and when Ariadne, later on, makes that revolution possible, and when Theseus carries it out, it is too late and Crete won't have any more history. The bull turns from an emblem of prosperity to a symbol of ruin, because Pasiphae falls in love with it and the child born is monstrous.

Pasiphae is different from Europa: the woman impregnated by a god or by a sacred animal no longer generates founder-heroes like Minos, but monsters like the Minotaur, simply because times have changed, and along with the times, everything else; the Great Mother, mistress of natural order, had to give over to a more differentiated and complex psychic organization.

So now the union with the totemic animal is perceived by the collective consciousness as a step backward, a perverse and guilty action, because it goes against the fundamental law of life: the necessity for change through successive deaths and rebirths. The sacred animal has become a sacrilegious hybrid because the Cretan collective consciousness felt at that point that the woman-bull union, which had been the main axis in its conception of cosmic energy, was a guilt that rejected humanity in a half-animal condition in the intricate darkness of the origins.

Also, from a psychological point of view, we systematically see the hypothesis of constant change for all life forms confirmed, and when this does not happen in harmony with its form, we witness regressive phenomena or, in other words, when a conscious attitude,

MARINA VALCARENGHI

which has given meaning and value to the life of a human being, no longer has its function and is not sacrificed, it poisons the personality by restraining it in a regressive spiral.

A few years back I had a male patient who tenaciously gripped the idea that women were inferior beings (to men, naturally); his unconscious hammered him with images of great offended goddesses, of women *full of light* and of old wise women, but he remained grasping his conviction like a macao to a coconut tree. The moment had arrived for that man to knock down the dictatorship of masculine consciousness in order to immerse himself in the depths of the feminine principle, but like Minos, even if in a different atmosphere, *he was not able to kill the old to give life to the new,* and he was very careful not to let down his guard, to remain a rigid toy soldier, desperate and elegant.

The masculine principle—which had also been the fulcrum of his equilibrium and his success—progressively became a more and more precarious support and then untrustworthy and finally regressive: at this point obsessive rituals, sleep disturbances, anxiety attacks, loss of appetite, and loss of weight manifested themselves. My patient convinced himself that he was ill, and he dedicated himself to incessant pilgrimages to doctors of all sorts. Nevertheless, he didn't abandon analysis with me, continuing to provoke me about the inferiority of my gender. Then one day we had a conversation that went like this:

"You are angry with me."

"How come?"

"You should tell me; anyhow I believe it's because of my opinion about women and because deep down I continue to think that what you call the feminine principle only serves to make idiots out of men."

"I'm not angry, but I am sad, because your appearance tells me that you truly risk becoming ill now."

"You see? This is being a woman: you are very good at expressing your feelings, but you are not capable of moving a finger. You are sad, now, but what are you doing to get me out of trouble?"

"Nothing."

"What, nothing?"

"Nothing. And what are you doing to help yourself?"

"Nothing."—And after this word, which came out despite himself, he resentfully added: *"But there's this difference, that you're sad."*

"It's true, this is a difference, that I'm sad."

And sadness had to be the first feeling capable of lighting up the contact: after that session a period of depression ensued during which the toy soldier was finally abandoned. Much later, recalling that meeting, he said he felt in my words a confession of impotence which was also a provocation, and he added that when he got home afterward, he felt like a child of my sadness.

Minos, like many human beings from all eras, was not able to affront the immense sadness that certain sacrifices drag with them. And thus the Minotaur was born.

THE MINOTAUR

The Minotaur has the head of a bull and the body of a man, and thus, in symbolic terms, he lives with the senses and feelings of a human, and with the mind of an animal. His regressive character seems to express itself in the incapacity to think like a man and to reflect on himself. His tragic innocence is double: in one sense it is the lack of guilt, in another a lack of reason; he is a stranger to his origin and his form, and he cannot be accused. He is also a stranger to his fury, his thirst for blood, and his terrible silence, because he doesn't have *logos,* that is, the words, memories, and thoughts, which are part of every human being. Thus he is innocent, not because he is a stranger to human passions, but because he doesn't recognize them: his feelings and impulses simply happen, but they don't put him in relation to anything or anybody, and he is condemned by his condition, even before the shame of the Cretans, to complete solitude.

The Minotaur seems to be delineated as a hybrid with which the Greek imagination expressed anguish in the face of a regression, which conserves human impulses and feelings without being able to know, reflect and communicate.

On a social level, regression strikes Crete, and, not being able to move ahead, it is inexorably pushed backward, sinking in the incapacity to renew itself and thus to produce culture. But, in a completely analogous way, the regression influences the individual personality as well, forcing it to turn back and to trust very precarious balances.

For all of these reasons I don't think that the Minotaur should generically mix himself with instinct, and that he opposes Theseus, the champion of solar thought, as an antagonist: the man-bull is not an animal, he doesn't exist in nature and he can't be an instinct: his meaning and tragedy are in the unnatural condition of being a hybrid, which reveals the pathology. Regression does not allow a man, or a social group, to *go back to how it was before*, but it rejects in the unconscious (individual or collective) a few aspects of the personality. So it is not the state of nature that Ariadne is called to condemn, but the push backward which obscures consciousness and imprisons her in the labyrinth of drives.

The infancy of humanity, for example, and the earliest infancy of every human being, has lived, and continues to live in the state of nature, in the absence of conflicts and in the pre-conscious beatitude of being part of a whole which contains. But in that context, solitude, humiliation, and monstrosity, which come into play when a man or a social group are not able to internalize the complications and the conflicts of adulthood, don't exist. The Minotaur comes to light when a human being or a social group is not able to sacrifice something under the pressure of something innovative; in other words, regression gets a foothold when, in front of a transformation process, the erotic energy to carry it out is lacking.

In the psychological case of Ariadne, the Minotaur represents an endogamous and regressive animus (they are brother and sister): an animus like this is not usable for awareness and it costs a lot, since it destroys young, creative potential, its voracity dissolves much new life. Frequently I meet Ariadnes who nourish and hide their Minotaurs: they are convinced that all men resemble their internal image of animus, and thus the monster from Crete, and they affirm consequently that men are violent, primitive, and inferior—an inevitable evil.

Having a useless masculine character available to the conscious, it is necessary for these women to exhibit a suffocating hegemony from the feminine principle, impeding the more evolved and intelligent traits from their animus to emerge and assert themselves. Often the mothers of these women resemble Pasiphae, both in their vital force and in their savage unruliness: they scorn and annihilate their husbands (they also cover them with symbolic cockroaches) every time their men try to evade their control, and their daughters learn that men are important, but women are worth more, and women can always find a way to dominate them.

Often these personalities are equipped with imagination, generosity, and deep feminine thought, but they lack mental discipline, precision in reasoning, lucidity in examining a conflict, and rigor in moral responsibility. "I hate confrontation," they say, for example. "It's something men do, you need to be aggressive and love power." They deny the value of aggressivity, but they don't know how much violence and competition they put into play to hold everything in their world under control. These women are convinced that they have developed the masculine traits of their personalities because they study, they earn their living, and they are able to make it by themselves, because a still dominant subculture induces them to confuse traditional gender roles with the form of the masculine and feminine psyche, and with their reciprocal and often unconscious dynamics.

A patient of mine, for example, when faced with facts of life, was often beyond reason and moral sense—of *any* moral sense—and thus beyond any kind of choice; she denied the consequence of her conflicts until—caught in a corner—she resolved them on impulse. She was periodically inspired by plans for vengeance, attacks of political fanaticism, or violent sexual jealousies, without any reflective meditation that could in some way succeed in being present in her conscious, and did not realize that she didn't have a thought or feeling, but that she was actually possessed by them. The evolution of her consciousness had been blocked much earlier in the passage from an existence prevalently instinctive to the life of feelings and conscious thoughts; this neurotic block had stopped her from going ahead in the more complex articulation of her personality, and consequently she rejected by regressing. Instinct, left to fend for itself, was a crazy compass incapable of orienting her; that woman lived her adult life, with the complexity of relationships and objectives it contains in this way, without understanding it. And since she lacked lucidity, moral criteria, critical discernment, and firmness, she caused pain both to herself and to those around her.

"What can I do, that's how I am," she used to repeat whenever she stumbled upon the mess of her existence. She certainly wasn't that way and yet she was that way, because she wasn't able to retrace within herself the unconscious and lost fragments of her animus.

This woman had a low opinion of men and considered them primitive and brutal, like the Minotaur, but without realizing the existence of her own projective mechanism. She fell in love with men and dedicated a lot of her time to seducing them: the fascination and intense vital energy she gave off made her desirable, but her mental disorder, and above all, the coldness of her feelings, exposed her to abandonment, so that her mental state was always oscillating between the satisfaction from a desire for power and the desperate fury of someone who has lost what she desires, but deep down scorns. Dominated by her Minotaur, she could not acknowledge and love a man, and perhaps she intuited this. What she couldn't know was how archaic her animus was and how taurine was her head.

Minotaur also belongs to the masculine psyche, as a regressive aspect of the ego: a man who becomes blocked, in the evolution of masculine thought and feeling, fixes his stage of consciousness on instinct, which, with time, inevitably becomes ill and rejects him in a regressive context. This, for example, is the condition of many young men, who have not learned either from family or school to construct the foundation of thought, firmness of will, moral sense, or the habit of reasoning, of transforming a passion into commitment, or an idea into a project. So they, like fiery bulls, transform themselves into Minotaurs, rather than men, and they go through life pushed by contradictory drives, inspired by great vital energy, at times illuminated by sudden ideas and large, vague aims, with mouths bigger than their hearts or brains, ready to devour everything—like the Minotaur—even their own youth. They make plans in which they have no faith; when they argue they don't know how to listen, they immediately raise their voice; they don't follow the line of the discussion, they are not rigorous either with themselves or with others, but they don't live happily, like perhaps in their early childhood, and at this point, like the Minotaur, they feel the weight of solitude and the anguish of passing time.

CHAPTER 7

The Labyrinth

From the most remote past, and in every civilization, human beings have drawn labyrinths, intricate courses which create and protect a center, like an abstract model of a universal sentiment which induces one to lose oneself and, if possible, to find oneself again. Although it is a spontaneous image, the labyrinth is not a simple form, because it derives from the complication of the spiral; as we can observe in figure 1 (page 128) the double spiral has its origin in the spiral, and then the superimposed one (the symbol of yin and yang) and then the crossed one, which is the origin of the swastika. Multiplying and complicating these figures, we find the labyrinth whose expansion toward the outside (or the inside) can go on infinitely.

The spiral form is the result of two opposite forces—centripetal and centrifugal—and it represents, together with the cross, the simplest graphic model of the union of opposites that the human imagination has ever been able to produce or recognize in nature. In its unwinding through the tension of opposite forces, the spiral develops a movement and thus a field of energy, a metaphor for the

Figure 1. The labyrinth. Top left: a spiral; top right: the double spiral; bottom left: the yin and yang; bottom right: the crossed spiral—the origin of the swastika.

meeting of physical and psychic opposites: inside and outside, contraction and expansion, dissolution and creation, shadow and light, conscious and unconscious, and so on.

The activation of the spiral's energy—observable in physical phenomena in the movement of a nebula, a vortex, a waterspout, or in the structure of an atom—is noticeable in the psychic field when contact between two opposite polarities gives origin to a new circuit of energy: for example, when an introverted subject activates an unconscious extroversion, or when a feeling psychological type develops the opposite intuitive function, it is possible to verify how, within the whole personality, not only a potential which until then had remained in the unconscious awakens, but also a new energy which derives from the meeting of an already constellated psychic polarity with the opposite, until then latent, polarity.

If the labyrinth constitutes a complication for the infinity of the spiral, it is also, above all, the image of movement and energy, and it expresses in its physical and psychic form that law which Heraclides had already intuited and from which every element is defined, starting from its opposite, in an eternally repeated and elusive comparison from which incessant, transformative energy has its origin. But the labyrinth, any labyrinth, can be seen as a whole, whose origin is its center, and which contains it; or, the other way around, like a point which begins and returns in itself, continuing to be nothing other than itself. The physical universe follows the principle of rotation, like the embryo grows in a spiral around the umbilical cord, and like blood which departs from and returns to its pulsating center. In this sense the center of the labyrinth seems to become an immobile, ideal point, the fulcrum, around which movement is activated.

Often, in fact, in the most ancient iconography, the meander and the labyrinth are linked by figures of movement and transformation. For example, incised on the back of a scarab, on the side of a ship, in the tunnel of a temple, near a swimming fish, on the belly of the Great Mother, on the shoulders of a walking man, around the sun, and on tombs, sarcophaguses, and funeral dressings, as if since then humanity has perceived in those forms the description of a profound experience, more than the model of natural realities. The spiral and the labyrinth are certainly found in nature in images, such as a coiled snake, a shell, a vortex, the meanders of the brain and the viscera, but considering the surprising analogy in the way of representing these forms in all cultures, it is possible to think that Kerenji is right when he writes that "the true source of forms is in the most intimate depths of the human soul,"[1] more than in the suggestion produced by natural models.

It is a widely held opinion that the cult connected to the labyrinth has its origin in the stone age, inside the natural caverns with their meandering paths and that it was celebrated by priestesses who presided over funeral rites and human sacrifices. This would be ascribed, at least in a first phase, to the cultural area of the Great Mother who, symbolically containing all opposites, embraces within herself the alternation of life and death in the natural cycle as well. Confirming this hypothesis there is the first known labyrinth-spiral, a Paleolithic talisman in mammoth tusk ivory, found in Siberia, inside a cave used for funeral rites.

This primitive ritual form was still celebrated in Crete in the Minoan epoch, inside natural caves, by priestesses covered in animal skins as in the Neolithic era; now, considering the refinement of the Cretan civilization, it is possible to explain the survival of that cult starting from the symbolic intensity which its forms (cave, darkness, meander) revealed to the followers; it must have still been linked (as still happens in many contemporary dreams) to the immortality of nature in which one is born and dies and from which one draws, as from the unconscious, inspiration and wisdom. The idea of the labyrinth, as a symbolic place of life, death, and rebirth, and thus the eternal flowing of matter and energy, is still traceable in different and far-off mythologies, as in sepulchral representations from all eras, and in the memory of the first monumental labyrinth constructions in Egypt, which, according to historical testimonies,[2] were royal tombs.

1. K. Kerenji, *Nel Labyrinto* (Boringhieri, 1983), p. 89. Translation mine. Tr.
2. See Herodotus, Strabone, Diodorus, and Pliny, the Elder.

From time immemorial and with the same symbolic value, the labyrinth was also tattooed during particular initiation rites in Africa and in New Zealand; in this case the men and the women believed that they *incorporated* in some way the significance of the symbol, thus guaranteeing immortality after physical death.

According to an analogous Maori (New Zealand) tradition, after death the soul meets a horrible witch who, devouring the tattooed spirals, says, "Go on to Maura, the land of the living at Bouro, the land of the dead," then, touching the eyes of the soul of the dead, she gives it the "vision of the spirits." But if she doesn't find any tattoos, the witch devours the eyes of the soul, blinding it and impeding it from finding immortality.

In a culture very far away from both Africa and New Zealand, in the Sumerian culture, the religious epic of Gilgamesh reminds us that Humbaba, the underground demon who guards the underworld where the seven terrors Gilgamesh must face are, has a tattooed labyrinth on his face.

In Rome, the labyrinth of the Cestian pyramid has the inscription: "Down down with a slow step to Orcus," suggesting the hesitating, winding path toward the unknown. But in the Aenead, in the Latin world, we can observe the most explicit and complete description of the idea of death and rebirth linked to the labyrinth: when Aeneas, having reached the coast of Cuma, approaches the cave of the Sibyl, and he finds himself before an entry portal on which Daedalus had incised the story of the labyrinth of Crete: and that same portal signals the beginning of Aeneas' trip in the underworld.

In more recent times, at the turn of the century, in Norway, on the cliff of Montensvaes at the fjord of Varanger, and in the locality of Grebbeatad, it was the custom for sailors who survived a shipwreck to construct labyrinthine rings by lining up stones in proximity to a cemetery: feeling that they had passed through death, and, thus, in a certain sense they were reborn, they described their experience following a tradition, but in a completely unconscious way, through a symbolically representative construction.

Two of the most ancient labyrinths which have come down to us confirm a contiguous meaning to the one described above, an *archetypical whole* referable to "mystery, the world of the occult, revelation, divination," still so alive in the unconscious of contemporary humans. The labyrinths are incised on two Mesopotamian clay tablets from 2000 B.C., together with cuneiform inscriptions which speak about animal viscera offered in sacrifices and of a "palace of viscera" *(ekal tirani)*. For psychological investigation, the two incisions offer a cultural representation from a natural fact, which serves to attribute meaning and value to that internal, dark and winding path, which is hidden in the body and which guarantees life. In the viscera a process destined to remain internal and secret takes place; the punishment, if this is not the case, is the death of what lives. But if the labyrinth of the viscera hides the complex mystery of life—which at the beginning of culture must have been upsetting, just think of the physiological phenomena linked to the belly—feces, urine, menstruation, sperm, conception, birth—the only choice is to try to reveal it.

And, in fact, the attempt to decipher in the signs of the viscera the codes of internal transformation, and to expand the meaning, by symbolic extension, to the facts of life, constitutes a constant aspect in the religious traditions of the most ancient Mediterranean cultures. The killing of animals, and even before of human beings, was the sacrifice which allowed for the bringing of the viscera to light, and thus to be able to see and interpret them, and it constituted the concrete manifestation of an idea in which death subtends life, so that it is necessary to die to know. Divination revealed what was hidden, what is difficult to decipher because it lives *inside,* and, thus, finally also what is unconscious.

We know, for example, that the particular conformation of animal innards offered in sacrifice constituted an omen that the seers revealed upon the founding of a city, as if that natural labyrinth described the particular, intricate unwinding of events through which it would or wouldn't be possible to pass from chaos to order, from nothingness to the foundation of a community. Perhaps, in a successive phase, this ritual repeated or reactivated the universal cosmic creation because, in choosing and delimiting a space, it was separated from chaos and made sacred by a purpose.

Inner truths, hidden potentials, and forbidden and blocked paths exist, which are not knowable with reason, and which were explored through ritual sacrifice and divination in antiquity, as if it were necessary to go inside to know. This idea of the labyrinth, associated with the viscera and the occult world which it reveals, is tightly intertwined to the idea of sacrifice: an *inside* exists which can be brought *outside*, a light whose origin is in darkness, but because there is a life which is born from a death.

Starting from the observations thus far made regarding the origin, the form, and the history of the idea of the labyrinth, it seems possible to me to hypothesize that it has been stratified in the collective unconscious as an image and an archetypal experience of a path, and of movement within a mysterious place where, through the dynamics of opposite energies, a magnetic field is activated which offers space for the search, sacrifice, and the awareness of a center. If we lose sight of this ambivalent and dialectical aspect of the labyrinth, it will no longer be possible to embrace the symbolic complexity of an image which contains opposites in a continuous growth. In its form it is the end, because it is the beginning, it is mystery because it is knowledge, it is fear because it is a search.

Probably the strong symbolic bond between the labyrinth and death, which has induced some scholars to limit its meaning to an allegory for the underworld, derives from the universal perception of death as the most radical and mysterious transformative experience, which draws a sort of symbolic trace valid for all other passages. Men, in fact, *didn't die* before they were aware of it, because death, too, is at the end of one of our *conquests*. Homer calls human beings "mortals" and Aeschylus "those set like the sun," because human beings, when they become aware, are defined by mortality; thus there exists an indissoluble intertwining between life and death where one is the foundation and the guarantee of the other, and where both fix the extremes of a line which winds up in a spiral in one direction and unwinds in the opposite direction infinitely.

If the symbol is the link between image and meaning, then it is possible, on the basis of what I said earlier, that the symbol of the labyrinth (which still appears in dreams today) describes the space of the unknown, of the unconscious, of the future: sometimes what we don't know *outside* ourselves, that is what we don't possess *inside* ourselves, is what we don't know *after* ourselves.

Labyrinthine dreams, which I have been able to observe over time, present a constant analogy between spiraling movement and transformative tension, describing a cycle which has a beginning, a middle, and an end: the image begins from a point, it expands, it becomes more complex, and it dissolves in another point.

Entering an interior labyrinth, human beings accept feeling alone in a dark and mysterious place whose meanderings they do not know and cannot control; from that moment on, the direction they take will no longer be in their hands nor in their era; but if it is a question of a voyage in the dark, without points of reference or a route, to succeed in revealing a mystery and then to find the light once again, every time human beings face a labyrinth they accept losing themselves in the hope of finding themselves again in another form, and with different knowledge.

The center of the labyrinth is the end of the trip, and at the same time a new point of departure. It is also the secret nucleus that the intricate path hides and protects, and only those who find the way can recognize it in time. From that immobile moment of passage, which is the center, the path inverts, because that moment is the aim of the search, and it signals the transformative passage: from before to after, from inside to outside, from contraction to expansion, from tension to abandonment. The center transforms the chaos of the search into the cosmos of the new direction.

There are three conditions for conquering the labyrinth: the first is to recognize it, the second is to accept to play, the third is to experience the solitude.

Recognizing the labyrinth means knowing the moment has arrived (or has returned again) to enter in the depths of oneself to try to resolve a problem, a crisis, a torment. It means thinking: "Here we are, a traditional compass, the actual signals are of no use, I have to go all the way into my darkness to discover a new light. Will I be able to do it? And will I be able to find the path to bring back the richness of this experience?" Recognizing in time one's own labyrinth is less easy than it seems, since the entrance often deceives because in dreams, literature, and life it assumes reassuring forms: sometimes it is the door to a library, the corridor of a hospital, a game situation, a walk in the country, a wide staircase where a human being tranquilly ventures, and then, gradually or all of a sudden, everything changes and one is already inside the labyrinth and the only possibilities are to either accept or refuse the risk.

Perhaps because of these deceitful aspects, many people slip into the labyrinths of their lives without even knowing it, with the carefreeness and the boldness of someone trying out a new game, and subsequently find themselves prisoner to an undertaking above their own strength. For the same reasons, other people are so terrified of finding labyrinths behind every door that they do not go in anywhere, remaining immobile, and ending up adapting their existence more or less to that of a mineral.

Only experience and attention help human beings intuit when the dark and disquieting form of the labyrinth meets with their life, and when it is time to search inside for the courage and the humility to face it. And passion is also a large support, because the labyrinth, at least in my experience, never offers an exclusively mental undertaking: intellectual curiosity is often part of the game, but we enter the labyrinth for necessity and desire; I have never seen transformation without eros. When new patients, facing that extraordinary labyrinth which is the psychoanalytic path, communicate that their motivation is intellectual curiosity, I ask myself how much time has to pass before knowing if a passion strong enough to overwhelm the defenses and to allow the journey to begin will come up.

Apollo ordered Theseus to be guided by the goddess of love, and Ariadne gives the thread to the man she loves: it doesn't seem difficult to me to understand this insistence on feeling, from the moment when, if the labyrinth becomes the meaning of life in a particular difficult situation, it is clear that life cannot be in mental knowledge. But the love which guides in the labyrinth is not that of Narcissus; one doesn't go to the underworld to show how brave one is, nor to draw personal advantages: Aeneas, Dante, Ulysses, Gilgamesh, Inanna, Psyche, Kore, Theseus go to the underworld moved by different and apparently contrasting passions, but they are all joined by a common denominator: the love of change and the knowledge of its laws.

The second condition is to accept to play the game of the labyrinth and this means none other than inventing an anti-labyrinth: the center waits for those who know how to use Ariadne's thread, and those people can unravel the ball of thread from one turning to another, with the patience to follow the path and the fear of making a wrong turn, without deceiving themselves by observing the labyrinth from above, and thus predicting it, but accepting to experience the labyrinth from inside and thus to discover it slowly. To accept the game of the labyrinth means to trust in that mental form which I have defined, in another part of this book, as *feminine thought*: it is the hesitating thread of inductive thought that recognizes the path along the way, and which enters the most remote areas where reason has no play and where only acceptance of the problem can lead to a solution. It is a thread which proceeds following at times opposite directions: "and if only, if instead" and it surpasses obstacles as they appear, elaborating flexible plans, adapted each time, finding the way to defeat the deceit with the same weapons. Ariadne's thread seems to me, from this point of view, to be the most perfect symbol for feminine thought: soft, smooth, silent, it can reach great depths by recording and remembering every passage.

The third condition for conquering the labyrinth is to accept the solitude: Theseus doesn't include his companions in the under-taking, because any truly creative undertaking requires introversion, and also because the uncertainty to go through is different for each person and cannot be shared. But perhaps there is another reason which is hidden in the difference between the relationship with oth-ers and the relationship with one's own internal search. A relation-ship is always activated by the ego as the center of consciousness, but in the labyrinth the ego no longer has energy for other people, because such a large part of the *libido* is concentrated in the searching. The characteristic tension always weakens the ego, at least temporarily, and is oriented toward a completely personal center. Thus a man, finally coming out of his labyrinth, can conclude: "Now I know that my life will take this direction," but none who hear him will ever know through which obscure meanderings, in which frightening uncertainties and following what intimate truths, he has reached his conclusion.

I have observed how many people have difficulties in entering the labyrinth of an internal search, precisely because of the fear of psychic solitude, as if it were intolerable for the ego to temporarily absent itself from the sight of others to face internal life. There is certainly an egoic discomfort in this necessity to always radiate toward the outside, and to impose one's own ego at the center of the attention of others, and yet this type of ego-reference seems to me only a symptom, behind which I have traced, with surprising regularity, a dependence relationship with the mother. From this point of view, the unwinding of the Cretan myth seems very interesting to me: Ariadne in fact separates herself from the maternal world when she meets a man (the image of her animus) who, loving his own mother, was able to leave her. On the basis of my clinical experience, the terrible insecurity linked to maternal dependence does not seem to allow for the detachment from a personal or collective You, the risk being the shattering of the identity.

The important transformative experience, which the image of the labyrinth expresses, requires, as does any initiation experience, an ego strong enough to resist the emptiness of solitude and the impact with the unconscious.

Regarding this, the last page of Hermann Hesse's *Narcissus & Goldmund* seems particularly illuminating. Goldmund, at his last meeting with Narcissus, close to death himself, and marked for life by his dependence on his lost mother, desperately murmurs to his friend: "But how will you die when your time comes, Narcissus, since you have no mother? Without a mother, one cannot love. Without a mother, one cannot die."[3] But it is possible to separate from a mother, only by *having her inside oneself*: the internalized experience permits the detachment from the real figure and restores strength and security to the ego. Otherwise the two fundamental experiences of life—love and death—are not possible, because we only succumb to them.

THE LABYRINTH IN DREAMS

A woman, who came to see me, had suffered a trauma from the age of eight months when her mother, who had two sons in addition to my patient, took into the house another baby girl the same age, and she nursed and took care of both of them. The cohabitation lasted for more than a year, damaging the fusional phase of the maternal relationship, and inducing my patient to have a strong dependence on her mother in a love-hate relationship. The principal consequences of this trauma were revealed over time in the impossibility of abandoning herself seriously to a man, for the fear of having to submit to another betrayal, and in the development of a narcissistic neurosis which forced her to propose herself as generous, strong, available, and capable of excelling on social and professional terrain. To reach these aims she had cultivated a well-equipped animus, leaving, however, a much more personal masculine complex in the unconscious, oriented toward objectives less socially valued, and in any case more introverted. On the other hand, her feminine

3. H. Hesse, *Narcissus & Goldmund* (New York: Bantam, 1971), p. 315.

ego had been struck by a fear of loving and being betrayed, depriving her of the capacity to abandon herself to a man and to express the warmth and passion which were hers. The motivations for analysis weren't obvious, but after a short while, behind the secure and winning face of the queen bee, a more hesitant, but more authentic and profound trace appeared. One day she told me this dream:

THE LITTLE GIRL IN THE LABYRINTH: *I am in a social situation, perhaps a party, with a lot of people, lights, and animation. I see my friend S. and a man who, in reality, I had met a few days before for work. We leave and, from the lights of the party, we enter the dark streets of the city, streets which I don't know. I have the feeling that I am alone now, and I find myself near a circus encampment, or perhaps a camp of Gypsies, where a woman, a real witch, proposes a game of cards. It is necessary to pay 3,000 lire to begin and I pay it, but a little boy (or a little girl?) takes the money away, I take out another 3,000 lire and also this time the child takes the money away from me. So I get very angry, really angry, not only because I can't play, but because I know that the old witch and the child are in agreement to cheat me. I run away, feeling it is a dangerous situation and I find myself in a place which resembles (or perhaps it is) a hospital, full of corridors and doors; I walk quickly to cross through because I still feel a sense of danger, until I find myself in a small construction of iron grating, circular or octagonal, like a gazebo, but which seems more sacred and solemn, and it makes me think of a baptistery, even though baptisteries are not open structures. I go out of it and I realize that, next to my baptistery, there is another one, the same, where a little girl is closed in who says, while I move away, "Come back, after, and remember that I am in number 4." So then I notice that the street number of her construction is 4 and mine is 3. I hesitate, perhaps I want to help the child, but I am in a hurry, I want to get out of there and I go. At this point I am in great haste, and I go up a staircase at the top of which there is an unprotected terrace, from which it is easy to fall. Maybe a man had fallen and died. There is no way out, I turn to go back, and I wake up.*

In association my patient told me that S. was a close friend of hers, a personality very different from hers, sweet, introverted, and passionate, and that the man was young and from southern Italy, calm, reflective, very masculine, but above all, very handsome and fascinating. "He is one of those men," she said to me, "who are very kind and even gallant, but definitely are not to be dominated."

"The kind who scares you a lot?"

"I like him and I am very scared."

Thus the dream opened in a collective situation, extroverted and noisy, rich and happy, typical of her life, but her unconscious energies, S., and the man from the South, make it so that she moves toward her labyrinth.

After a series of dark and unknown streets, which announce a different and mysterious path, there is an important passage: the cheating of the witch and the child; the unconscious, through the fairy tale image, recalls the betrayal of the mother, accomplice to another child. The witch and the step-mother, in fairy tales as well as in dreams, give body to the negative maternal manifestation which rejects or betrays, and consequently my patient feels deprived of energy (the money), but above all, she senses their mockery, the ridicule and that terrible feeling of exclusion. She can't play according to the rules because the rules have been upset: the mother is a witch and the other child is a thief, so the symbiosis becomes impossible because the relationship was loaded. That woman can't win the first game of her life, and she will neurotically compensate for that wound, deciding to win in any case and always for the rest of her existence.

Anger pushes her away in an attempt to escape from rancor and humiliation, but she continues to feel in danger, and she ends up finding herself in a hospital (another moment of her labyrinthine path) where she cures herself, and resolves the trauma by turning it into a neurosis. Thus, she learns to manage herself, to move ahead quickly and determined, to feel self-sufficient and capable of getting out of the *impasses* of life. But inexorably, and without her knowledge, the labyrinthine path guides her toward her center, toward the essential nucleus of the problem, the two circular baptisteries which constitute, since they are places for baptism, the symbolic space for rebirth in a new life. The dream affirms that the woman's ego seems at first to have passed this test, because the reference number is 3, but it also recalls that an unconscious image has remained imprisoned since infancy because the number is 4: my patient was unaware of her childhood trauma, or she had minimized it, examining it with her adult-woman-consciousness and limiting herself to seeing the 3. That is the number which includes her and her two brothers, and, thus, the acceptable condition, but, for a long period, in her unconscious a little girl had remained prisoner of the 4, and thus of the trauma of the *extra* child. So the little girl, the baptistery which locks her in, and the number 4 constitute the center of the labyrinth, the symbolic place that has to be acknowledged and resolved in order to take the path to return.

In the dream, my patient can see the suffering of that little girl, and also feel the impulse to help her, but she is not yet able to slow down the imminent rhythm of her life to open herself to the pain and feel it as hers. The weak and losing aspect, that stimulates the solidarity as a strong woman when it refers to her neighbor, becomes difficult to accept when it refers to herself. Consequently, the center of the labyrinth has been seen, but not yet surpassed. The dreamer believes at first to have succeeded, but then she realizes that it is impossible to go out, that she has entered a dead-end, one of many spread throughout the labyrinth. Her unconscious knew this and had transmitted it through the words of the little girl: "Come back, after, and remember that I'm at number 4." It is inevitable to return to where her past, a prisoner of defeat and rancor, waits to be liberated.

The liberation of the little girl will signal the end of narcissism, of the compulsion to please and to win, of the obligation to be successful and will coincide, in the end, with the liberation from the maternal complex. Only after this undertaking will the friend or the unknown man find space inside her, assuming forms still unknown, but which will give a different value to her life.

Another woman told me this dream one day:

THE LABYRINTH OF EROS: *First I go with someone in a narrow street, I see a colorful shop window and it reminds me of a cooperative run by young people, just opened, which sells shoes at good prices. The girl I am with knows them and doesn't want to be recognized by them. I go in, the window is colorful, with tree trunks, feathers. In reality there are no shoes, nor a shop, but I only see a descent by means of a ladder, the rungs fixed and solid, made from tree trunks, toward an outdoor excavation site: there is earth and grass, and at the end there is a well. Everything is very orderly and controlled and as I descend I meet with busy young people—the ones from the cooperative—in couples or groups, who seem busy constructing this labyrinth which perhaps will become their*

*cooperative. They don't look at me and I have the feeling of being
an intruder, and I don't know if it is good or bad that I am there.*

*From the last room, the one with the well, on the same level
one enters into another room. I approach it, and I see a bed, and the
curly hair of someone asleep, I think it is a male, a boy. At this point
it seems to me that I have pushed too far in, to I go back and return
to the surface.*

In analysis my patient searched for the security of good shoes at a
reasonable price, an identity which allowed her to go along her own
path. But what path, toward where, if that woman had never
known a passion capable of giving a direction to her life? What will
she do with the shoes if she has no aim or doesn't know she has
one? Someone taught me, a long time ago, that "it is better to know
where to go and not know how, than to know how to go and to not
know where." My patient's search seemed to orient itself toward
the second possibility.

She was a cold and intelligent woman: her body, her soul, and
her mind had never really burned for anything or anyone. So the
dream forgets the shoes and, instead, in the shop window there are
tree trunks and feathers, natural images of very heavy and very light
things, telluric and aerial, all strange to this woman, who didn't
know the weight and the value of her roots. She wasn't trusting
enough to abandon herself to the wind and fly. The girl who accompanies her, the image of an *alter ego* linked to the analyst and the
awareness of the unconscious (the girl knows the people in the
cooperative), stands aside leaving the dreamer to have her solitary
adventure. Instead of selling shoes, the cooperative is constructing a
labyrinth which resembles an archaeological dig. It contains in itself
the past and the future: it is a question of a well-organized network

of paths and rooms, open to the sky, in the middle of earth, grass, and at the end, water.

The death which that labyrinth promised was the death of the young cerebral and patinated woman, with a much more attractive *persona*, but a little fatuous, with a pleasing body, but cold ("The ideal would be if sex didn't exist," she once said to me). At the archaeological site, in the far off past, she would afterward rediscover her farm origins—the contact with air, the earth, and water, and, through these elements, with nature, matter, the body, the life of instinct and pleasure. She would accept falling in love and accept growing old (she had a horror of old people) and finally understand and forgive her mother.

That labyrinth didn't lead only toward the past, however, but also contained an omen for the future, for there was a *divine youth* with curly hair asleep in the center of the last room. As in the tale of Psyche, Eros sleeps, still wrapped up in unconsciousness, but he is alive and he has been seen. The image is so numinous that the dreamer thinks: "At this point it seems to me that I have pushed too far in." In that phase of her life, the center of the labyrinth—and that is the passion of Eros—assumed the vague physiognomy of a future still far away and unimaginable. When would he wake up? And when would he pierce her with his arrow? And in what direction would it set her existence? And more: would she be able to follow him? Would she accept the sacrifices which passion requires?

From another patient I received this dream:

THE LABYRINTH AND DEATH: *I am in a wide valley surrounded by trees, in an English-style field—a beautiful spectacle. In the middle of the green field there are many groups of small ruins, very ancient, I think I am in Rome, and the ruins make me think of the* ancient Romans; I am holding my son, who is a little younger than he is now, by the hand. The ruins are really entrances into tunnels, which lead into ancient cities, catacombs, which are immense: the walls are made of dark red, dusty earth, but everything is clean, or so it seems to me. To go in we attach ourselves to railings and we descend the steps; in certain moments there seem to be people, in others not, but I become aware of my capacity to estrange myself from everything, while I look at what is around me and think.

I don't even see my son, even though the sensation of his hand in mine is present for the whole time. I don't know if Claudio [the son of a friend of the dreamer] is with us, or if he is already there, but at a certain point I see him sit in a chair, fall onto a table and die. I think of how to not scare my son and how to tell his mother.

Upon exiting from underground, I reascend the steps and grab onto another railing, my son's hand is still in mine, and my mother is also by my side as I proceed on big sheets of old, white rock; far away columns are visible. A Milanese family, whose son is a schoolmate of my son, passes by. One of them starts to tell me about the daughter, ugly, pudgy, and small like the son, who had been given a contract to act in a TV movie. I reply distractedly, I think of the dead child and his mother, and it bothers me that my mother rejoices with the other woman for something so stupid as television success. Then I think that they don't know, and, if they don't know, why should they be worried or sad?

Finally we move on, and I find myself in a room similar to the one where Claudio died; his mother is in front of me; I tell her what happened; then we go into the other room, where there is the body of the child, and I feel guilty because I don't know how to explain how or why Claudio died. His mother approaches him, she caresses his hair, and asks and looks for a scissors to clean his nails: he has *to be seen clean and orderly even dead. I realize that, even if she talks about her son as dead, in reality she is not accepting the situation, so I take her by the shoulders, I shake her and I tell her that now she needs to cry, that she can't pretend it's nothing serious, I tell her to bring out the pain that she has inside, and as I speak, my voice rises, until I am almost screaming, and to cry becomes an order, an intimidation, and while I am yelling, she begins to shed big tears.*

Again in this dream we find a labyrinthine progress in the archaeological dig, and the descent into the viscera of the earth: the patient speaks about catacombs and tunnels formed by walls of earth, and of her capacity to estrange herself from everything. The child who dies in there is not hers, or perhaps it is better to say that it is no longer hers. It is the model of an impossible life plan for which it is necessary to observe the end: it consumes itself, it fades away, except that one wants to go all the way to see.

But something is born, and it is born in two different moments: in the economy of this dream and in the awareness of the pain that any end brings. At first the dreamer can no longer speak of other things, because she had been able to witness death, she is aware of it, and it is at the center of her attention. The people she meets speak of futile things, but as she immediately acknowledges after, "I think that they don't know and, if they don't know, why should they be worried or sad?" The *others* have no weight, and there is no sense in revealing that death to them: in this moment the psychic solitude in front of the labyrinth is fully acknowledged.

In the second part the dreamer shakes Claudio's mother and asks her, in a dramatic crescendo, not to pretend it's nothing: the part of her that is the mother of the dead child has to accept the mourning, because behind that pain, that future which has faded away, there is a suffering which also has to be acknowledged.

In the center of the labyrinth, in this case, there is the depression for what was not possible to experience, or for what was not experienced well, for everything that is finished; for what, in her existence, couldn't grow and express itself. And so the way out of the labyrinth is through crying.

Sometimes, instead, for some people, entering the labyrinth means facing the hell of a large shadow. In disseminating ruin in one's own and in other's lives, in destruction, in the systematic capacity of annihilating oneself in everyday life, it is sometimes possible to recognize that one has lost oneself. As far as I know, in my life and that of other people I have known and loved, I have been able to recognize this terrible form of labyrinth: some become alcoholics, some drug addicts, some shoot and at times kill, some follow an infallible vocation to lose, some wound themselves and the person they love, some lose themselves in paths too far from their own; in every case a tremendous violence subtends this *cupio dissolvi* and the negative energy that sets it in motion. If a human being is able to reach the center of this labyrinth, which in this case often means hitting bottom, then the boa's twisting becomes possible, the energy changes sign and returns to the light.

But the result is uncertain, even in this case: if it is possible to hit bottom and return, finding the path of regeneration, and thus dying and being reborn for oneself, or if it is inevitable to remain entrapped in the spires of the labyrinth, finding one has gambled and lost to the forces of the shadow, this is the enigma that only time is capable of unraveling. Only time is capable of recognizing the existence (or the absence) of the energy necessary to face transformation. This energy truly seems to be the great unknown, the true nucleus of mystery of every internal passage.

THE OBSESSIVE LABYRINTH

The labyrinth also makes its appearance in obsessive rituals. When this happens, instead of being a transformative passage, the labyrinth constellates a dead-end path just for itself; it is a mechanism that springs to entrap existence: obsessive people, in fact, self-impose behaviors that have the single aim of furthering them from this objective, without letting them forget it. We see useless behaviors and gestures, at times self-denigrating, often repetitive; on a social plane we can recognize them, for example, in military organization, bureaucracy, and in prison structures, all spheres characterized by obsessive pathologies. In these contexts, the labyrinth is artificially constructed in order to get lost; the center is not lost from sight, but it is not reached, because the neurotic block is, above all, the lack of freedom, in this case the freedom to reach the goal. Staying in this internal prison generates an anxiety that is sometimes very intense, analogous to that of a person really imprisoned.

A woman, during our first session, was so constantly occupied with the contents of her purse and her pockets (Did she have the money to pay for the session? Did she have her keys? Her check book? And her driver's license?) that she was almost unable to speak. She got lost—and she defended herself—in her labyrinth of obsessive thoughts, and at the same time she manifested an authentic anguish for her helplessness to tell me what she wanted from me.

Another woman told me that obsessiveness rose in her only when she was going to enjoy herself; in these cases a "click in her brain" sprung, as she called it, and, whenever she was ready to leave her house, she was forced to go around checking things, always the same things, three times. Were the lights turned off? And the gas? Was the stereo switched off, and was the refrigerator running? Was the safe closed and covered by the painting? Were the appliances turned off? Sometimes, when she had already left, she had to go back to make sure the front door was locked, that no window had been left open, and that there was a bowl of water for the dog. She hated this behavior, but it was much stronger than she. Sometimes the labyrinth became so winding that it slowed her down until she missed a train or an important meeting.

Naturally, in dreams it is possible to observe the labyrinth as an obsessive ghost, but I don't think that it is recognizable every time that a normal path becomes blocked by an obstacle. In fact, these cases seem to be a question of an oneiric description of a simple psychic resistance; in order to talk about an obsessive labyrinth, there has to be a complex and intricate path, something to reach, and one loses oneself along the way, as for example in the following dream of a male patient:

THE BALL IN THE CENTER: *I have to go to Rome, but there are no planes because of the fog. I run to the train station to catch the only train which will get me there in time for my appointments, and I ask my secretary to accompany me because she can take her time parking the car near the station. When we arrive, they tell me that the trainworkers are on strike, and that my train isn't going to leave. So I decide to drive to Rome, but to do this I need another car which goes faster, which is in a garage at the opposite end of the city. Finally I leave and I drive toward the outskirts of town to get onto the highway, but they are working on the road and I am detoured onto side roads that I don't know. I try to keep the right direction, but the fog and all of the necessary detours make it difficult. Finally I turn onto a wide, asphalted road, which I am sure will bring me to the highway, but then it begins to get narrower, it becomes paved, then a dirt road, and finally a foot path. I continue to follow it and the path turns into a one-way country road; at the crossroads there is only one sign: Milan. I have no choice because I am really lost.*

Immediately after having told me this dream, my patient said, laughing, "This shows that not all roads lead to Rome!" But he was the first to admit that his obsessiveness and haste were the worst enemies to his reaching his objective.

The sadistic aspect of the obsessive ritual, which has unconscious origins in our patients, is rather almost always planned and conscious in public institutions. Many years ago I went to an interview with a prisoner who was subjected to a particular surveillance; the aim of the warden of that prison—to impede that conversation—was legally impossible because of the permit I had. So a labyrinth was constructed around me, irreprehensible from the formal, legal point of view. I was subjected to being frisked, then my identity was minutely checked, calling Milan for confirmation of the authenticity of my documents; then I was sent to an area to check the material (books, newspapers, and food) that I wanted to give the prisoner, and this operation was carried out in the same manner, flipping the pages of each book, each newspaper, with exhausting slowness. The passage from one control to the next was interspersed by long waits, for which, with a lot of courtesy, warrant officers and other officials apologized. Finally, after having taken one hour and forty minutes to carry out a series of tasks which in other prisons had never taken more than ten minutes, I was accompanied into the interview room where I waited some more, before the person I was waiting for arrived. At that point, the young and innocent prison guard who had accompanied him told me that the warrant officer in charge informed us that the time allotted for the interview—according to the regulations between noon and 2 o'clock—would expire in ten minutes. My prisoner friend and I had lost our center, both victims of the obsessive and sadistic labyrinth which others constructed around us.

The Court House of Milan, for example, is another public structure where the labyrinth expresses its form in the architectural design, even before the way its offices function. It is contrived in such a way that it is natural to get lost, and the citizen's aim becomes a treasure hunt rather than a bureaucratic incumbency. Enormous corridors, exactly alike, doors which look like elevators and elevators which look like doors, tunnels that lead to stairs which lead to other tunnels, where the doors that open are only apparently numbered in a progressive order, because, finally having reached number 232, near the goal, the next door is number 7. Where is number 240? Other enormous corridors, other stairs, other tunnels, other well-hidden elevators which conceal the treasure from the indiscreet glances of the common citizen, so that when one finally waves a penal certificate, one has the sensation of having won a war more than having exercised a right.

THE DANCE OF THE LABYRINTH

The hypothesis that the meander and the labyrinth have always been connected to the idea of movement is confirmed by a prevalent opinion in the anthropological sphere, for it is said that the labyrinth, before being built, was danced.

Jill Puirce, an English anthropologist, writes: "[T]he essence of the labyrinth is not its outward form, its delineating stones and hedges, but the movement it engenders. The spiral mandalic movements of the dance predate even the labyrinth itself."[4]

---

4. Jill Puirce, *The Mystic Spiral* (London: Thames and Hudson, 1974), p. 30.

K. Kerenji holds the same opinion: "All of the research about labyrinths has had to start from dance."[5] And Pausanias, for his part, wrote in the second century B.C.: "At Knossos they didn't show the trace of the Minoan palace, but Daedalus', a place for dance, on white stone."[6]

The origin of the labyrinth in movement is a suggestive hypothesis which is also based on innumerable examples of labyrinthine dances as manifestations of the meeting of opposites in rites of passage.

In Hindu culture, for instance, the dance of Shiva represents the winding and unwinding of the world, the contraction and expansion of matter and energy, through a series of movements in which the human body becomes the labyrinth. The Mevlan Dervishes, initiated to Sufi thinking, express in one of their most ancient dances the pace of a double spiral with descending and then ascending vortexes, which they carry out by bending down to the ground and then turning around themselves and then lifting themselves as high as possible, in the symbolic search for contact between the energy of the sky and the earth.

Still today in South Africa they dance the *deumba* (the dance of the python), in which old women kneel in the center, immobile, like a fulcrum around which the young girls of the Barenda tribe, lying down in a circle, leaning against each other, move in a spiral, winding and unwinding in a labyrinthine figure, following the movements of the python; raising themselves rhythmically and falling to the ground, entering and exiting the spiral volutes, as they physically describe the biological cycle of death and rebirth.

---

5. K. Kerenji, *Nel Labirinto*, p. 55.
6. Pausanias, I 40, 3. *Guide to Greece*, Peter Levi, trans. (London & New York: Viking Penguin, 1984).

Another example of the danced labyrinth is traceable in the *Maro* dance of Ceram, in Polynesia. As K. Kerenji writes:

> The Maro dance is still today performed only at night; men and women participate. A man leads the group of dancers, who follow, men and women alternated, with joined arms, as is prescribed. In a multicolored procession, the formation of the dancers expands and forms a circle; when the beginning and end of this circle are joined, then the line winds up in spiral around the first circle, until it forms a multiple spiral. Once this figure is constructed, the group of dancers moves in a circle counterclockwise, with measured steps, stamping the terrain with their feet on the melody of a three-voiced song. Maro is still today danced almost exclusively on ceremonial occasions, and without doubt it is tightly linked to the representations of the trip of the dead.[7]

The center of the Maro labyrinth is, in fact, a door behind which the queen of the dead hides, and the aim of the dance is to reach it.

In the Aaland islands, the oldest generations still conserve the memory of the *Jungfrudans* (the dance of the virgins), in which the young men competed, running through corridors and tunnels inside deep natural caves, trying to be the first to reach the maiden seated in the center.

It has also been possible to reconstruct documentation of other very ancient labyrinthine dances in the New Hebrides, in northern Europe, in Greece and in southern Italy. The characteristic rhythm of the labyrinthine dance in Greece was called *geranos*, that

7. K. Kerenji, *Nel Labyrinto*, pp. 41–42. Translation mine.

is, "the dance in crane style," perhaps because the participants proceeded in a line linked together, resembling a group of cranes at the moment of seasonal migration.[8]

At Delos, in particular, the labyrinthine dance was part of the sphere of the cult of Ariadne and Aphrodite joined in a single figure. According to legend, Theseus triumphed over the labyrinth thanks to Aphrodite's favor and Ariadne's intervention. In honor of the goddess of love, the young men danced the labyrinth with their companions for the first time at Delos, following Ariadne's instructions. This detail of the myth could make one think that the Delian dance, as it has come down to us, was the same as the one performed in the labyrinth at Knossos. We know that it went from left to right, around an altar made from the left-side horns of bulls. Recalling that the left is the symbolic direction for death, it means that the path unwound toward death to meet it, and then turned to the opposite direction, toward the beginning of a new life.

The name *geranos*, which makes one think of a flock which rises in flight and the rope tradition almost as though it were necessary to keep oneself anchored to the earth, and the oscillating and repetitive movement of the dance (forward and back, left to right), suggest that this particular dance induced a semi-hypnotic state in which consciousness could feel grasped and pushed by an unknown energy, so that it would "fly" like a flock of cranes and almost lose itself in a daze which perhaps resembles a state of *trance*. If this was the case, it can be better understood by the clinical case referred by C. A. Meier and summarized by K. Kerenji:

> It is a case of *ambulatory automatism*, that is, of a circular motion effected in a sleep-walking state, but with

---

8. K. Kerenji, *Nel Labyrinto*, p. 60. Translation mine.

a lucid memory, rather with manifestations of hyperamnesia. In substance, to use the term which for the Romans indicated circular ritual processions, one could speak of a *circumambulance*. The movement first went toward the left, then, upon reaching the center, toward the right. This experience was repeatedly accompanied by the phenomenon of levitation. Who experiences it, feels the impulse to rise up from the ground, almost as if a strong wind was blowing; one must hold oneself firmly and anchor oneself in some way to the ground; and also in this case there were similar manifestations (I am citing to the letter the clinical description). The patient was absolutely not crazy; she didn't get lost, she didn't *lose the thread*, and during the whole process she acted in a state of *double conscience*. To not fly away and to not lose contact with this world, she grasped onto the garden gate, or a holly bush. Wasn't the cable which held the Delian dancers perhaps for this purpose? Or rather did it react to the two needs, that of executing with precision the figure and simultaneously that of keeping one steady? Perhaps the dancers of the geranos also experienced free flight in such a violent manner that they were forced to hold each other's hands, so that they could remain anchored to reality? The intensity of their experience should absolutely not be underestimated. . . . At the end of this *circumambulation,* the woman found a gigantic ammonite in the grass; she was incredibly attracted to it and fascinated by it. She remained immobile looking at it, as if she were enchanted, not being able to remove her gaze from it; she had the strong feeling that that object was exactly what she had "looked for." One finds the pure form of the spiral in ammonites, the original form of the labyrinth.[9]

In 1979 I happened to assist one of these very ancient spiral dances in the village of Olympos, in the Carpathian mountains. This island in the Dodecanese was still a stranger to tourism at that time. August 15th was the day of the village's celebration. After the religious ceremony of orthodox rites and ritual distribution of bread, olives and honey, even to us strangers, the dance began.

The men and women lined up Indian style, and they all each held the corner of the apron[10] or the edge of the jacket of the dancer in front of them, as if on the one hand they didn't want to lose the thread of the dance, but on the other they intended to establish and maintain contact. The steps were short and oscillating, perhaps three forward and two back: the gait was very slow, and the repetitive music, which accompanied the dance, slowly induced, in both the observers as well as the dancers, a sort of hypnotic state. The dancers structured their path in a very complex double spiral, which, in the end, formed a labyrinth: first the spiral wound up on itself in a contraction, then it untwisted toward the outside in a phase of expansion, first to the left, toward the depths of the underworld, then to the right, toward the heights of heaven.

The dance went on for the entire afternoon, but my friends and I were incapable of tearing ourselves away from what we felt was a very ancient rite and not only a village dance. The dancers were silent and absorbed, and I felt, in that living labyrinth, a magnetic circuit of extraordinary intensity.

---

9. K. Kerenji, *Nel Labyrinto*, pp. 61–62. Translation mine.
10. At Carpathos in 1979, women still wore the traditional costume: a long ample blue or black dress of cotton and a colored apron.

Only a few years later, rereading *The Iliad,* did I realize that I had witnessed Ariadne's dance. Describing Achilles' shield, Homer tells what Hephaestus has sculpted on it:

And then the renowned smith of the strong arms made
  elaborate on it
a dancing floor, like that which once in the wide spaces
  of Knosos
Daedalus built for Ariadne of the lovely tresses.
And there were young men on it and young girls,
  sought for their beauty
with gifts of oxen, dancing, and holding hands at the
  wrist. These
wore, the maidens long light robes, but the men wore
  tunics
of finespun work and shining softly, touched with olive
  oil.
And the girls wore fair garlands on their heads, while
  the young men
carried golden knives that hung from sword-belts of
  silver.
At whiles on their understanding feet they would run
  very lightly,
as when a potter crouching makes trial of his wheel,
  holding
it close in his hands, to see if it will run smooth. At
  another
time they would form rows, and run, rows crossing
  each other.
And around the lovely chorus of dancers stood a great
  multitude

happily watching, while among the dancers two
  acrobats
led the measures of song and dance revolving around
  them.[11]

Homer observed that it had to be a long procession, because, after a short while, the dancers were in double lines, one in front of the other *(επι στικασ αλλελοισιν)*. And this necessarily happened when the formation was forced to change the direction of the dance with an inversion of the spiral movement, or when it formed circles within the complicated figure of the labyrinth. In this way, he who found himself at the head of the procession began to move in the opposite direction and parallel to the others who followed him.

Homer's words, however, bring up at least two questions: why was the labyrinth constructed for Ariadne's dance and not for the Minotaur? And why was a dance, which is not a warrior subject, sculpted on Achilles' shield? Remembering that the life of the Greek hero was to end under the walls of Troy, I believe that the dance on the shield translates this destiny into an image: Achilles' imminent task was to face the most profound transformative experience of human life. The labyrinthine dance confirmed, on that shield as well, the ideal image of a sacred and protected space. Here is where the great mystery of the life and death of the individual takes place—within the vast circuit of an incessant transformation of matter and energy.

But then, if this was probably the meaning of the Cretan labyrinth, and if Ariadne was sovereign, and if it was only afterward that it hid the Minotaur, then what exactly does this myth want to tell us? Kerenji (in his work, *Nel Labyrinto*) comes very close to the

---

11. Homer, *The Iliad*, Book XVIII, v 590–605.

center when he affirms that Ariadne is the goddess of death and transformation. He takes a Cretan clay tablet written in Linear B, deciphered in the 1920s by the English architect Michael Ventris, which says: "Honey to the mistress of the labyrinth," and "Honey for all the gods," as his starting point. The scholar, recalling that honey was the food of the immortals, identifies the mistress of the labyrinth, and thus Ariadne, a goddess, if the palace was constructed for her. It could be, but it could also be that Ariadne was imagined to be a mortal creature, a priestess to the goddess. In any case, through her sovereignty over the labyrinth, Ariadne has become the symbol of sovereignty over the unconscious, as well as death, mystery, and infinity.

Homer does not speak about the labyrinth, but about *koros,* a place for dancing; but the most ancient Cretan tablet uses the term "labyrinth" *(labyrintoio):* this term is probably derived from the word *labris,* which in the ancient Anatolian language[12] meant "double axe," and the double axe is drawn and painted innumerable times inside the palace at Knossos, with the intent of symbolically describing the simultaneity of opposites which define themselves one with the other. Once again we meet life and death, matter and energy, the infinite world of opposites, in an instrument etymologically connected to the labyrinth. But this object also constitutes one of the most ancient signs of the sovereignty of the Mother Goddess, the ritual instrument for castrating the priests and taboo for the masculine world, to the point where, in the most ancient Anatolian civilization, men couldn't touch it.

So the Cretan labyrinth specifies its particular identity as a place sacred to the Great Mother, of whom Ariadne is an incarna-

---

12. An Anatolian civilization is tightly linked to the Minoan one, and might have originally been part of it.

tion, or a priestess, or both in different moments. It is a dark place, like the maternal belly which gives life, and like a cavity in the earth which receives death, a place of movement and transformation, like a vortex and a serpent, a place which hides the mystery to decipher like animal viscera; a double place, as the double axe from which it takes its name. It is the place where opposites meet, it is the place of totality and infinite energy.

The Cretan labyrinth is the center of a cult in which the sovereignty of the feminine principle is expressed in the phase of individual and collective psychological evolution when it absorbs its opposite, the masculine principle.

Ariadne dances with her companions. She experiences the labyrinth as a place for the cult; but when the time for differentiation arrives, the masculine principle has to become autonomous, and the bull must be sacrificed. If this doesn't happen, the Minotaur is born, and from that day on there is no more dancing. The labyrinth changes from a temple to a prison, to guard in Ariadne what couldn't be transformed.

Once I dreamed I was in a clearing in the woods: I was wearing a dress of red lace, and I was very young; I was dancing alone and the steps and the twirls slowly brought me deep within the woods. I remember an extremely beautiful light among the leaves, very soft and sweet. All of a sudden I saw the entrance to a stone cave, dissimulated by moss and leaves. It was really only a dark cave, but in the dream I thought: Here it is, this is the palace of Knossos. Like the young Ariadne, in the dream, I went to rediscover the lost palace, the one built for the dance a long time before and then transformed into a place of repression. So it was necessary to kill the Minotaur and save Theseus. But alone, without Ariadne, Theseus has gone crazy, and patriarchal culture has lost itself in another labyrinth, inhabited by other monsters, colder and less innocent than the Minotaur. Who knows if women, dressed in warm and feminine feelings (like the red lace), will know how to enter into the darkness all the way, according to the ancient dance, another time, but with a different understanding, so they can subdue the masculine shadow and bring the *anima mundi* back to life? In the dream I stop at the threshold, enchanted with looking.

The image of the labyrinth, and the dance that repeats it, seem linked by both archetypal and formal solidarity. It is as if men desired to express the hesitating and winding path of human searching, of the continuous transformation through the body, in a dancing, rhythmic movement that expresses the possibility of the eternal repetition of a cycle in its endless shape. If the labyrinth is an allegory for the human condition in its resolutive moments, the dance describes the way of accepting it. One doesn't run, or stand still, but one proceeds with rhythm and measure, embracing the mysterious sinuosity of the path, and the beginning and the end of the trip, since every end is none other than a new beginning.

CHAPTER 8

The Choice: The Theme of Relationships

To examine, from a psychological point of view, the meaning of the meeting between the two protagonists of the myth, it is necessary to imagine Ariadne's unconscious animus in Theseus; that is, the complex of masculine functions she was not able to recognize and develop. Symmetrically, it is also necessary to imagine Theseus' unconscious *anima*, the complex of feminine functions unknown to him, in Ariadne.

From this point of view, the myth is interpreted as a large collective dream, and the story of Theseus and Ariadne is a representation of an internal meeting. Here a man and a woman, recognizing and loving in the other a part of themselves which, until that day had been foreign to consciousness, become involved in a profound transformation.

According to the information deduced from this myth, women had no autonomy at the origin of Athenian society, and they lived, oppressed and protected, in the shadow of patriarchal order. They receive the unknown man who the father leads to their bed, they bear and raise a child which they will have to send away without knowing why, they keep secrets they don't understand, without ever asking, or discussing, apparently not even seeming to think. They are eternally daughters, and are accustomed to an almost animalesque obedience. In Troezen and in Athens, women, reduced to this state, don't count, and they don't count their way of thinking or feeling (the feminine archetype), simply because even the memory of the feminine archetype has been lost. Feminine thought, feeling, and instinct, pushed back into the unconscious by the Attic people, reappears in the destructive shadow of Medea, the enemy of men and always defeated. Or it appears in the pliant and infantile feeling of Aethra, incapable of recognizing the autonomy, meaning, or dignity of her own existence.

Theseus thus becomes a man orienting himself to the unilateral development of masculine functions, because his unconscious anima doesn't find correspondence in the primitive feminine behaviors of the maternal model. At 16 he puts on his father's sandals and follows in his father's footsteps; he grasps the sword and recovers its lucid and cutting force; he becomes combative, courageous, determined in action and thought, and progressively assumes the aspect of the *solar hero*.

At this point Theseus, since he is male and strong, returns to Athens, the center of the patriarchal organizational principle, to be recognized by Aegeus and to completely express his young man's energy. And suddenly he finds himself before the first real conflict of his life: here there aren't any bulls or brigands to defeat, like en route to Athens; here he must decide the meaning of his life and the fate of the city. Should he accustom himself, like the others, to the idea that the periodic tribute of human lives is normal, or should he acknowledge the drama of Athens and give it a name? And after: should he organize an expedition risking, if defeated, the definitive slavery of Athens, or should he leave alone, risking only his own life? There is no sense, there is no *logos* in continuing to allow oneself to be invaded by guilt for the death of Minos' son, for this death has already earned a tragic price. It becomes inevitable that he must leave to face the monster alone, because combat with the monster is not war, but a duel where one wins and the other dies. Theseus' thoughts proceed in a straight line to the conclusion: become one of the victims, try to kill the Minotaur, and keep the undertaking a secret. Behind the thought there is a passion, since eros is the etymological and semantic nucleus of the heroic condition, and in Theseus' soul thought fuses with a feeling that brings emotional tension to the undertaking. It is a question of the desire for justice and the moral strength that encourages him to satisfy it. In spaces even more profound, it is instinct which guides his behavior, because, if consciousness had its beginnings in a drive, which only at a certain point becomes conscious of itself, then feelings and thoughts about freedom and justice are, even before, instincts, an irrepressible drive against everything that opposes one's own movement. We see this phallic instinct again in the darkness of the labyrinth when, in hand-to-hand combat, it is clear that each struggle is a struggle for life; everything else exists, but it's before or after, and in any case it's beyond the Minotaur's and Theseus' bodies.

On the basis of these considerations, the young prince, facing his undertaking, unites the three psychic activities within himself in their most completely masculine forms. He is fighting for survival, to express a value, and to affirm the weight of reason.

And it is exactly in this stranger from the sea that Ariadne recognizes her internal image of a man, which she didn't know: Theseus is different from Minos and from the men of Crete, he doesn't depend on women, he doesn't deceive his god with a false sacrifice; he can fight if he judges it necessary, fair, and reasonable to do so; and he transmits with his glance, his body, and his way of doing things a tranquillity and a firmness, which, for Ariadne, was unknown and yet inexplicably familiar. Theseus is part of Ariadne. He presents himself to her consciousness animated by a passion which, when in contact with thought, delineates moral conduct. Ariadne doesn't know this way of being, nobody taught it to her, but she recognizes it inside herself when the moment comes, and she falls in love with it.

As in the myth of Ariadne, and in the feminine psyche, the mechanism that makes the transformative dynamic spring from the maternal bond to the meeting with the animus is passion. Passion makes life subjectively worthy of being lived, not only because courage is born from the union between desire and fear, but also because the force of passion, can lead a woman away from that emotionally important center which is the maternal world, the origin and essence of her feminine identity. The gods make Ariadne fall in love with Theseus, and they place a choice before her.

The theme of choice, and thus of conflict, seems contextual in feminine psychology in the meeting with the animus. Women influenced by maternal complexes, or dominated by an archaic or regressive animus, or one modeled after dominant values in the collective conscious, have difficulty in deciding. They lose themselves in anxiety, continuing to evaluate the pros and cons, to weigh the risks, to try to conciliate desire and opportunity. They go around the conflict because they are incapable of recognizing the lucidity of the masculine archetype within themselves.

The choice often involves a particularly painful situation, as in Ariadne's case, when the father has been psychologically subordinated by the mother: on the one hand a woman wants to be autonomous and morally responsible for her actions, on the other she is blocked by the risk of not succeeding. In these cases, if the principle of psychic inertia takes the upper hand, the entire personality is repressed into the darkness of the labyrinth, and desire does-n't meet with judgment.

Ariadne also has to choose because she has to kill in any case: either she has to kill a regressive energy, which has accompanied her during her entire life, as a brother, or she has to kill another energy, lucid and impassioned, but foreign to her whole existence. She has to kill either the monster or Theseus—the old or the new.

Ariadne offers Theseus her ball of thread, and in a more ancient version of the myth, she accompanies him inside the labyrinth, illuminating it with a crown of light. In either case, whether she enters or not into the labyrinth, it is still she, the divine maiden, who guides Theseus. The entire identity of a woman is gambled when she meets with the masculine principle, and it is always a high risk encounter (as is an encounter with a man). Ariadne follows her internal law, violating her father's law, and risk-ing death, because at the end it is Ariadne who dies. Yet another ancient legend tells of the profound value of transgression and also of the necessity for sacrifice.

I believe that the small, luminous, Cretan princess, the sensu-al, topless dancer, the woman who holds the crown of light and the ball of thread in her hands, represents one of the most linear images of feminine heroism in mythology. At the same time, she is one of the most complete forms that the feminine archetype has ever assumed in manifesting itself to human consciousness.

An anxious woman once came to see me. She always talked about *her needs*: her need for money, love, and so on. Her agenda was repulsive and vaguely intestinal, and suggested the almost phys-iological urgency of her drives. Run through by contradictory dri-ves, she felt paralyzed, and nothing ever happened in her life: she was afflicted with a serious form of oralness, for she ate and talked, talked and ate.

One day, during one of her flood-like monologues, among other things she said, as if incidentally: "Because you have to understand this need of mine."

I interrupted her: "I don't think that is possible."

"What, you don't think that's possible, why?"

"Because I don't want to."

"What do you mean?" And her language had, all of a sudden, become essential.

"You need me to understand your numerous needs; in this way you ask me to be an accomplice to the insecurity and the anxiety which brought you here, and this need of yours doesn't meet with my desire."

"But everyone," answered my patient, angered "has needs, even you!" About two months later she brought me this dream:

THE BLACK SAILOR: *There is a riot at the port. I try to escape, but curiosity holds me back, and I see a black sailor fighting with a short, fat man, but very violently and forcefully. At a certain point, the sailor pulls out a knife and I see it glisten as he points it to the throat of the other man. They stand still like that, then the police arrive, and they take the short man away, and now I know that he is a pusher and a drug addict. The sailor turns and looks at me, exactly at me, and he is smiling. There is a top on the ground. It has a spiral design in different colors on it. The sailor bends down and makes it spin in front of me; he makes it spin very fast, and he looks at me. The top outlines a strange path back and forth, then it spins left and right, and then it goes back to the starting point, as if it were following an imaginary labyrinth, and it seems beautiful to me, with all the colors that fuse together. At the end it stops in front of me, and there is a lacerating scream like the siren of a ship.*

A man came from the sea. He was so unconscious as to be physically dark, but he fought against the dependence of the pusher/addict, against the contract, against the chaotic complex of needs that blocked the dreamer's life, and he delivered this "bad man" to the forces of order, which removed him. Then the black sailor showed her the movement of the spiral and the labyrinth: it is up to her to decide, not unlike Ariadne, whether to accept the death and life hidden in that image. It is also up to her to decide whether or not to hold the gaze of the young black man. I asked her how she felt about the sailor.

"He was very handsome," she answered, "strong, young, tall, a little like one of the Harlem Globe Trotters, but his gaze, while the top was spinning, was strange, a little tender, a little ironic, almost the gaze of an old man, yet very attractive. There was an understanding between us, but I don't know what type."

The responsible and aggressive masculine feeling, which the dream had brought to light, could perhaps have helped that woman combat her drives, and, at the same time, the infantile dependence that had made her suffer so.

I remember another woman, about 40, who came to me because she had fallen in love (mutual) with a boy twenty years younger than her. This feeling had upset her whole life, perhaps at that time a little drowsy, but her confusion now was absolute. She loved her husband, her children, her work, but she also loved that boy, and she felt cruel, ridiculous, and cowardly because she couldn't make a decision. It was only when she realized that falling in love—whatever the circumstances are—is never a crime—that it was possible to begin our work. It was still a question of choosing, but on the basis of an awareness, as profound as possible, of her own identity.

During the course of her analysis, an adventurous and transgressive side of her animus came to light, which, because of her upbringing and the presence of a seriously depressed father, hadn't been given space in her life. The character of the young man corresponded, in her eyes, to the image of the unconscious animus, as enunciated in her dreams. The love that tormented my patient could also constitute a symptom of her uneasiness, and her attempt to compensate.

I will never forget the fear which shook her body as sobs and which overwhelmed feelings and thoughts. She was afraid of experiencing something absolutely new, of not finding the way, of not being able to, the fear of *too late*, the fear of the unknown, and fear of the many foreign and unknown things that seethed within her.

One day she sat down in front of me, looked at me with clear eyes, and said: "I'm leaving next week, on my birthday." She had told me, a while before, that when she was young she had longed to leave alone for a trip *to the end of the earth* with only a sleeping bag, but she had never dared to do it. She was going to go now, knapsack on her back, to mediate her life. She was not going to the end of the earth, she wanted to have a month of wandering, a leave of absence from her job; she had a long conversation with her loyal and intelligent husband. It was an initiative trip. The meetings, the adventures, the discoveries of that period of solitude profoundly affected her, and upon her return she said: "The problems are still there, but I am not as afraid as before." That woman now faced a *real* choice: the boy was no longer the projection of her animus, he was only *that boy* that her husband faced as an antagonist, and she, on the other hand, by now in love with her internal man, could renounce the one who had been his symbol. Over time she extended her activities to a social sphere which had always impassioned her, discovering therein interest and satisfaction, and she rediscovered a mature and profound feeling for her husband which she had never felt before.

Returning to our myth, we can now see how the men on Crete are the ones who count little, and they live, notwithstanding appearances, psychologically subordinated to the women and are fatally inscribed in maternal order. Minos and Daedalus obey Pasiphae, or they must submit to her witchcraft; rational thought, the sense of responsibility, and strength are not winning values, and they remain submerged in the shadow, from where they appear periodically as fury and overbearingness.

Where is Minos' sense of responsibility, who first asks a god for help and then deceives him? Where is the lucidity of a man who places his desire before the prosperity of his country? And finally where is masculine instinct if he agrees to tolerate a headless and bloody monster in the heart of the city? Minos keeps the Minotaur hidden in the labyrinth and, to assuage his voracity, periodically offers the Minotaur his enemies as a meal.

In psychological terms, Minos interrogates himself about the future of Crete and, when the voice of his conscious tells him that it is time to sacrifice the past, the maternal culture that the bull represents, to guarantee the future, he is not able to carry out the sacrifice of a part of himself. He tries in vain to hide this defeat from his conscious. The regressive symptom which derives from this is accepted for the most part, and Minos lives with his sense of guilt, pushing it away into the unconscious and projecting his guilt onto others. First he can't find the strength to renounce, and after he can't find the courage of expiation.

Ariadne's masculine functions, modeled after the characters of her father and the Minotaur, are weak and violent. They are completely useless in affirming themselves in the world; consequently the strength of her identity remains anchored within the feminine archetype. Her way of thinking is inductive and analogical. Her way of thinking tends to connect with, rather than disarrange, the items of knowledge, to understand them as a whole and to conserve the trace and memory of its own flowing. Thought is more profound than rigorous, and orients itself toward completeness rather than precision. Like the light of the crown, it illuminates the path a little at a time, step by step; slow and close-fitting to the search, it serves to go deeper in rather than to observe.

Ariadne's way of feeling is oriented toward the undertaking through a relationship. She doesn't try to convince Theseus to renounce his intentions. She unites with Theseus *to carry out the undertaking,* sharing the value, but her activity, more than killing the Minotaur, is turned toward saving Theseus. She doesn't need the oracle to know what she has always *known.* She knows that love will show her the way, for feminine feeling seems naturally oriented toward union, and *in holding together* she expresses the most profound loyalty to her principle.

Feminine instinct guides Ariadne to act to save. It also gives her the strength to wait, to recognize the right moment to get to work. Feminine instinct doesn't serve to attack, but receives and transforms. It is less impetuous in as much as it is sensible and perceptive.

In this passage of the myth it is possible to also observe differences between receptivity and passivity. When does Ariadne ever passively submit to the behavior of other people? She thinks, decides, and acts of her own free will with initiative and a determined mind. Only a very unilateral masculine attitude could confuse these two irreconcilable functions of the conscious. Being passive means submitting to others' actions while being receptive means choosing an action, even if it is not a penetrating one, and consequently exploring, transforming, and creating as a result of this awareness.

It is precisely in Ariadne's archetypal complex that Theseus recognizes his own anima. He falls in love with his anima; he falls in love with a way of being that he had not known either in his step-mother or in his mother, a way of being autonomous and reflective, full of strength and warmth. Theseus feels he can never be as he was before because Ariadne's energy has pervaded and transformed him. There are other forms of knowledge besides the sharp blade of rea-son, there are other ways of perceiving sensitive reality. Feeling can take on a goal and a relationship at the same time.

It becomes inevitable to renounce the dictatorship of the mas-culine principle and recognize, in his own anima, the guide who saves his life. There seems to be, in the life of every man, balls of thread which are better not to lose. Following the goddess of love, many men, like Theseus in the myth, end up finding themselves. In many male dreams the beloved (the girl who knows the path, the saviouress), represents a metaphor for the anima, without which a man is lost.

A man, no longer young, always profoundly depressed, came to my office. Because he had hepatitis caused by psychotropic drugs, he couldn't continue to follow the treatment he always used for his depression. He was not without a sense of humor (he used to call me Magicarenghi), and supported by extensive and profound study, he searched, without hope, but with my help, to establish contact with his anima, the feminine energy capable of transmitting mean-ing and vitality to his experience. One day he brought me this dream:

THE WOMAN OF THE SPRING: *I am looking for something and I don't have much time, and if I don't find it, something fatal will happen. It's something connected to nature, to the earth, of which I know nothing, and I don't even know what to call it. I feel like Petrarch who I think of in the dream: "Alone and thoughtful the most deserted fields I go moving with a slow and heavy step...." There is absolutely no one to ask for help, and I feel lost. All of a sudden I hear the murmur of water, like a small waterfall. I follow that sound, I approach it, and on the path, under a tree, a source springs; you (the analyst) are next to it and you smile at me as if you were waiting for me. You have a glass in your hands, you fill it with water, and you offer it to me saying, "Here, this is the water of life." While I drink it I know that this is what I was searching for and now I am saved.*

In association he said to me: "I discovered cool water!" But we both remembered the fairy tale where the three sons of the old king go around the world looking for the water of life, the only medicine capable of curing him.

A manager, very concentrated on his professional goals, and basically a stranger to the rest of the world, brought me this dream one day:

I have to leave on a trip for work, but a lot of obstacles detain me, unexpected and forgotten things, and I have the feeling that something is not going right; it's a bad day. Finally I am in flight to New York; I am calmer because I know who I have to see and why, and I have all the necessary documents with me. The plane lands, but when I get off I realize I am in the countryside and not at Kennedy airport. There are no taxis, the people slowly disappear here and there, and I am left alone. A car driven by a girl approaches: she is black, pretty, and with a smile she asks me where I want to go: to

Manhattan—I tell her. She signals me to get in and I do, because I don't see any other alternative, and a trip which seems very long to me begins. I see villages, woods, deserts, train tracks, and immense cultivated fields: they seem like pieces of different trips I have taken in the USSR and Africa, spliced together on film. I am afraid that I will never arrive at my destination. I am nervous and desperate. Every now and then the girl turns to me and says, "Be patient," or "This is how it's done," or "Calm down." Slowly as time passes, however, I feel more at ease and I realize I even desire that woman, and it's as if I knew that she, even if she doesn't say it, knows her business and knows the road. So I relax and begin to look around. When you get down to it, I have seen many things in my life without having really looked. I observe the landscapes, the scenes of everyday life, a child on a bicycle, a policeman with a whistle around his neck, two lovers, and I feel calm. I want to make sure to remember everything I see, and to be able to feel the emotion I am feeling now. All of a sudden I see the towers of Manhattan, and she, without asking me anything, takes me to the right address, but instead of leaving she goes up with me to the headquarters of the company. We go into the managing director's office who, to my great surprise, shakes her hand with a lot of consideration and invites her to sit down. The girl, nodding in my direction, says to him, "This guy let himself go." And this phrase seems to make them both happy.

At this point in the myth, Theseus and Ariadne are in front of each other: the strength and the sword of the young hero will be indispensable in defeating the Minotaur, but without the little princess' thread and her light there would be no memory of Theseus today. This type of encounter, which operates in the union of opposites in the psyche of a human being, is simple by nature. It is unexpected and sudden, just as a meeting of love, and it opens the soul to lacerating conflicts.

Like every true privilege, one must also pay the price for the union of love; thus Theseus will make his father die of pain, and he will abandon Ariadne on the beach at Delos, and Ariadne will betray her brother. It is not possible to understand their reasons if one does not consider that in the human conscius, a psychological evolution can be perceived as a betrayal. The conscious suffers in betraying its own history, and at the same time it feels love for the new things which arise, activating a conflict, generating guilt, and activating transgressions which are of fundamental importance for the construction of a personality endowed with depth and autonomy.

If we consider the different versions of the myth of Ariadne, we notice that all of them hide a common secret: the return, through death, to the orbit of the feminine archetype from which the young girl had been separated in meeting Theseus. It is as if death constituted the expiation of a sense of guilt which rebalances a broken equilibrium.

On a symbolic level, to die in childbirth means to be punished for the union with a man. Artemis' arrow has the same meaning. The marriage with Dionysis, and the metamorphosis into a constellation, attenuate the weight of the sense of guilt, and accentuate the sacred value of Ariadne's sacrifice, conserving all the same the almost magnetic reference to the feminine psychic circuit. Dionysis, as we have seen in the first part of this book, is the androgynous god-bull connected to the world of women and to the culture of Crete. To marry him means to return to the symbolic dimension of the maternal world, which the island represents. The constellation into which the Cretan heroine transforms is named Aridela, which means "very pure," that is virgin, meaning in the Greek sense "not married, of being one with oneself." At the end Ariadne dies, but the light of feminine thinking, which had illuminated the path inside the labyrinth, becomes eternal light for everyone who lives under the sky.

This common message, which the different conclusions of the myth contain, speak to us about a sense of guilt whose origin is in a too radical separation. After having killed her brother, Ariadne suddenly and forever leaves the island and everything it contains. This departure, which doesn't leave space for mourning, or bidding farewell, seems too rushed, nor are there promises of return. Yet there was a brother to grieve, the abandonment of a mother, the disobedience of a father, and a relationship with that place and with her past. No woman can ignore everything without becoming ill. Transgression is necessary, but it becomes a boomerang if it is not possible to pay the price.

And more, in a woman's psyche, the continuity of contact with the feminine archetype is of fundamental importance for the forming of the personality, especially after the meeting, so creative and dramatic, with the masculine principle. Thus an oscillating progress becomes necessary over time, which every time guides toward the animus and then withdraws back toward the feminine world. I have often observed a woman's periodic need to withdraw into herself, a need whose strength varies depending on the strength of the relationship with a man or the interior masculine world, as if it were necessary to have a pause to recharge and begin to withstand the tension of opposite forces again.

I will be able to go into this oscillation more deeply with the myth of Demeter and Kore, but here I limit myself to observing the absence of this wave-like progress in Ariadne's life, a movement which reminds me of the tides of the ocean, when the water pushes ahead covering everything and then, withdrawing, it leaves behind many wonders, like shellfish, shells, and pebbles spread in the sand.

Yet it happens that not even the periodic return into the interior feminine world can stop a woman from losing herself. Sometimes the contact between the feminine ego and the animus can't withstand personal difficulties, or if it is interrupted due to a lack of energy, or if it is broken in the face of social incomprehension, or by fact of destiny, then a woman becomes ill and sometimes goes crazy, or even dies, because the contact with the masculine interior world is so creative and vital that, once it is primed, it can no longer be interrupted, the risk being the ruin of the entire personality.

This is the case of many women in history and in mythology: Dido dies when Aeneas abandons her. Camille Claudel goes crazy because her family and her social sphere can't understand the necessity of her art. Virginia Woolf commits suicide, Karen Blixen lets herself die, and Sibilla Aleramo pays an immense price for her expressive freedom. And like them, there are many other anonymous women, whose pain has been forgotten. And the stronger the animus, the more greater the risk, and I don't think the reason can simply be traced to a cultural element: the persisting, diffuse distrust toward women who express masculine contents; I think there is also something else, something very deeply rooted in feminine psychology. Women have the temptation to fall into a *participation mystique* with what they are doing, and this tendency becomes proportionately less consciously controllable as the situations concern unconscious contents of the animus.

So the end of Ariadne's myth denies the triumphant image of the *coniunctio oppositorum*: the meeting with the masculine principle can liberate a woman from a maternal complex, but it doesn't constitute a guarantee for the life of theh psyche. The embryo of the union of opposites is contained within the unconscious of every person, as the seed of a tree contains its future form. Every person, during analysis, finds himself or herself before *the other,* and the task is to recognize, love, and search for possible integration with it. But there are other risks: one doesn't always, in my opinion, keep in mind the danger that the animus represents; it is a mistake to believe that, once the image of the masculine principle has been constellated, all the rest ends up in the best possible way. The myth of Ariadne is there to remind us of this: no internal experience for a woman is more erotic, *numinous,* but also more terrible than the meeting with the animus—not unlike an encounter with a man.

PART 3

———

Hades and Persephone

CHAPTER 9

From Kore to Persephone

The myth of Kore-Persephone, Demeter and Hades, and the birth of the "Eleusinian Mysteries" are told in the Homeric Hymn "To Demeter." The Homeric hymns are ancient Greek compositions in honor of a god, which celebrate the story, the activities, the mental state, and personal characteristics of the god addressed. The origin of these poems is uncertain, the most ancient ones are probably from the tenth century B.C. and they were passed down orally, or in rhapsodic form, until, around the fourth century B.C., they were collected as we know them today.

Thus having a direct source of great literary value for this myth, I have decided to not summarize it in my own words, but to propose that readers become familiar with the original version, which conserves intense dramatic vigor together with a surprising sweetness.[1]

---

1. "Hymn to Demeter," in *The Homeric Hymns*, Apostolos N. Athanassakis, trans. (Baltimore: Johns Hopkins University Press, 1976).

THE SEPARATION AND THE ABYSS
(LINES 1–39)

Kore

In this myth, the narrative and psychological center is in a meeting, and the complexity of the reactions this meeting stirs up. And, also in this case, the spell to be broken is the one which closes feminine identity in the original world of the mother, and which simultaneously isolates masculine personality in the univocal adhesion to the patriarchal world. Liberation begins in the discovery of the other, and in the reciprocal, contradictory fascination that activates a new energy.

While the myth of Theseus and Ariadne places the accent on the dynamics of thought and feeling which unite the two protagonists in an indispensable and triumphant collaboration, the story of Hades and Persephone stresses the role of instinct, and its numinous force, in the meeting between a man and a woman, like the meeting of two complementary energies within a single personality.

At the beginning of the poem, Kore is playing in a field with her friends, completely immersed in maternal, protective nature, unaware of the masculine world, and completely defenseless before it.

In Greek, *Kore* means "maiden," and in the Homeric text this word is always written with a lower-case letter, like a common noun, and used alternately with the term "zugatra" (ζυγατρα), "daughter."

This is all that we know about her before her abduction: in psychological terms Kore thus seems to outline a virginal character common to all women in adolescence and, later on, in those particular phases of life when one becomes a maid again because a new love is about to begin, or when there is about to be a new manifestation of the animus. Sometimes the two things happen together and they bring up great fear.

Kore is not a woman, nor a goddess, nor does she preside over any function, nor does she have tasks, or a story; she doesn't even have a name. Kore is a virtual presence, a possibility which expresses itself in the still time of waiting. Something must and will happen, but in the meantime nothing seems to disturb the absolute calm, the celestial beatitude of the fusion of the daughter with the maternal world. The maiden is there, among the flowers, and then, all of a sudden, she disappears, to return definitively different.

From this point of view, Kore is different from the other traditional virgin goddesses, whose virginity is eternal and whose sovereignty is expressed in a specific series of feminine psychic functions. In fact, there is no need for contact with masculine energy, because Hestia can express protective concern for the house as the center for relationships and the sacred place for hospitality. Nor does the animus have any role when Artemis manifests her impetuous and slightly savage energy that orients her to solitude and creative inspiration, nor when Athena recognizes the vein of an inductive and nocturnal knowing within herself.

These three important virgin goddesses present themselves immobile in their archetypal context, while Kore seems to represent a phase of passage in feminine evolution, the brief, traumatic movement from one psychic condition to the other, a *before* which foresees an *after*. And thus Kore's meaning seems to be to exist to be taken.

On the other hand, if Kore is the tranquil little girl in the phase of self-conservation in the maternal world, she is also, immediately after, the lost and despairing creature who succumbs to abduction, and crying, invokes her father. She takes form as a phase of passage, and also as the incarnation of a conflict between desire and the fear of the encounter with the masculine principle.

Desire breaks the spell of the unconscious time of waiting and causes the god from the remote depths to rise. Fear induces her to experience the meeting as though it were a dark abyss, which deprives her of points of reference. Every time the desire/fear complex, facing the irruption of the animus, shatters a psychic virginity that generates the drive to abandonment on the one hand, and on the other, the anguish of loss. The passion which derives from it dissolves the preceding equilibrium, the wholeness of the feminine principle, inducing the loss of oneself in order to rediscover oneself different. Kore no longer exists because, at that point, Persephone exists.

There is an early detail in this abduction which is worth considering: Kore, while she is being abducted, invokes Zeus, an invisible father *"And she raised a shrill cry, calling upon father Kronides, the highest and the best"* ("To Demeter," lines 20–21). Why doesn't Kore, in harmony with her psychological condition, call her mother? Perhaps because, in a patriarchal society, if the order is disturbed or if an injustice is committed, one asks the father for help, when the animus is unconscious. Psychic virginity thus places a woman at the mercy of the masculine principle and delivers her to the patriarchal authorities in a defenseless and psychologically protective dependence relationship. "I can't defend myself—it is as if a woman spoke thus—but the Father, he surely is powerful and he can save me."

In a society marked by a decided masculine dominant character, a woman had no choice but to trust in patriarchal power as is affirmed in everyday life, hoping that it is benevolent and protective like a good father. Or she could recognize and abandon herself to her own masculine energy in a painful and healthy relationship of love and death.

The phase of passage and the conflictual tension which derives from it, as represented by the character of Kore, open themselves for the first time during adolescence, through a complex transformation that is both physiological and psychological, but which seem to symbolically repeat, in the life of every woman, every time that a man, or a content of the animus, still unknown, irrupt into her life.

Kore, in fact, manifests herself in a constant and systematic way, even in the dreams and behaviors of adult women who not only have experienced intense love relationships, but who have already integrated significant aspects of their animus. In these cases, Kore represents that particular, cyclical feminine disposition to let herself be taken by new passions, and present, little-structured characteristics and scarce defensive capacity are comprehensible, because it is precisely this fragility which permits the animus to take position and invade the field. Every woman becomes Kore again whenever it is necessary to experience a transformative event. It is a dialectical process with mysterious rhythms.

This means that the particularity of Kore in feminine psychology consists in the tendency and the reconstruction of a psychic integrity destined to shatter every time. Thus, Kore seems to incarnate the virginal aspect, defenseless, that always new and yet eternal feminine principle, the psychic situation deprived of any power, naturally seductive, in which one finds a woman who is really about to meet the animus—or a man.

It is a moment, in Kore's time: a moment in which panic and desire overwhelm the conscious, and it is clear that nothing exists except that desire and that fear. It is the time of the words of Juliet of Verona, or Francesca when she reads with Paolo, or Isolde when she meets Tristan.

Yet, if one doesn't pass through Kore, one doesn't truly become a woman: the trip to the Underworld, to the depths of the animus, seems to be the real apprenticeship for conquering a psychic and emotional maturity.

When all of this doesn't happen, Kore still doesn't exist, because, by her nature, she is a phase and she can't last forever. In other words, when a feminine personality, in the course of its evolution, becomes blocked in the passage that Kore describes, it can no longer be psychologically defined by the archetype of the maiden. If the transformative movement doesn't conclude, Kore dies anyway, even if she isn't born as Persephone and a neurotic nucleus of resistance takes form instead, which substitutes the evolutionary passage. In this case, the feminine personality becomes rigid in a compulsion to repeat a way of being which, instead, because of its nature, is limited in time.

Facing this neurotic crystallization, it is only a painful and pathetic caricature of the maiden which appears, a condition which the myth doesn't foresee, because it goes against the evolutionary instinct.

Thus if, because of custom or convenience, one speaks about *woman-Kore* or *woman-puella*, when we refer to that neurotic feminine complex, it is a good idea, in my opinion, to keep in mind that it is neither a question of Kore nor of puella any longer, but of the dramatic incapacity to complete the passage toward Persephone, and thus of the impossibility at that point to comply with either one or the other of the two psychic conditions.

These observations don't seem irrelevant to me when they are translated into a clinical context. They contribute, I believe, to explaining Jung's theoretical and therapeutic severity regarding women immersed in the maternal world and impermeable to the masculine principle. Jung's position in front of this feminine complex seems to me, yet again, courageous and innovative, because, during the time he lived, the *women-Kore* were considered ideal women, precisely in virtue of their neurotic suffering which, as we have seen, delivers them to dependence on the patriarchal world.

The neurotic attribution to this feminine model has brought, as a consequence, the neurotic attribution to a model of masculine priapism, at that time (and sometimes still today) hegemonic in the collective conscious. It is worth rereading his words:

> These bloodless maidens are by no means immune to marriage. On the contrary, despite their shadowiness and passivity, they command a high price on the marriage market. First, they are so empty that a man is free to impute to them anything that he fancies. In addition, they are so unconscious that the unconscious puts out countless invisible feelers, veritable octopus-tentacles that suck up all masculine projections; and this pleases men enormously. All that feminine indefiniteness is the longed-for counterpart of male decisiveness and single-mindedness, which can be satisfactorily achieved only if a man can get rid of everything doubtful, ambiguous, vague, and muddled by projecting it upon some charming example of feminine innocence. Because of the woman's characteristic passivity, and the feelings of inferiority which make her continually play the injured innocent, the man finds himself cast in an attractive role: he has the privilege of putting up with the familiar feminine foibles with real superiority, and yet with forbearance, like a true knight. (Fortunately, he remains ignorant of the fact that these deficiencies consist largely of his projections.) The girl's notorious helplessness is a special attraction. She is so much an appendage of her mother that she can only flutter confusedly when a man

approaches. She just doesn't know a thing. She is so inexperienced, so terribly in need of help, that even the gentlest swain becomes a daring abductor who brutally robs a loving mother of her daughter.[2]

As the crux of the main axis of his theoretical construction, that is the *coniunctio oppositorum*, Jung couldn't but find in the contact with the animus the individuative orientation of the feminine personality; but the relationship with the personal animus delivers a woman from dependence on the masculine world forever and creates the foundation for her psychic autonomy.

The myth itself declares how much this process derives from instinct because it is Gaia, the Great Mother Earth, who precisely on that day gives birth to narcissus, the perfumed flower, "for a girl with a flower's beauty," under which Hades hides. And Kore can't but fall into the trap which Nature has laid for her. *"She was dazzled and reached out with both hands at once to take the pretty bauble; Earth with its wide roads gaped and then over the Nysian field the lord and All-receiver, the many-named son of Kronos, sprang out upon her with his immortal horses."* ("To Demeter," lines 15–18). Instinct does not only seem to push toward the meeting, but it also seems to demand the *marriage with death* as an event necessary for the radical transformation of the feminine psyche.

What the maiden wants is the narcissus, but what she finds is death and, afterward, a rebirth; in feminine psychology, a sudden, emotionally upsetting impact with the masculine world seems to be necessary—and I verify this in clinical practice, in order to shatter

2. C. G. Jung, *The Collected Works*, Vol. 9, Part 1: *The Archetypes & the Collective Unconscious*, Gerhard Adler, et al, eds. R. F. Hull, trans. (Princeton: Princeton University Press, 1968), §169. Also see "The Mother Complex," and "The Psychological Aspects of the Kore."

the fusion of the original relationship with the psychic maternal world.

As in the myth of Ariadne, it is only love's passion which, revealing a conflict and demanding a sacrifice, allows the union with *someone or something else*. But why a marriage with death? What explanation is there for this fear of death, so recurrent in the feminine unconscious of our time?

The first meeting of love with a man, not unlike the first contact with an unconscious animus, shatters her psychic integrity. A man has already experienced this in childhood when separating from his mother. Until this moment—meeting in love—feminine consciousness is oriented toward identifying, and not comparing, itself within a relationship, following the scheme of a maternal, fusional relationship. It is true that the unconscious animus (and sometimes even a man) break up this equilibrium by imposing a conflictual tension on the feminine psyche. It is also true that in this process a woman runs the risk that the unconscious, and not only a far away myth, continues to define the entire identity as mortal and destructive.

And it is a risk to move from one fusion to another. There is the fear of not being able to maintain the ego as the guide of the personality, of not knowing how to sustain the tension of the meeting with *someone or something else*. A woman could reflow into a dependence on the masculine world instead of on the maternal one, re-emerging, in the most serious cases, in the *participation mystique* experienced with the mother at the beginning of life.

When this risk comes to pass, it becomes very difficult for a woman to face the dialectical comparison that subtends any relationship. It is completely *natural* to remain anchored to the nostalgia for a complete infantile paradise, wrapped up in safety from any fracture, where the subject and the object of love are a single thing.

Experience with the masculine world, so desired and feared, so vital and necessary, is thus transformed into a psychological dependence that can lead to the loss of one's own identity. That loss can mean that the entire existence is an existence in function to another, when the other is a man, and where the ego is at the mercy of the animus, when the other is the masculine archetype.

The abduction of Kore tells us about this risk, and the time in which it can occur. Her desperate invocations to the father, while Hades drags her away with him, express the awareness of this risk and the anguish before an event decided on by the gods, of course, but stronger than consciousness and pregnant with an uncertain future.

There is nothing so mysterious and intense for a woman as masculine energy, but it truly seems to activate a magnetic field in which it is easy to feel lost.

The narcissus and Hades, in the symbolic context of this myth, seem united in order to stress, on the one hand, the extreme beauty and inevitable anguish of an abandonment, while Nature serenely contemplates the omen of a fulfillment: "*A hundred stems of sweet smelling blossoms grew from its roots. The wide sky above and the whole earth and the briny swell of the sea laughed*" (lines 12–14).

Nature cannot but accept what she herself wanted: if Gaia makes the narcissus bloom and if it, at its root, hides abduction, it means that nature's fusion with the maternal world has to break up at a certain point. That means, in the natural order of things, that enchantment dissolves to make space for the trauma of the meeting with the other, for the panic, and for the passion that opens and matures the body and the *anima* of a woman. It is the earth which generates the narcissus and which opens before Hades, because it is nature that constructs and transforms its balances.

Is it possible that another meaning hides behind Narcissus who gave the name to the flower, the youth who, in Greek mythology, dies for love of his own image? Why that flower, blooming for the first time that day?

It is possible that the narcissus doesn't only constitute the snare which pushes Kore into Hades' arms, but it is also present to signal an obligatory passage toward that meeting. Kore, as Jung stressed, is inclined to incarnate the projection of her animus because she has to compensate her own fragility. By feeling confirmed by the other, she trains herself to play with the passion of the other, being very careful to not put her own into play when the "other" is a man. She gets used to projecting onto the opposite sex the potentials of the animus when the other is the masculine unconscious.

But behind narcissistic self-contemplation, behind the apparently innocent games, sometimes there is a man, and thus, not without cries and desperation, narcissism is destined to fall in order to make room for a relationship.

Narcissism is a psychic condition characteristic of adolescence, but perhaps it is also a necessary moment of passage, or less possibly, every time a woman has to reckon with a new aspect of the animus which comes up in consciousness, as if in that moment it were important for her to feel confirmation and reassurance for herself, to find the courage to abandon herself to something unknown.

So the narcissus can be either an obstacle or an ally, or both, because it is behind that symbolic image—like self-contemplation, but also like self-reflection—that one finds the strength to overcome the relationship with oneself in order to be able to sustain the encounter with the other. One can recognize that in the end there no longer exists something ephemeral to receive, but something profound in which to let oneself go.

Because it is part of the natural order, the abduction of Kore is not a rape. The ancient Greeks certainly weren't afraid to speak about sexual violence. In mythology heroes and gods frequently give in to their impulses; in these cases the threatened maidens have no choice but to succumb to a metamorphosis or some form of violence.

None of this happens in our myth where, instead, Hades asks Zeus, her father, for Kore as his bride, and then he takes her away in his royal coach, but without any sexual violence. In fact Kore doesn't escape, she doesn't change form, but, though crying and invoking her father, she allows herself to be abducted.

These details of the episode—which are repeated with slight variations in the dreams of all women (in my experience without any exception) are the evidence of the harshness of the internal conflict that opposes passion in the meaning of death in the desire of a woman to be taken.

THE ABDUCTION: *I am driving home taking the usual way, and a car comes up next to me. In the darkness I see a man driving; he doesn't seem particularly interesting, but in any case I look at myself in the rear-view mirror[3] to see how I look. While I am distracted doing this at a red light, he gets out of his car, opens mine, and in the wink of an eye, he lifts me out, he pushes me into his car and he drives off. I scream in a desperate way, but nobody hears me and he smiles without speaking and drives calmly. It is a nightmare and I wake up.*

---

3. In the detail of the mirror, narcissistic self-reassurance, of which I spoke in the preceding pages, is recognizable, and which often immediately precedes the trauma of the meeting.

THE CHASE: *A man is chasing me and I am running away, but I always feel him behind me; I take off my shoes to run faster and I continue to run, I feel his breath come nearer; it is terrible, even if nothing happens, I wake up all sweaty.*

THE MAN FROM THE MOUNTAINS: *I was hiking and I felt good and tranquil, which only happens when I am in the mountains. My friend L. was walking about 20 meters ahead of me. At a certain point, I see a human shape about 50 meters to my right in the valley. I call L., who doesn't seem to hear me because she doesn't answer. At my call the shape doesn't move: I am afraid that someone has had an accident, even if, at that distance, it could simply be a black windbreaker among the shrubs. I decide to go down and, slowly as I approach, I see that it is a man, perhaps fainted or dead. I look at him from close up and I don't see traces of blood, but he doesn't seem to be breathing: I bend down over him and suddenly he opens his eyes, which are very dark and beautiful; he opens his arms and he hugs me in silence. I feel an incredible fear, but I remain there and I am not even able to yell.*

In these three dreams, analogous to hundreds of others I have collected over time, the common characteristics in the abduction episode of the myth are evident: the unknown man, his strength, the pursuit (or the trap), the panic, the desire, and the sexual undertone.

In all three cases, the dreamers felt fragile and helpless when facing an unknown man, yet they were the ones who dreamed them and they were the ones who dreamed of the impossibility of resisting. All three of these women, like innumerable others, had to subsequently recognize the necessity of actuating the masculine force of aggressive instinctiveness in themselves in order to defend their aspirations and their values.

I have often heard objections, on this point and on this subject, from my patients, that aggressiveness is a masculine characteristic to reject, because the weight of many centuries of oppression against women induces them, in the majority of cases, to confuse aggressiveness with violence and the capacity to assert and defend oneself is confused with the desire to annihilate. But, even when this difference is recognized, often the reluctance to concretely activate their own aggressive energy persists, as if they found themselves facing an ancestral law which cannot be transgressed.

Certainly, until a woman is able to recuperate her aggressivity on a conscious level, she experiences a subordinate role, with little possibility for self-assertion, or she must, alternatively, have a man defend her, a shield against the aggressiveness of others. In any case, since this form of instinctive energy cannot be eliminated but only repressed, it always ends up reemerging in feminine behavior that assumes the shape of the shadow. The world is full of women who can't assert themselves, who can't truly defend themselves, but who don't do anything but complain, protest, harm those close to them, or curse destiny.

On the basis of my experience, the feminine unconscious, in a systematic and relentless way, asks for respect, dignity, and autonomy for women's lives, proposing in dreams the union with an internal, aggressive companion, strong and decided, capable of defending her: and this is the phallic instinct.

Demeter

Demeter carries within her very name a maternal destiny, and she constitutes the most profound inheritance of the great goddess of the origins of patriarchal culture. Her archetypal identity manifests itself in that psychic territory where fusionality reigns and it encompasses all opposites—thus the masculine and the feminine.

Demeter's psychic virginity is eternal, opposite to Kore's, because she doesn't belong to a man, since, as a mother, she already contains him within herself.

What counts for Demeter is to create, nourish, make grow and transform following the natural, cyclical model. Eros is thus oriented toward maternity, while sexual union seems to constitute only a means, which is inscribed in the endogamic circuit through the relationship with Zeus' brother.

The encounter with masculine energy as *something other than the self* is outside of Demeter's psychic field, and it is constituted as an unconscious potential destined to surface in the conscious of that part of herself, different from herself, who is called Kore.

In the Greek imagination, Demeter reigned over the earth, the wheat, the biological rhythms, and also over the mystery of natural life. Its eternal cycles—gestation, birth, nourishment, and transformation—all close in maternal instinct in an isolated space. In this space a woman is, as is said, *one with herself,* and thus alone and complete at the same time.

But Demeter also reigns over the immense mystery that wraps nature up in the eternal flowing of matter and energy, over everything that cannot be explained, but only perceived and symbolically described; in this sense, and as the protagonist of the Eleusinian Mysteries, Demeter is also the goddess of initiation knowledge.

Her power manifests itself, according to the tradition of the Middle-Eastern mother goddess and the Indian goddess Sakti, in creation and destruction according to a periodic rhythm, and her image can be the reassuring mother with an ear of wheat in her hands, or the savage witch who is in a chariot driven by lions or surrounded by wolves.

On the basis of these considerations, Demeter seems to enucleate herself as symmetrical with respect to Kore, and in some way she constitutes a double, as if the two characters had originally been a whole which at a certain point were separated, revealing a polarity of opposite inclinations, and as if they were destined to meet again in the end, in a new form, no longer fusional, but dialectic. The symmetry of the two characters could perhaps be summarized in the following outline:

Demeter	Kore
Mother	Daughter
Strong	Fragile
Active	Passive
Mature	Young
Powerful	Helpless
Independent of the masculine	Overwhelmed by the masculine

The fragmentation of an archetype—as it is known—is part of the process of the development of consciousness which tends to distance itself from the unconscious; the differentiation of the archetypes is due to the variety and multiplicity of attitudes that the conscious can assume within the same individual, even if—as I have already said above referring to Jung's words—it is possible to hypothesize a second phase of evolution in which the archetype tends to become one, but with the consciousness of its own complexity.

The original singleness has its origin in the mother, both in biological life as well as in psychic life, and when the archetype differentiates itself, the maiden takes form from the Great Mother, but this scission doesn't constellate any dramatic nucleus as long as the maiden remains inscribed within the maternal world.

In feminine psychology, this situation seems very evident to me. A woman dominated by the maternal archetype feels strong, autonomous, tranquil in her occupation, because she belongs to her world and she controls it; her masculine contents are prevalently unconscious, and her relationships with men are not profound. Her instinct is more maternal than sexual, her feeling is receptive, her thought is inductive: we are facing a manifestation of the feminine archetype in its completeness, but also in its isolation.

In this psychic context, the Kore Complex occupies a small space, and the woman's life is latent; it refers to a phase of potentiality and of waiting, of which I have already spoken. In this type of suspended existence, there is no drama because the scission between the two aspects of the feminine are not yet, so to speak, operative.

The conflict begins when the animus erupts from the unconscious to shatter the calm of the closed circle of the Feminine, demanding vital space and taking what he wants. It is true that the animus is enucleated from the Great Mother, but it progressively conquers autonomous positions, takes power, and opens a conflict because in a woman it separates the maiden from the mother, and it imposes the force of its diversity.

At this point, which always signals a traumatic and delicate passage, the animus has to find the way to progressively establish contact with the conscious personality, without making the conflict chronic, but also without installing itself as the guide of the ego. And the possibility for this contact can't be but Kore, the weak link, the defenseless aspect of the chain of the feminine archetype, and thus the one open to the risk and the desire of the relationship. In other words, a content of the animus can attack that side of feminine consciousness which is disposed to fall in love with it. As I said before, the penetrative features of feminine personality don't have the opportunity for development if they aren't objects of passion; but the passion of love, in every woman, doesn't overwhelm the *mother* but the *maiden*.

This is not different from a love story: passion strikes a woman in her dimension of the eternal maiden, and in losing oneself in a man every one of us women, even the strongest and the most mature, rediscovers in herself the fear and the pleasure of feeling swept away. Every woman feels abducted when she falls in love, and deep down it is Kore, in each and every one of us, who goes looking for trouble.

Demeter and Kore thus seem to constitute themselves, on the basis of these observations, like two poles of the feminine archetype, in whose oscillation the possibility for renewal and the meeting with masculine energy begins.

Hades

But why, in this myth, is Hades the god of the first encounter? I believe that it is not only the fear of the unknown or the risk of the *participation mystique* that induce one to see a fatal danger in the unconscious animus, but also and above all the part of the shadow that it brings with it.

In Greek mythology, Hades represents the dark, subterranean side of the original divine triad of Zeus-Poseidon-Hades. He was so powerful and numinous that in antiquity it was forbidden to pronounce his name, and he was called Pluto instead, because of the immense wealth that is hidden under the earth and, analogically, for the infinite knowledge which lies in the unconscious.

He lives underground and he is the god of the dead: his sovereignty extends over all that is shrouded in secret, over the mystery of invisible transformations. His territory is wrapped up in darkness and inhabited by shadows, yet it is a territory full of life, where germination takes place, where the earth moves, where fire and water can meet. In psychological terms, Hades reigns over the unconscious, over all of its knowledge, but also over all of its shadow.

Because of this, when he comes to light and invades the psyche, the masculine unconscious brings with itself an immense richness contaminated by the shadow, and, thus, an evolutionary potential, a widening of psychic horizons, an aggressive and creative tension impregnated by violence, schematism, abstraction, and overbearing unilaterality. Hades offers a new and rich kingdom to the feminine psyche, but he overwhelms with his will and he behaves more like an invader than a shining prince, and the shadow which accompanies him is so dark that sometimes, when he appears in feminine dreams, his face is not even representable, and assumes the semblance of a faceless thief, for example, or a ghost, a black shadow, a figure wrapped up in a cape, a voice, and so on.

But it is not possible to forget that the animus belongs to the feminine unconscious, and the overbearingness, the sectarianism, the violent unilaterality which he brings to light, were already part of the unconscious feminine psyche, and they can finally be recognized and faced. The recognition of the shadow constitutes a considerable part of the elaboration of the animus and, during an analysis, it is often the origin of lacerating conflicts because those contents, repressed and rejected by the conscious, emerge charged with negative energy and they make a woman intolerant and spiteful.

To succeed in embracing and then transforming those traces of the shadow is part of life's work, as the myth in its unwinding indicates, but first the subject, not unlike Kore, feels dispossessed, no longer the mistress of her own identity.

This is a very delicate passage in the evolution of feminine consciousness, because it is possible that, instead of following the natural evolutionary process indicated in the myth, the feminine ego places itself in a position of dependence on the animus, renouncing the control of the personality. In this case, it becomes an autonomous complex, at the origin, as we shall now see, with dangerous consequences.

But what part of the masculine principle is Hades in the psyche of a woman? And what part of her relationship with a man? I have asked myself these questions many times over the past few years, every time that I recognized his image in a dream, or in the life of a patient. What is *the underworld* for a woman?

Hades arrives as a man on a horse, and abducts the dreamer, or he arrives as a black man who pushes the elevator button, making it plunge downward, or as the stranger who, with sharp words, induces her to leave with him, or as a nocturnal thief who steals the most precious jewels from the safe. All of these dreams, innumerable, and in every case dreams of women, have in common the feeling of physical fragility before an unknown and overpowering energy. Often these dreams include the theme of darkness, of plunging downward—the night, basements, elevators, black men, an overflowing river, a precipice, and sometimes even death.

All the images of these dreams, innumerable and constant in time, are foreign to thoughts and feelings which are animated instead by a masculine force almost always linked to sexuality. The oneiric complex, "black man, precipice, darkness, force, fear, sex, upset," which Hades represents in the myth, seems to refer to the instinctual masculine complex.

But what does it mean for a woman to integrate masculine instinct into her own conscious sphere, given that it obviously can't influence her sexuality? For a woman, it is a question of recuperating a force, precisely that force which, still projected, in the dream is the origin of her fear. In other words, it is a question of the capacity of asserting and defending one's own way of being. This is energy concretely translated into aggressiveness, enthusiasm, tenacity, determination to build and to destroy also, if necessary. It is a force which imposes respect for oneself, and which permits one to assert one's own personality and values.

To make this discourse more concrete, in the setting I often use the example of a garden. Each one of us possesses a terrain—more or less big, more or less in a good position, rich or scarce in rain, appropriate for cultivating this or that. Each of us has to make that terrain into a garden: some will grow stately oak trees and rows of lime trees, others simple flower beds, vegetable gardens, tranquil zones of shadow where one can relax.

But whatever type of garden it is, in order for it to exist, it is first of all necessary to know how to defend it. If we accept that it is dirtied, stepped on, and ignored by those who pass by, if beggars, thieves, loafers and envious people can enter, disturbing our work or discounting our efforts, then our garden will soon become an abandoned terrain good for every passage and every conquest. But only we can defend that garden, because nobody will help us: it exists in the measure in which each person takes on the responsibility.

To defend it, it is necessary to screen it off, equip it with gates, so we can allow who we wish to enter, when and how we want. Only then does it have meaning to cultivate, and we can attempt new experiments and get to work.

The great majority of women, of all ages, who have come to my studio, weren't aware that they had a terrain, nor that they had the task of turning it into a garden. Or, if they knew of its existence, they didn't think they had the right (the duty) to defend it, nor did they think they could impassion themselves with its cultivation.

Very often the women's gardens are centers of mad *maternage,* where the needy of all sorts crowd around, offering opinions and advice for the cultivation of others, imagining how nice it would be to have a little space and time to grow a flower, as long as it was not stepped on after, but who knows where the seeds are.

Over time, women have been induced to think that this is the meaning of their garden: a space open to incursions, more or less barbarian.

Masculine instinct in a woman seems to take shape as aggressive energy which restores self-respect, one's own psychic territory and thus one's own identity (Kore doesn't exist before she becomes Persephone), permitting creative passion and meaning in one's personal daily actions to take shape.

But a woman cannot make the penetrative energy of the masculine instinct her own except by falling in love with it, as happens in meeting a man. In the myth of Kore, like in the myth of Ariadne, Psyche, Ishtar, like in every myth where a woman descends to the underworld, it is passion which guides, and for passion which one dies and is reborn.

Hades thus lights up Kore's anima and he makes her die of fear. I have recognized Hades uncountable times in feminine analysis, and in the words of many woman I have found almost the same words as in the Homeric hymn. Innumerable times I have heard them say: "I am an abyss, I am afraid of falling, I feel myself sinking, I lose my head, I feel small and weak like a baby, I am terrified of losing who I am, I feel myself being dragged away, far away from a part of myself."

One time a patient of mine, making love with a man to whom by then she had been married for a long time, had the sensation of losing herself, of sinking into an abyss; "It was a feeling of death," she said to me, "yet it was very sweet and I wanted it and didn't want it at the same time; it wasn't an orgasm, it was a sort of an estrangement, as if he took me and carried me away from myself."

These sensations are so violent and definitive, and they transform the body and soul so radically, that many women unfortunately cannot permit it for themselves, and they stop themselves at the margins of passion.

In the first part of this book we saw how the feminine sexual drive can have an existence that is autonomous from feelings, and it can induce a woman to *lose her head*, but in that case the conscious abdicates in the face of its own desire, in the face of the dragging violence of the drive, and the relationship with the man doesn't necessarily assume importance. The archetypal context is thus still that of the Great Mother.

Here, instead, it is a question of a different way of *losing one's head*: in this case, a woman doesn't abandon herself to her instinct, but to a man (or to her animus) and it is the emotional violence of contact that makes every woman a child. What makes her weak and lost is that overpowering energy in which it is so terrible and so sweet to let oneself go. In this case, sex plays its part *within* the relationship, and it is a dangerous game, because the other has in his hands not only the body, but the soul, and the entire personality of a woman. A dangerous game, but perhaps because of this, a most fascinating game, if there is the courage, on the part of both, to go all the way.

There doesn't seem to exist a torment and a pleasure more intense for a woman than to feel possessed: a mysterious energy, whose origin is hidden in the most archaic layers of the psyche, reemerges from the shadows and, taking the body and the soul of a woman, it drags her with it, offering her an immense, unknown richness. This, briefly summarized, seems to me to be Hades, and thus the descent into the underworld, far from constructing a neurotic nucleus, seems perhaps the most radical transformative experience in the psychic life of a woman.

Perhaps there is something—which is also a possible meaning of this passage in the myth—that in a man a woman can never know, but only desire and fear. There seem to exist psychic truths which are stronger than our capacities to understand them. The animus is not, however, a conquest of reason: when a woman falls in love with a plan, an idea, a craft, then it is possible for the phallic energy to enter her and bring her to completeness, and it is good as long as this process is not obstructed.

In the myth, in fact, nobody intervenes in the abduction, and those who see it say nothing, not only because it is Nature which has provoked this event, but because, by nature, it has to be completed.

It is only feminine consciousness that, after the time of toil and passion, can find its unity again, and thus the mediation with the demands of the animus. Kore will find Demeter again, but not forever and in any case she is no longer Kore, and the period of waiting is by then the period of transformation.

Like in the myth, many women's dreams talk about an abyss, and about a man who is at the bottom, and the immense danger that falling brings. Dreams of the abyss sometimes signal a *borderline* condition but, because of the above considerations, more than the possibility for a psychotic nucleus, it seems that they simply talk about the fear of the instinctive energy of the masculine archetype. Sometimes the meaning of the dream is rendered even more obvious by the presence, in opposition to the man, of the dreamer's mother, like in the first of the following two dreams, or by an image of the Great Mother.

SUPERMAN'S ABYSS: *I dreamed I was in line with a group of people, perhaps tourists, a few strangers, or maybe the place was abroad. We go down long staircases, as if we were tied, in an Indian* line, *like roped when you go hiking on ice in the mountains. Every now and then, in the center of the stairwell, I see a surface of black rock which opens itself. It is just a moment, but it is sufficient to see that beneath there is an even bigger empty space, and then another and another; it is an abyss which perhaps arrives at the center of the earth or who knows where, but it is scary. I am afraid of being sucked in and perhaps I see a man, a sort of 007, about 40, athletic, strong, handsome, who is standing on the edge of the chasm which opens and closes. Perhaps it is he who provokes this opening and closing? He is a secret agent, and he is not afraid, he is a sort of Superman, he seems to fly above the chasm. I realize that my mother is no longer with me; before she was there, now she's gone. So I approach a middle-aged woman, an Anglo-Saxon type, a stranger, perhaps she is our guide, and I tell her in English, "I've lost my mother." I am anguished and she replies in Italian, trying to reassure me, she tells me that my mother has gone far away, to the East. I don't know how to find her again, and I am anguished, and besides I see the abyss which opens, and I am afraid, terrified.*

ALICE'S CHASM: *I am in a car on the road that goes to my house in the country; after a curve, all of a sudden I see a man (a black man) who signals me with a small flag to stop: I think there is work on the road nearby, or that the machinery has to complete maneuver and I stop. The man approaches the car, he opens the door, and he invites me to see something. I follow him, and after a few meters I see that there is a crevasse in the middle of the path, and just as I am about to thank that man for having saved me, the crevasse suddenly opens wider and wider, it opens under my feet, and the unknown man takes me in his arms and jumps into the chasm. I scream with all my strength, but I know that no one can hear me; he holds me tightly, but without hurting me, and I realize that the fall is slow as if we were in an elevator. It seems that it never ends, and in the darkness I feel completely at the mercy of that man, who instead seems to know what he's doing. At the end we fall onto a field and there is light again, like day, and I feel like Alice in Wonderland, and the man says to me smiling, "Was it really necessary to yell so much?"*

DEPRESSION
(LINES 40–275)

The Search

Kore's imploring voice goes to Demeter's heart, who feels it break in two, overcome by desperation. Every time, when meeting the masculine principle, from the first moments a woman feels that the mediation that will subsequently take place within the personality will not be capable of wholly restoring the past, because something ends forever, something that is at the origin of the meaning of death. A part of the personality abandons itself and permits the encounter, but another part rebels and forms the basis for future mediation.

This ambivalence constellates a very profound nucleus of feminine psychology, and it is the origin of behaviors apparently contradictory, yet fundamental for the equilibrium of the personality. If Kore didn't let herself be abducted, the fusional dimension would never shatter, provoking pathological situations; but if Demeter didn't rebel, the symbiosis would tend to shift onto the Persephone-Hades relationship, with just as serious consequences.

But there is another motive for Demeter to despair, and it is in the sudden awareness that the masculine principle is already so strong and autonomous that it can lacerate the solidarity of feminine identity. At that point he has nothing more to do with the passive instrument of phallic fecundation dear to the Great Mother; he is no longer the son-lover, the reproduction slave or the simple object of desire, but he has assumed the disquieting shape of a figure capable of overwhelming the control of the feminine ego. Hades finds Kore in Demeter, and uses force to take her for himself, so that Demeter is exposed before him and before herself, and she understands in the same moment that she has lost her absolute power over her own identity. The man, the animus, becomes *the other, the different*, against whom one measures oneself, but only after having succumbed to contact.

And finally the third motive for agony for Demeter is the solitude and the abandonment in which she feels herself sink. Nobody tells her about the event, neither the gods, nor men, nor the animals "wanted to" tell her the truth, because all of nature collaborated to break up the fusion between the mother and the maiden, to make room for the union of opposites.

For nine days and nine nights, without either eating or sleeping, Demeter wanders about the earth wrapped in a black veil of mourning; no image constellates the pain yet or is aware of it, and the conscious finds itself in the dark, deprived of meaning and an aim. The pain in that moment is a scream without cognition, at the edge of madness.

Nine is the number which refers to maternal gestation, and it represents the crowning of an effort, the conclusive phase of a natural process; in proposing this periodicity, the myth seems to want to tell us that Demeter's desperate behavior is natural, like a gestation, and it contains within itself the possibility for change, as if the rejection of the truth found a space to allow for its own subsequent transformation.

This reactionary phase, that doesn't want to hear reason, is normal after any serious emotional trauma, and it becomes pathological only when it doesn't conclude in *natural* time. That means, in psychological language, in a certain period of time, variable from person to person, and from case to case. I think it is the analyst's job to be able to understand a little at a time when it is time for the reactionary phase to conclude on the basis of the subject's psychic constitution and the emotional intensity of the experience, encouraging, as much as possible, this process.

Translating the episode into psychoanalytical terms, it is a question of a rejection phase induced by a sudden weakening of the imputable ego, who in turn, provoked the scission as a result of the violence of the emotional shock.

Falling in love, or the contact with a new form of the animus, at times is sufficient, in the feminine personality, to cause an emotional trauma.

In this case the scission of the personality is first noticed as an unbearable weakening, against which all possible resistance is activated, and it corresponds in the myth to Kore's supplication and to Demeter's search. The rejection of the trauma induced one to deny it, and to reconstruct the preceding wholeness.

Many women, over the course of time, have told me that they realize they are reactive, stinging, and unbearable with their companions, and they don't know why: "It is as if I hated him, but that's not true," "He is stronger than me, I have to punish him," "I withdraw from sex and this makes me suffer, too." It is possible that phrases like these hide the fear of facing a relationship which can get bogged down in a dependence dense with unknowns and pain.

One time a girl, very young and very much in love with a foreign man, renounced leaving with him: "He is so strong," she told me, "and I love him so much, that his life would take me away from mine and I couldn't be anything except a part of him, and I don't want to, and maybe I wouldn't even be able to."

"I have to break up with him immediately," another, more mature woman said to me one day, "otherwise this relationship ties up my hands and I can't allow a man to overwhelm my life, modifying rhythms and plans which I have planned with a lot of effort over time. I'm risking becoming one of those unbearable women who only live for their man; I already realize that I think of him continuously, I have lost my energy and I seem to be growing stupid." Soon after, with the voice of a frightened little girl, she confessed that she was so in love, and so physically involved, that she concretely felt the risk of losing herself in that relationship, and that this awareness made her happy and desperate at the same time.

While I listened to her, I recognized the double presence of Demeter and Kore in her words, the revolt of one and the panic of the other, the same ambivalence as Violetta in the first act of *La Traviata*, or Juliet in her nocturnal monologue, and I verified once again that natural, double reaction facing the pull which had lacerated my patient's ego. Only time, consuming those emotions, could make space for the relationship.

For a man it certainly isn't like this: his identity doesn't separate before a woman and not even before his anima because, beyond neurotic contexts, he doesn't run the risk of sinking into dependence. He also doesn't need to prime such radical defensive strategies.

Now we will examine this complex of panic and revolt, told in the first part of the myth, no longer in regard to a man, but in regard to that unconscious part of the animus that concerns masculine instinct, and we will see significant analogies between the two situations.

Many women—usually unconsciously spiteful and competitive—declare that they don't want to be *like men*, that is, according to them, violent, cruel, schematic, cold, ready for everything, and so on. Limited to the examination of the shadow of the masculine principle, and refusing to recognize the strength and to feel the attraction, they take precautions against the unconscious risk of a relationship with the animus, as dramatic as it is fertile. Kore struggles and cries, Demeter rebels, until Hades is only a black and bad man.

On the other hand, though, these same women desire to assert themselves, they would be only too happy to give form to their ambitions, they want to count, to be heard, and to have success in their undertakings, even if they don't always admit it; from this point of view they hide a legitimate, natural and dignified desire for masculine aggressiveness, without which the affirmation of one's own identity is unthinkable, in whatever social sphere. They hide this desire from themselves, and often, especially nowadays, are convinced of saving the purity of their souls, while all they are doing is following a tradition of the feminine collective conscious which, in homage to patriarchal culture, has since time immemorial deprived women of the right to descend into the field to fight. And so, continuing alternatively to desire to be aggressive and determined, and refusing themselves to be so, too many women still continue to be overbearing and whiny. They don't listen to the warrior Bradamante, who is hiding within them, and they believe that fidelity to the feminine principle consists in this while, in the name of fear, they celebrate the most definitive betrayal.

For example, a woman realized, in the course of analysis, that she wanted to work in a social sphere which required moral responsibility, organizational ability, capacity to face conflict, and a good dose of aggressiveness. So it was a question of developing aspects of the masculine principle relative to thought, instinct, and feeling. These features of the animus pushed inside her to find expression and to help her in the work she loved. And she herself searched for this masculine energy inside herself, while at the same time she was afraid. And if she lost her femininity? And if she was not able to do the things well? And if she became cold and mean? And if this new field of interest imbalanced her life? And if she was not able to mediate between everyday life and her passion? And if she had placed too many expectations and too much energy in it? Then it was better to renounce it immediately.

Also in this case it would have been necessary to wait for the rejection crisis to complete itself, before a period of depression could orient her toward her new task and at the same time toward the serene acceptance of the limits of her work.

Sometimes this reactionary phase is experienced through apparently non-pertinent symptoms: sudden bursts of crying, mood swings, aggressiveness, emotional hypersensitivity, insomnia, loss of appetite, eating disorders, and so on, as if the entire psychosomatic organism betrayed, in the symptom, the initial phase of uneasiness that the emotional relationship with the masculine world generates in a woman.

Depression

At dawn of the tenth day, Demeter sees Hecate, who grasps the torch, the sign of the moon goddess, approach her, and tells her that she didn't see Kore's abduction. If the moon didn't see it, then the sun must know and so, without having yet broken her silence, Demeter goes with Hecate to Helios.

In the first part of this book I tried to analyze the instinctive sphere governed by Hecate in Greek culture and still today in the collective unconscious; in contrast to this episode, in particular, Hecate seems to me to describe a self-protective characteristic of the feminine principle, which closes a woman in herself to help her live through a difficult moment.

But her power is as smooth and therapeutic for the feminine gender as it is disintegrating and awful for the masculine gender, because Hecate, as we have already seen, is an enemy of men.

This image is of great interest precisely because of its ambivalence: from a psychoanalytic point of view it is, on the one hand, a part of the force which tries to hold a woman back from the risk of dependence on a man in a situation of total autonomy; on the other, it is also the energy which can definitively send a woman away from the masculine world, inducing her to nourish feelings of aversion and vengeance.

Hecate is the light of the moon, she is the daughter of the night, she is the protector of women, the good witch who cures, but at the same time, she is also the nocturnal goddess of death who sucks the blood of men and poisons them, she is the disintegrating energy of masculine consciousness, the sworn enemy of love and relationships, the goddess of sex, the mistress of Circe and Medea, the shadow of the Great Mother.

And in all this complexity Hecate operates, from this point of the myth on, next to Demeter. In fact, she at first helps the goddess come out of the state of shock to look reality in the face, but after she will become the overbearing and vindictive witch against the masculine world.

At the beginning of the myth only Demeter exists, one with herself, intact and intangible in the closed feminine universe; Hades' incursion breaks up this identity, splitting her and taking into his power the most fragile element. Hecate's arrival (the third character of the triple goddess of the origins) starts up a dialectical movement which seems very important to me because it helps, with the good and the bad, to save the autonomy of the feminine principle, though accepting the evidence of a completed fact.

And thus it is precisely this character who will allow Demeter to recompose in a different synthesis the relationship with Kore. Analogously, in certain passages of the life of the feminine psyche, Hecate's characteristics will protect a personality against the risk of a too radical exposure to a love relationship, or to the power of the animus.

The psychological complexity and interest of this figure reside precisely in the ambivalence of her relationship with the ego: on the one hand, Hecate reinforces the trust in feminine autonomy, on the other, she starts one toward the awareness of the relationship with the other. And perhaps in this continuous, subterranean oscillation one plays, in the life of every woman, with the possibility of opening up to passion remaining oneself.

Helius, the symbol of solar consciousness, replies to Demeter, "You shall know," and his words, which announce a divine marriage willed by Zeus, open Demeter's heart to "a pain more awful and savage." Now, in the light of consciousness, the goddess knows what she has lost and where. In her heart, a sadness descends which makes her unrecognizable: her appearance at this point is that of a lonely and unhappy old woman, the mirror of an internal truth which no longer allows her to live among the gods. Thus a long period of depression begins for Demeter, which seems possible to divide into three phases.

Even depression,[4] especially in feminine psychology, is not always the same: it can happen that it opens a defensive emptiness in the ego when facing pain, but it can also be that, instead, it hides an aggressive shadow which has no room for fighting in conscious

---

4. In this case, the term "depression" means a reactive depression to an event, and thus of episodic character, and not the depressive pathology.

life. In the second case, as soon as the repressed aggressive tension is liberated, we almost always see an hysterical symptom appear.

In my opinion, Demeter's phase of depression is the second type, which resembles that strange calm that precedes a storm, when the air is charged with tension but nothing is moving yet.

And nothing moves because the awareness of the helplessness that imprisons the aggressiveness has spread, and I don't believe that it is difficult to understand how this mental state historically and culturally is intertwined with feminine psychology. The helpless desperation winds up in itself and creates a vacuum of energy: Demeter no longer looks for Kore, she no longer asks anybody for anything and she submits to her disorientation wandering in silence and under a false appearance.

Here a few ways of being which I have met with many times in this phase of depression are recognizable: letting oneself be ugly and slovenly, curling up in bed, hiding the face against a wall, with the chin on the chest, in a silence which obstructs any communication, wandering here and there without an aim, feeling strange in every environment and alone everywhere.

This empty and lifeless space delimits perhaps the most difficult moment of depression, difficult but necessary, at least as far as I know. The surrender of the ego before the force of events, the helplessness acknowledged in stopping the pain, in correcting an injustice, in restoring life or freedom, result as healthy for the maturation of consciousness, but sometimes they open a hemorrhage in the vital force which only time, in the majority of cases, is able to heal. For Demeter as well, as the Homeric poem says, a lot of time is necessary and also the patience to let it pass.

Time and patience, in this particular situation, costs more than anti-depressants, but in the end they are more effective, because they start the subject separating herself slowly, not from the symptom, but from the nucleus of the suffering, allowing one to continue facing the pain, instead of feeling submerged in it. In other words, the phase of depression, also in this initial period, is not necessarily a neurotic obstacle to get rid of, but it can mark an important passage within a characteristic path, and as such, in my opinion, it must be respected.

This position, supported on one side by psychoanalytic doctrine, seems to clash with a dominant in the contemporary collective conscious, engaged in exorcising depression, just like all that belongs to the negative sphere: illness, defeat, old age, death. The imperative that thus derives is: "always young, always healthy, always beautiful, always successful, and always in a good mood," or "I'm OK, you're OK," according to the "pop" American psychology.

It is understandable how much a similar socio-cultural context is fertile terrain for the growth of those explosions of irrationality (superstition, witchcraft, and all kinds of occult practices) which so arouse the curiosity of the media: in this unnatural and distorted form one attempts, in fact, to close the accounts with the sphere of the negative (not of mystery) which continues to reappear. The inability to accept oneself as fragile and helpless before the forces of pain brings to light an overbearing and infantile desire to keep life under control, to be able to predict it, or to deviate its course.

But this pathetic arrogance, called neurosis by some, while social underestimation and sometimes even therapeutic tenacity direct themselves instead against the depression of who, defeated, wants to look her pain in the eyes.

This diffuse haste to eliminate depression doesn't seem in the end something to share either from a therapeutic point of view or from a moral point of view, because it induces one to confuse, and thus exchange, even in psychotherapy, a phase of depression with endogenous depression. More than ever I am convinced that both forms should be treated in different ways because the causes that generated it are different (and if one is very attentive, so are the manifestations).

As for the phase of depression to which I am referring, it is a reaction to an event, and I believe that the administration of psychotropic drugs should be exclusively limited to cases in which a risk for borderline has manifested. And, incidentally, this timely recognition is one of the difficulties of our job.

In the contrary case, the anesthesia of depressive suffering constitutes an undeserved and prescriptive interference on the part of the psychotherapist which, in reality, is translated into a lack of respect for the patient and a lack of faith in the regenerative capacity of her pain. This type of depression is often announced by a dream, for example with a vacuum of energy, a fall of blood pressure, an electrical blackout, an escape of gas, and so on.

THE METHANE GAS METER: *I am at the window of my house in the country and I see the farmer, who occasionally works for me, arrive with his truck; he stops by the edge of the lawn and spills a truck load of earth over the gas meter, which in the dream is also the distributor of the methane, and so it can't remain covered up. So I run down quickly, yelling at him to take away that earth immediately, but he calmly begins to speak about this and that, and he doesn't even dream of doing what I said.*

The dreamer was a man about 40 who had lived life with his head down, intensely wanting security and well-being for himself and his family. In the dream the earth falls on the flow of his energy: there is no way to distribute the gas, nor to know how much there is, nor to stop it. The farmer, the tranquil man who knows the ways of the earth, buries, at least for a while, a source of energy which has been sacked and needs rest. There was a great fatigue in that man. He was used to managing his life, without taking the time to stop and reflect on his solitudes, renunciations, and defeats. The dream, despite him, and thus in a conflictual context, started him off in a period of depression which would require him to reconsider his life.

PRESSURE 20: *I am at my doctor's, who is a woman. She is measuring my blood pressure and the pressure is 20. I almost don't believe it, but the doctor confirms it: "Yes, it's 20, luckily," and so I recognize the voice of my analyst.*

Hypertension signals an energy vacuum that corresponds to a phase of depression in which there seems to be no more blood, and thus no more libido. But in that woman's life, a large repressed pain demanded at that point to be received. It stifled her strength and stunned her extraverted and reactive personality.

The prevalent feeling in my patients, who perhaps for the first time cede to a phase of depression, is the fear of not returning. From the point of view of the unconscious, the truth seems to be the opposite: depression, having used up its time, generates new energy, while the extroverted, reactive desperation on one's own libido induces states of anxiety and anguish which tend to become definitive.

Returning to our myth, Demeter's first phase of depression, her mute wandering, ends at the fountain of Eleusis where she meets Keleos' daughters, before whom she breaks her silence, confiding in them her experience in the form of an analogy.

Telling them her fantasy, Demeter confesses her deepest truth: the pirates abducted her and now she no longer has a goal or an identity. When a communication seems too painful, then one recounts something *similar, which is understandable,* regarding the sense of the suffering. For the first time after Helios' revelation, Demeter speaks of her experience as something that cannot be modified: Kore is lost, and with her the sovereignty of the feminine principle; it doesn't make sense to argue with this, but one can ask something and Demeter asks pity and help from Keleos' daughters.

What the mother goddess asks for, in order to be able to continue to live, is to take shelter among women, in the protective atmosphere of a domestic hearth. She also wants to take care of a house and a baby, to be able to carry out the series of simple daily actions that help maintain contact with reality, because they are elementary and necessary habits, and because the repeated gestures are always the same, and are a millennial experience in women's lives. In this reassuring context it becomes possible to drink, to smile, and to begin a period centered on the concrete things of life.

Uncountable times in feminine analysis I have met with this psychological condition: as we have seen, the fear of losing oneself in love for a man, or the resistance to contents of the animus, allow dreams of abduction, violence, or theft to appear where male images represent a constant threat. Simultaneously, in the conscious sphere, the necessity for a period of isolation in the feminine world appears—the desire to stay at home, to see one's oldest and dearest female friends, to dedicate oneself to concrete and reassuring tasks. I believe this period should also be respected as a passage toward the acceptance of how much is still too dangerously *other than self*.

This attitude of the conscious is very feminine and consists in blocking active attention, in difficult moments, and I believe it is a question not of evading, but of keeping oneself in balance. Making the beds, ironing, preparing food, cleaning the house, taking care of children, are more solid embankments than one would think in the fullness of pain. In the end, it is a question of a spontaneous form of meditation in which mental emptiness is achieved through the automatic repetition of gestures which are always the same and don't involve the activity of thought, while they induce relaxation and concentration.

This attitude of the conscious is naturally not exclusive to feminine psychology: Jung, who in the solitude of Bollingen cut wood, lit a fire and prepared food, said that "simple things make simple and profound men."

A patient of mine, with a long borderline period behind him, told me this dream at the end of his analysis:

THE COPPER POTS: *I am with my girl friend in my analyst's kitchen. There is an old, white-haired man, with a wise and affectionate expression. From now on I will talk with him and not with her. I know that my analyst wants to give me a parting gift, and I say to my girl friend, pointing to some copper pots hanging on the wall, "You'll see that she'll give me the pots." Then my analyst comes in and she gives them to me, taking them off the wall. I thank her and I say, "I learned here that it is very important to know how to make a good minestrone."*

In this case it was not only a question of saying goodbye, or of the integration of the inferior function of an intuitive, or the recognition of the transformative capacity of analysis, but also the awareness of meaning and value in certain simple, habitual gestures.

Returning to our myth, it is thus in the closed circle of the daily concreteness of the feminine world that the recognition of the shadow takes place. In Metaneira's house, in fact, Demeter experiences the dark part of the feminine principle all the way, tightly intertwined with the problem of power, and thus with the moral problem. It is among women, in the reassuring atmosphere of domestic walls, that there is an opening through which the shadow is able to filter—from the emptiness of meditation, the monstrous creatures that the fine net of conscious thought had more or less been able to hold prisoner also appear. Demeter's shadow is Hecate, that is, the magic and demoniacal power, the capacity to alter the natural order of things on the part of those who wanted this order.

Demeter's stay in the Eleusinian House, which takes up only forty lines in the Homeric hymn, is wrapped up in mystery: Demophoön grows magically, without drinking, eating, like a god, and at night he burns in the fire "like a brand." Thus Demeter, the goddess of nature, carries out enchantments aimed at altering the natural order. Why? Doesn't this behavior resemble a dark desire for revenge, a manifestation of an egoic and competitive superiority, without any other end than the affirmation of one's own power? Nobody asks for immortality for Demophoön and besides, mortality defines a human being, because a man begins to live, and thus to die, when he becomes conscious of it; and instead it is the unconscious which restores a creature to biological immortality: the crickets are immortal because they don't know they will die, nor is time a dimension of existence for them. To offer immortality to Demophoön equals depriving him of humanity and history, it is a perverse way to exercise a power, to modify nature against nature.

In Greek culture, the immortals are the gods and rare human beings who experience extraordinary undertakings—thus one is born, or one becomes, immortal, but not for the caprice of a goddess.

A few scholars have connected the episode of Demophoön with the *Eleusinian Mysteries*, almost as if it constituted an anticipation, in form and substance, of the birth of the *divine youth*. I do not agree with this concept, for the profound meaning of symbolic immortality—the eternal youth—linked to the natural cycle of eternal returns is perceived and represented in the *Eleusinian Mysteries* as the fruit of a union of opposites, as the product of the dramatic and marvelous encounter between masculine and feminine energy. The earth can't repeat the immortal cycle of life by offering her fruits if the sky doesn't send the sun and the rain, and the same process is seen in internal life.

Only when Demeter gives in to the masculine principle and the mystery of the *coniunctio oppositorum* can the eternal youth be born, but until that day only unilateral and uselessly overbearing acts will take place, acted as challenges to the masculine world and like a desperate affirmation of the ego.

Humanity, in the character of Metaneira, rebels against Demeter's plan, and Demophoön remains mortal. And yet, if the myth reveals, in this episode, the need to extract all the poison, the demand to express a shadow, which, so often in the feminine psyche, dims the anger of a frustrated power, if it were so, it would be possible to trace in this passage the necessity to have experience of the dark side. And this necessity to recognize the shadow, not abstract, nor intellectual, nor descriptive, but harshly concrete, I find it, and I have found it, in myself and in my patients, over time.

Demeter is not elegant in this passage of the myth: masked as a poor, old woman, protected by a veil of haughty sadness, searching for pity and work, ready to tell lies and intent on clandestine magic practices, she does not offer her best. But this weakness, this ugliness and this overbearingness are integrating parts of the human condition. They constitute the dialectical polarity which allows for knowledge and experience of good and evil. Demeter experiences her dark side at Eleusis, as much as she is capable and as much as possible, accepting, as I believe that everyone must, to be full of it, because the shadow, in measure to what comes to light, is a part of the human knowledge of pain. Only in this way can one move ahead.

Many dreams over the course of time, many conversations, and innumerable facts have convinced me of the fundamental importance of the elaboration of the shadow in the course of existence. At the same time, these experiences have shown me how exclusively vertical, celestial tensions induce one to project one's own shadow onto others, and thus send us away from our own humanity. I will never forget the terrible dream a woman, dominated by an extremely violent, destructive shadow, brought me one day in tears:

DEATH THE DECEIVER: *I am at home with some friends. The doorbell rings: it's death, who is like a big, black shadow. I think that all told she is harmless, being so immaterial; and she herself reassures me that she hasn't come to take anybody. But a friend says to me: "Be careful, because she'll do us all in." "But no," I reply, "She herself said that she doesn't want to do any harm." So I invite her in while my friends go to make a crèche on a small hill on the lawn in front of the house. I look at the black shadow and I see her push an avalanche down toward my friends, which in fact buries them all. "Why?" I ask her, and she says with a smirk, "I really like to deceive people."*

In that woman's life, a radical and irremediable betrayal had marked her childhood, and the desire to betray and destroy were recurrent, but very unconscious, themes in her existence. So in the dream it was not a mistake, as she believed, to open the door and let that shadow enter. There will be problems if she doesn't see that death drive, but there will also be problems if she doesn't experience it, since it was a part of her: one can't make a crèche closing the door in the face of one's own hell. It is really too costly for everyone to pretend to be good and to project the bad onto others.

The first signs of liberation came, in the case of this patient, after this dream, in a progressive surrender to the shadow and in the boundless sadness that its invasion generated.

An emotion experienced all the way, a negative emotion, tends so to speak, to depersonalize itself; that is, to deprive the power of the ego, allowing a limpid pain to come up, where the thought, "I suffer and so I want to," gives way to make room for another, more simple, "I suffer."

MEDIATION
(LINES 275–470)

The Negotiation

With experience of the shadow, Demeter's depression ends in the Homeric hymn: only now is the goddess ready to accept the mediation that feminine nature suggests between the need for the integrity of the ego and the desire for abandon in a relationship. The poet, after the path of obscurity and mystery, now describes an image of shining splendor:

> . . . the goddess changed her size and form
> and sloughed off old age, as beauty was wafted about
>   her.
> From her fragrant veils a lovely smell
> emanated, and from the immortal skin of the goddess a
>   light
> shone afar, as her blond hair streamed down over her
>   shoulders,
> and the sturdy mansion was filled with radiance as if
>   from lightning.
>
>   (lines 275–280)

Purified by her infernal path, Demeter wisely organizes a plan which will reveal itself to be effective because she uses her powers, but openly, in the light of the sun, accepting to reckon with reality.

From the experience of the shadow, a new equilibrium of the ego has its origin, and this casual relationship seems to have a systematic character, at least in my observations. Once it appears in the conscious, the shadow slowly lightens its negative characteristics, still maintaining its energy potential intact, as if, after having been recognized and integrated in some way, it can *change signs*. This process becomes possible because the shadow also contains in itself corrective and therapeutic contents for the conscious, which, in the formation process, is not integrated, but which, coming to light, the shadow drags along with it.[5]

The shadow can, for example, bring with itself the desire to assert oneself, the mania to win, the desire to overwhelm and prevail and also, later, the possibility to mediate this young aggressiveness with the rights of others and the boundaries which life places upon us. First the desire for power is underhanded, hidden and negative, and thus charged with unconscious, negative, and in any case useless, tensions, like the episode of Demeter and Demophoön. But when the ego experiences power, it recognizes it for what it is; it sees the cruel, egoic, and also dangerous features, and it intervenes with a healthy deflation, which in some way purifies the personality, liberating, on the one hand, a natural desire for self-affirmation, and on the other, orienting the comprehension to the needs of others and thus to the possibility of negotiation. When one accepts one's own *psychic garbage,* one becomes more tolerant

---

5. On the shadow in particular, see M. Trevi, A. Romano, *Saggi Sull'ombra* (Venice: Marsilio, 1975).

toward others. And only when the shadow is no longer taboo is it possible to mediate it.

Demeter's first gesture, after having recuperated her appearance, is to ask for the construction of a temple in her honor, announcing the teaching of a mysterious rite which would take its name from that city.

But seeing that the cult would symbolically repeat the entire order of events in the myth, Demeter's words seem, already at this point, to know and to anticipate implicitly the outcome; that is, the search and the possibility of mediation within the masculine-feminine relationship destined to generate new life in both the biological cycle and in the psychic dynamic.

The goddess' second action, enclosed within the temple, consists in rendering nature sterile, thus threatening to extinguish men's lives, and indirectly that of the gods, seeing that they live in human consciousness.

Now Demeter rediscovers solitude and silence, but finally on an equal level with the emotion, recognized and accepted for what it is:

> . . . but blond Demeter,
> sitting there apart from all the blessed ones,
> kept on wasting with longing for her deep-girded
>   daughter.
>
> (lines 302–304)

She deprives the earth of her fruits, because she, herself, has been deprived of her fruit, and, describing the negative side of her experience, she reflects it: so the dialectical moment between death and pain become the object of mediation and a transpersonal event.

Depression, when it has found the way to follow its complete course, flows into the calm river bed of mediation and abandon, mediation and abandon from which new energies will originate.

The temple is the internal space where all of this can happen, and where Demeter, drying up the earth, accepts death, if this is to be her destiny. A goddess is immortal, but she isn't immortal in her meaning, and Demeter's meaning, is the creativity expressed by the feminine principle closed within itself. And this value is not possible to renounce, so Demeter, parching the world, starts a game in which she makes her declaration calmly, and waits for a response.

The impossibility for Demeter to live without Kore seems like a state of necessity, more than a choice. The goddess of the earth, in Greek culture, *is* the earth, and this if it dries up, it means that the goddess herself is dying. Sterility, in the context of this myth, is not blackmail, nor is it a manifestation of the violence of her dismay, and it isn't even the result of a profoundly embraced emotion. Sterility, in this case, seems to me to be the image of a psychological condition of the feminine personality; that is, of the impossibility to feel completely and definitively divided between a part closed within autonomy and another open to a relationship.

If it is in the natural order of psychic evolution that Kore moves away from the maternal world to unite herself with the masculine principle, it is just as much in the natural order of things that Persephone returns to reunite herself with Demeter. In this psychological characteristic, and in the behavior which derives from it, one of the principle differences between the masculine and feminine psyche manifests itself. It is very unlikely that a man would run the risk of losing himself as an individual, of losing his meaning and his autonomy in a relationship, while a woman, if she's not careful, if she doesn't make an effort for herself, always tends to identify herself in the other, because it is not natural to keep a distance from the relationship for reflection. The identification with the mother, experienced during childhood, conserves a vitality and always risks submerging feminine consciousness in the relationship with the animus or a man.[6]

A relationship, following the meeting with the masculine principle, is possible, for a woman, as long as there can always be a return, and that there is an oscillation between proximity and distance, otherwise the relationship tends to wear itself out because the psychic distance between the opposite energies is progressively annulled.

The index of this balance is Kore-Persephone, the maiden who becomes a woman by abandoning herself to the relationship, and wisely preserving feminine wholeness. Thus, it is Demeter who fades away, the earth becomes sterile, and all life risks extinction if the feminine archetype is not permitted to reunite. Zeus has to bend before this law.

This part of the myth is found in many women's dreams and life situations. When the importance of a relationship with a man, or the intensity of the relationship with the animus, risk overwhelming her, a woman first despairs, struggles, reacts with overbearingness, loses her head, and then, at a certain point, she calms down and falls into a state of melancholy in which it seems that nothing more can sprout within her.

The event has been recognized as stronger than the ego which submits to it, and a disconsolate introversion derives from it which truly resembles arid terrain. And the unconscious, in these cases, lets

---

6. Regarding this, see Silvia Di Lorenzo, *Modern Woman & Her Shadow* (Boston: Sigo Press, 1992).

images of sterility and sadness come up, like dusty deserts or rocky terrains, milk which curdles, salt on the earth, dried up plantations, and so on.

THE DESERT AND FEAR: *I am in bed with my boyfriend and our fusion is complete, as it happens between us in reality, and I feel transported by passion. The scene changes and I am standing at a windowsill where a basil plant has all of its leaves dried up and withered. Outside an infinite red desert extends; so I ask myself where I am, and I am afraid that I won't be able to find my city, and that I will die there. I am strangely calm, but I wake up crying.*

The analogy with the myth in this dream seems surprising. In the first scene there's a very intense relationship, something that transports. In the second, there is the desert and the fear of dying far away from the familiar environment: and these are the two dialectical poles of the feminine principle in the particular moment of schism which precedes the possibility for change.

Another woman, who worked hard and had success as an artist, brought me this dream one day:

THE BURNED PLANTATION: *I am in Louisiana, in a car, on the side of a country road in front of a hut where slaves once lived, and where now a black woman is crying silently. I approach her and ask her what happened. She makes a wide gesture with her arm, indicating the sugar plantation behind the hovel, and I realize that it is completely dry, as if the sun had burned it. It seems like a disaster and, continuing to look, I feel that the sadness of that woman becomes mine. Then I ask her what caused this terrible aridity and she tells me: "Passion kept the two women apart."*

In association I asked my patient if she had an idea who the two women were, and she, after a moment, and lost in thought, answered, "Me and her, me and the woman who is crying." And so even the passion that had separated them could find a name, the name of her artistic activity and her success which had radically divided her from the wholeness of her feminine identity, and which had exposed her at the same time to identifying with the animus.

In these cases, the fear women express in analysis is the fear of losing contact with their own passion, once the feminine circuit becomes reactivated. "If I return within myself, if I regain the pieces of my life before, I will also lose the magic of this encounter," "Doesn't a career, for a woman as well, require definitive and total immersion?" "A woman who decides to dedicate herself to science, and who makes this her work, has to accept the dispossession of herself," and so on.

The unconscious, like in the myth, affirms the contrary—the only way to avoid aridity and dependence, for both Demeter and Persephone, is to periodically rediscover themselves *one with themselves,* or, in other words, to reign over one's own feminine autonomy; just as the only way to escape a regressive fusionality is to accept the relationship with the masculine principle. Truly in this case *tertium non datur*: a woman is truly a woman when she knows how to be alone in full autonomy, and when she is capable of following a passion, or of losing herself in the arms of a man. And in the same way, a woman is truly a woman if she conserves the entire receptive capacity as something precious within herself, knowing how to integrate the penetrative energy which appears from the unconscious.

Neither of the two conditions alone is able to make a woman blossom, while it is precisely the oscillation of this archetypal bipolarity which constellates sexual identity.

Mediation

At this point in the myth, the only possible alternative is the end of life or Kore's return, and so Hermes arrives, who, as the mediator, appears to help a depressed conscious (likewise in the myth of Prometheus[7] because the possibility to hit upon an intermediate solution seems more acceptable when one feels weak and defeated.

Hermes reduces the importance of the egoic will, proposing a compromise which doesn't fully satisfy anyone, thus affirming the relativity of every human event. From this point of view, Hermes has a deflationary effect not only in the myth, but also in many dreams, one of which I am about to recall here, hoping it amuses the reader, as it amused my patient and me.

This patient was a man, narcissistic and inflated: his life was a triumphant march, he only had extraordinary adventures, the esoteric sect with which he was affiliated was the most obscure and most powerful, and the experiences which touched him never seemed to him simple and normal. If he fell in love he was Romeo, if he suffered he was Prometheus, and if he fought he was Achilles. Finally one day he brought me this dream:

HERMES AND THE RESTAURANT: *I leave my house to pee and I don't know where to go; I walk around here and there without finding the right place, then I begin to climb a mountain, always going higher and always discarding every possibility. The need to pee is always becoming more impelling, but always less possible. I move among peaks, steep rock faces, high summits. By now I scramble up with my nails and elbows, risking to fall with each movement, until I find myself completely blocked and without strength. At this point*

7. M. Valcarenghi, *Nel Nome del Padre: Appunti Sulla Transgressione Nell Analisi e Nel Mito* (Milan: Tranchida, 1987).

a winged youth materializes in front of me and says: "You want to pee: go back down because there's a restaurant with a bathroom."

Hermes brings one's feet back to earth and he represents a formidable corrective for an inflated conscious, but even in this dream he can only "materialize" when the subject is already reduced to desperation, or when the situation is blocked; in the phase of the *ascent,* he wouldn't have been convincing.

In our myth, Hermes mediates between Hades, Persephone, and Demeter, and he carries out his task upon Zeus' order, and that is in the sphere of the *law of the father,* in full respect for the given order: the mediation is destined to avoid definitive lacerations.

Hades is the first person whom Hermes addresses once he has arrived in the underworld; he communicates to him the order to bring Persephone back to the earth, calling the goddess with her new name for the first time. And, at the winged god's words ". . . Aidoneus, lord of the nether world, with smiling brows obeyed the behests of Zeus the king" (lines 357–358), and thus, for the first and only time, we here Hades' voice in the myth:

Persephone, go to your dark robed mother,
with a gentle spirit and temper in your breast,
and in no way be more dispirited than the other gods.
I shall not be an unfitting husband among the
    immortals,
as I am father Zeus' own brother.

(. . .)

Thus he spoke and wise Persephone rejoiced
and swiftly sprang up for joy, but he himself
gave her to eat a honey-sweet pomegranate seed,

contriving secretly about her, so that she might not
spend all her days again with dark-robed, revered
  Demeter.

(lines 360–364, 370–374)

In these words Hades is no longer the king of the shadows who suddenly emerges from the earth and takes Kore away from her mother, herself, and the light of the conscious. The unconscious and dangerous animus has transformed itself as it slowly becomes known. Hades now reveals a strong, attentive, and tolerant masculine character, able to understand and to support the femininity of his woman, and to permit the departure to avoid the repeating (and this time with him, a man) of the fusional dynamic. Hades doesn't want to *take possession of* Persephone, he wants to love and marry her, because the meaning of union is not symbiosis, in which one annuls oneself and becomes part of the other, but the creative tension that lights up when they both remain themselves. Hades has a cold mind and a warm heart, a condition in reality less diffuse than one would think, and because of this, because he reasons lucidly and encourages Persephone to leave, and because he loves her, he offers her a pomegranate, the symbol of love. And, to express all this, a slight smile is enough.

Hades, as a husband, is from this point of view the best possible, because he understands the reasons for feminine ambivalence, and he shares the responsibility for it but, at the same time, he does what he must to keep his companion tied to him.

Hades, as an internal husband, is just as enviable: having lost the archaic and violent features cultivated in the unconscious, he is by now the masculine substance of Persephone's personality, the penetrative energy oriented toward affirming one's own identity and facing experiences, rather than receiving them. In Hades' words, if now we see him as Persephone's masculine principle, we can embrace that right for sovereignty and love which, for the goddess, derives precisely from her marriage: it is the union with the animus that transforms the maiden into a woman and makes her mistress of her internal life.

> . . . *When you are here*
> *you shall be mistress of everything which lives and*
>   *moves;*
> *your honors among the immortals shall be the*
>   *greatest,*
> *and those who wrong you shall always be punished,*
> *if they do not propitiate your spirit with sacrifices,*
> *performing sacred rights and making due offerings.*

(lines 364–369)

But even when she is up there, in her mother's world, Persephone will no longer be Kore, because she will bring with her the awareness of union and its periodic repetition. The symbol of this indissoluble bond and this irreversible transformation is the pomegranate, the sweet fruit born from Dionysis' blood, and thus above all the image of pleasure and energy. But, in antiquity, the pomegranate was also sacred to three goddesses: for Aphrodite it was fertility, for Hera it was the matrimonial bond, and for Persephone it was death, summarizing in a common denominator the transformative continuity of the feminine through union, death, and fertility.

Thus when Persephone, unknowing, eats that fruit, which unites, kills, and fertilizes, and thus transforms, she can't return to how she was before, and Hermes' mediation will bring Persephone, not Kore, back to her mother, starting up that oscillation of the adult feminine psyche between one pole and the other, between the unity in oneself and the union with the other.

Persephone is she who exists between two lives, and she describes the internal image of the woman who is able to compare herself with the masculine energy of the unconscious and to transform herself with it. To sink into the unconscious and accept the laceration of the *marriage with death* seems to be the condition necessary to completely become a woman if, as I believe, a woman, like a man, becomes herself only when she has reckoned all the way with the other.

The transformation from Kore to Persephone, through the dangerous and conflictual passion for Hades, is a subject more than ever relevant in our work, for the growing importance that, after thousands of years of exile, the animus is taking in feminine life.

In the time of the founding fathers of psychoanalysis, the socio-cultural balance didn't orient research toward the meaning and value of the animus in the feminine psyche. In fact, if the animus is the psychic substance that pushes a woman to face reality and not only to embrace it, and thus if it unites phallic thought, feeling, and instinct in the way proposed in the first part on this volume, then, in the end, what could a woman have reasonably done with her animus until fifty years ago? Excluded from the economic, social, political, religious, artistic, and cultural spheres where decisions and changes are made, restricted within the family circle, or in marginal or supportive activities, what could the lines of development for her masculine features have been?

In addition, the animus, after thousands of years of coherent and systematic repression, would inevitably have appeared charged with a violent and vindictive shadow capable of discouraging, until a few decades ago, even the most confident analysts. Jung, himself, after having enucleated the concept of the animus and after having formulated the basis for the development for theory and clinical practice from this point of view, put aside the subject, as something ambiguous and cumbersome, while he continued to study for all his life the images of the anima. Considering the times, it couldn't be otherwise, and Jung, besides, must have intuited the masculine counterpart in women, once it appeared in the conscious, would have generated incalculable upheavals, not only psychological.

So when in 1939, writing about the psychological aspect of the figure of Kore, Jung bumps into the character of Hades, he takes leave of him in a few words:

> Man's role in the Demeter myth is really only that of seducer or conqueror.[8]

And, further on in the same essay:

> But the Demeter-Kore myth is far too feminine to have been merely the result of an anima-projection. Although the anima can, as we have said, experience herself in Demeter-Kore, she is yet of a wholly different nature. She is in the highest degree femme à homme, whereas Demeter Kore exists on the plane of mother-daughter experience, which is alien to man and shuts him out. In fact, the psychology of the Demeter cult bears all the features of a matriarchal order of society, where the man is an indispensable but on the whole disturbing factor.[9]

8. C. G. Jung, *The Collected Works*, Vol. 9, Part 1, §310.
9. C. G. Jung, *The Collected Works*, Vol. 9, Part 1, §383.

On this page which concludes the essay, the last line seems like a dissonant note, as if Jung himself, projecting himself onto the masculine character of the myth, intended to exclude himself from the event and from his analysis.

He recognizes that this event doesn't concern the projection of the masculine anima, because it concerns the mother-daughter experience which excludes men. But he doesn't take the next step, which consists in examining, from the point of view of the feminine psyche, Hades as a projection of the unconscious animus. Jung, after having given the coordinates for finding the point, that is the value of the animus, stops himself and leaves us the task of starting from there, as if being a man during his era made the theoretical investigation in the unconscious feminine psyche not completely opportune, and certainly premature.

"Man is an indispensable and disturbing element," he writes, and then: "Man's role is only that of abductor and rapist." This image, which Jung proposes, is only the projection of Kore's animus in the first part of the myth, that is the unconscious sexual counterpart when it appears in the conscious contaminated by the shadow. Not unlike the masculine anima which, when she finally makes her appearance, is weighed down by aftereffects of sentimentalism, afflictions and moody melancholy.

It is rather precisely through the contact with the *abductor* that Kore becomes Persephone, with the risk in the contrary case of remaining a maiden forever; it is only through the violence of the impact, feared and desired and succumbed to, that the animus transforms from rapist to bridegroom, and that a woman completely becomes herself, able to celebrate the sacred marriage within her being and within what she will become.

John Donne describes this complex feeling as a paradox in his beautiful poem called "Batter My Heart."

Yet dearly I love you, and would be loved fain,
But am betrothed unto your enemy:
Divorce me, untie or break that knot again,
Take me to you, imprison me, for I
Except you enthrall me, never shall be free,
Nor ever chaste, except you ravish me.[10]

During a woman's analysis, when the problem is that proposed in these pages, it is possible to observe, in dreams, the passage of the animus from abductor to bridegroom, and, sometimes to see both images simultaneously present in the process.

THE POSTPONED WEDDING: *I have to buy myself a dress for my sister's wedding and I have to do it today. But, as I leave to go to the store, I realize I am being followed by three boys; they don't do anything to me, they don't threaten me, they don't have a dangerous aspect, but I feel uneasy in any case and uselessly I try to flee.*

In this case it was the sister's marriage, the person closest to the dreamer. It is projected because it is not yet bearable. And it isn't even possible to buy the dress because a *residual* of the masculine archetype, incarnated in the three youths, still impedes her. Yet, at the same time, a marriage is imminent and no real danger impends in the dream.

THE QUARREL: *Two men are quarreling over me: one is my husband, the man I am about to marry (and in the dream the incon-*

---

10. John Donne, "Batter my Heart," in *A Treasury of Great Poems: English and American*, edited by Louis Untermeyer (New York: Simon and Schuster, 1942), p. 367.

gruousness is not that) and the other is a Nazi official. The Nazi has abducted me and keeps me closed up in a sort of dark bunker. I am desperate and prey to panic, when the door of my prison opens; but it is my husband I see, who smiling says to me, "What are you doing in here? Don't you remember we are going to get married?"

THE TILE: *I am in a strange prison: it is out in the open in a sort of courtyard and we prisoners, all women, have to stand perfectly still, each one on the surface of a tile which has been assigned to us. On one side of the courtyard there is a small building-office where our guards seem occupied with bureaucratic tasks, and they look at us distractedly every now and then. There is no barbed wire, nor walls, nor guards, yet no woman moves from her tile, as if she were glued to it. Me, too. At a certain point, however, it occurs to me that I could try to leave. I move from my tile and go away undisturbed. It was really so simple, who knows why I was so afraid.*

THE SURPRISE: *Outside, at night. I am walking in the street and I realize that a man is following me, so I turn the corner, and so does he. I cross the street, and so does he, so I speed up my step and then I run, and he continues to follow me. Out of the corner of my eye I see that he is very large and wrapped up in a large black cape. My heart is beating crazily, and at a certain point I think: enough, I can't escape like this, it's useless, I may as well face him. I turn and I wait for him; he approaches, opens his cape and I see M., a restless and complicated man, but I know and love him deeply.*

In all of these dreams it is possible to see a signal of willingness, on the part of the dreamer, to measure herself with a masculine energy experienced until then as something overpowering and dangerous.

The Return

Thus Persephone, guided by Hermes, returns to light and finds her mother again; then Hecate joins them, thus recomposing the triple goddess of the origins: the earth, the moon, the abyss, the magic, fertile and mysterious totality of being wholly and uniquely a woman.

But the incantation of fusionality is broken forever and Kore no longer exists. Demeter intuits everything hugging her, and her words go from doubt to certainty without need for a confirmation from Persephone:

> And as Demeter still held her dear child in her arms,
> her mind suspected trickery, and in awful fear she with-
>   drew
> from fondling her and forthwith asked her a question:
> "Child, when you were below, did you perchance
>   partake
> of food? Speak out, that we both may know."
>
> (lines 390–394)

And then without waiting for a reply, she asks the last, direct question: "With what trick did the mighty All-Receiver deceive you?" (line 404). Many times in the course of life, a woman pronounces these words in an internal dialogue, having to acknowledge to herself that she no longer completely belongs to herself, because a part of her is elsewhere, in love with something or someone and if for a man being in love is taking, for a woman it is belonging.

The pomegranate was sweet, and there was no violence in his offering it to her,[11] but Persephone looks for excuses before herself:

---

11. Regarding this, see lines 370–374 of the Homeric hymn, "To Demeter."

> . . . *Aidoneus slyly placed*
> *in my hands a pomegranate seed, sweet as honey to*
> *eat.*
> *Against my will and by force he made me taste of it.*
>
> (lines 411–413)

Or, perhaps, is this ambivalence true? Is penetration sweet and violent at the same time? When, for example, the passion for an undertaking requires rigor, solitude, and great determination from a woman, she feels it separate from the rest of her life, and so it is possible that she recognizes within herself a necessary violence together with an inexpressible sweetness of love for what she does. Or when, for instance, a man's glance leaves a woman without strength and helpless like a child, and yet she desires more than anything else that that glance never abandon her: isn't this also an ambiguity with violence and sweetness intertwined? Persephone has become a woman through the experience of all this, of all that the masculine principle means.

The return to maternal fusionality is impossible, and Demeter herself recognizes the necessity for a compromise, but it is Rhea, Demeter's mother, the incarnation of an ancestral feminine power, who commands her to accept the mediation, arranging that Persephone will stay in the underworld for one third of the year and in the sunlight for the other two thirds. As Demeter had foreseen:

> *Whenever the earth blossoms with every kind of sweet-*
> *smelling*
> *spring flower, you shall come up again from misty*
> *darkness,*
> *a great wonder for gods and mortal men.*
>
> (lines 401–403)

Like wheat, her allegory, Persephone comes to the light at the beginning of spring and rolls back into the darkness during the autumnal sowing. The mediation, accepted by all, makes life be reborn on the earth, just like an analogous agreement, internalized by the feminine conscious, permits life to resume with the awareness of what happens at the two different levels.

Thus concludes a transformative event of the feminine personality, in which the contact with the unconscious animus first caused a dramatic schism, and of the two parts, one fell into a depression and experienced the shadow, and the other abandoned herself to a relationship, accepting the meaning of death. And the synthesis, as we have seen, causes a recomposition with different equilibrium.

But what happens when the whole series of evolutionary passages (separation, estrangement, desperation, depression, encountering the shadow, and mediation) aren't completed, or if they become blocked at a certain point in the progression?

We find ourselves facing a series of possibilities, more or less seriously pathological which generate very different consequences in behavior, depending on the phase in which the blocking has taken place.

Blocks Facing Separation

The first possibility is that there has never been a mother-daughter separation; in this case, the feminine personality results as immersed in fusional dependence on the mother, or on the world of women in any case.

These cases are considered by Jung in his writings on the maternal complex, and they manifest themselves in the identity, the projection, and in reactive defenses regarding the mother; in all three situations in the dependence on her image. In the first case, we are facing the repetition of the typology of Demeter who invades the entire psychic field. As Jung writes:

> . . . To her the husband is obviously of secondary importance; he is first and foremost an instrument of procreation, and she regards him merely as an object to be looked after, along with children, poor relations, cats, dogs, and household furniture. Even her own personality is of secondary importance; she often remains entirely unconscious of it, for her life is lived in and through others, more or less complete identification with all the objects of her care. . . . Women of this type, though continually "living for others," are, as a matter of fact, unable to make any real sacrifice. Driven by ruthless will to power and a fanatical insistence on their own maternal rights, they often succeed in annihilating not only their own personality but also the personal lives of their children.[12]

Demeter-women are strong and organized and they constitute a point of reference for their environment, but their dreams, when they address this aspect of their lives, describe great efforts, solitude, and power anxiety. A few fragments just to illustrate:

I am riding my bicycle uphill, but my mother, my brother, and the cat are also on the bike.

I put each of my children in a different box that has a label with their names on them, then I line them up in order near some jars of

---

12. C. G. Jung, *The Collected Works*, Vol. 9, Part 1, §167.

---

jam. The boxes are transparent and they have air holes; I think that it's OK like that, for today I/they aren't in danger.

I feel terribly lonely, everyone needs me and they are always asking me for something; I am tired and I complain to my mother, the only person who can understand me, and she replies: "This is being a mother."

I dreamed that I woke up because I felt wet, and I discover that my breasts are full of milk, but the milk is coming out uncontrollably, wetting everything, and I don't know how to close the taps and I am terrified.

In the case of the projection of identity, feminine personality stays anchored to the mother on whom it transfers the entire maternal complex. As Jung writes:

> Everything which reminds her of motherhood, responsibility, personal relationships, and erotic demands arouses feelings of inferiority and compels her to run away— to her mother, naturally, who lives to perfection everything that seems unattainable to her daughter. As a sort of superwoman (admired involuntarily by the daughter), the mother lives out for her beforehand all that the girl might have lived for herself. She is content to cling to her mother in selfless devotion, while at the same time unconsciously striving, almost against her will, to tyrannize over her, naturally under the mask of complete loyalty and devotion.[13]

---

13. C. G. Jung, *The Collected Works*, Vol. 9, Part 1, §169.

At times these women, instead, are not able to reach any stable union nor any affective autonomy; their great love stays mother-mistress, with whom often they live forever, or who they ask in any case for help, advice, orders, and prescriptions.

In the most serious cases, a woman has such a tight symbiosis with her mother that she can't bear her mother's death. She may even potentially consider suicidal intentions, or she expresses very self-destructive behavior in some way. In the neurotic portraits of this type, often the dreams merge images of supreme beatitude and mortal risk, as in the following examples:

TENDERNESS AND THE EARTHQUAKE: *I am in bed with my mother, who is being tender with me like when I was a child, and I am very calm, but all of a sudden there is an earthquake and a large crack opens in the floor; I am afraid that we will fall in.*

THE MIRROR AND THE SHADOW: *I am wearing a dress of my mothers' and I look at myself in the mirror, pleased, I resemble her a lot, I am almost the same as her. But in the mirror I see a shadow behind me which is about to attack me.*

MOMMY AND THE SHOOT-OUT: *My husband goes out, but I prefer to stay at home with my mother (as often happens in reality). He is against this, as usual, but I am not going to change my mind. At a certain point we hear gunshots very close by, perhaps in the garden, and we throw ourselves on the floor, hugging.*

THE LAKE AND DEATH: *I immerse myself in calm, glass-like water, perhaps it is a lake; there are swamp reeds and insects who buzz: the water is dark and I am completely alone. I swim slowly and, leaving the shore, I see the trees which line the shore and I dis-*

tinguish the willow trees from the oaks. It is an extraordinarily beautiful, immobile landscape, and it transmits a profound calm and almost a sense of beatitude. It is absurd, but I think that I never want to come out of there. At a certain point I hear, from the shore, some pebbles roll and some branches break, then the sound of masculine voices getting closer. The enchantment is broken, and I realize that I am nude and I am afraid for what could happen.

The third possibility—when the separation has not taken place—is the reactive defense against the mother. In this case, as Jung writes, ". . . a fascination which however will never reach the point of identification. . . [14] takes form, rather, it becomes a rejection: these are the situations in which a daughter doesn't love, respect, or share with her mother, or she doesn't feel understood or accepted as she is. The separation is thus rendered impossible because of the endemic hostility which closes the two subjects in a relationship of conflictual dependence.

In neurotic contexts of this type, a woman often finds herself coping with disturbances in the instinctual sphere—frigidity, amenorrhea, anorexia, bulimia, and in certain cases even neurotic sterility. At the same time, in cases like this, the development of compensatory masculine behaviors is frequent, although it has little or nothing to do with the animus. It is a question of reactive and spiteful manifestations, wrongly believed to be appropriate, to shatter maternal power. They rightly belong to that complex which, in the first part of this book, I defined the collective animus, and they refer to dominant models in the social conscious.

If, in fact, a woman is not able to psychologically separate herself from her mother, she can't truly enucleate her principle of

14. C. G. Jung, *The Collected Works*, Vol. 9, Part 1, §170.

relationship with the masculine, and thus she can't even recognize it. If Kore doesn't exist, Hades has no motive to leave the underworld to go abduct her.

The oneiric universe of these type of women is populated by old, evil women, witches, fatal swamps, poisonous or suffocating snakes, insects, wicked nurses, and all these images impede the dreamer to follow her path, to meet a man, to complete a task, and so on.

Often, at the beginning of analytical treatment, the suffering, in this type of neurosis, is particularly unconscious, just as the distance between the subject and her animus is unconscious. In almost all cases, these patients are convinced that they have developed the masculine traits of their personalities, when in reality it is only that they know how to manage, more or less deftly, in the world of men. And the two situations are truly profoundly different. Hades has never abducted them, because they are too busy defending themselves from their mothers, and they can't simultaneously risk their identities on two fronts.

Peace, even relative, with the maternal world, and a consequent detachment, are necessary so that the energy which allows these women to abandon themselves to the animus and, if ever, men, can appear.

In all three of these possible variations of mother dependence (identity, projection, and reaction), the relationship with the animus, though in different forms, remains a projective relationship.

In the first case, the conviction of the racial superiority of the feminine archetype induces the underestimation of men and the masculine principle; a mental form of benevolent superiority derives from it, which in daily life translates into oblative and obliging behaviors in regard to their husbands, sons, brothers, lovers, male friends and colleagues: these women pass through and nourish a masculine territory which they don't know, and which deep down they scorn, but without which they cannot do because it incarnates the symbolical place of their projection.

In the second case, in which the maternal complex is projected onto the mother, the relationship with the animus is one of subjection, because, by remaining the daughter, the masculine reference stays inevitably anchored on the father. In this type of neurosis, women express fear and trepidation toward masculine authorities, in comparison with whom they feel fragile and inadequate. With great difficulty they are able to recognize the right to exercise power and authority and even more rarely do they decide to transgress an order given. In their dreams, school principals, bosses, chaplains, managers, government ministers, and police officers appear, all melancholy images of an unconscious desire to decide and command, sometimes to oppress.

Finally in the third case, reacting to the maternal world, masculine characteristics develop, with a compensatory value, innate in dominant models of the collective conscious. Hardness, violence, obsessive rigor, organizational capacity, which doubtless is of assistance in daily life, doesn't liberate the more authentic and personal masculine aspects which remain anchored to the unconscious animus.

In these cases the prevalent attitude toward men is of alliance and friendly collaboration, because these are women who feel more akin to men and who play more willingly in their territory, without realizing, in the majority of cases, how painful it is to feel exiled from one's own.

Blocks Facing Abduction

The second possibility is that the separation between mother and daughter has occurred, but an encounter with the animus has not been able to happen: in this case Kore flees from abduction. Women who are part of this neurotic context are always able to find a way to stop themselves at the edge of the abyss, and they keep themselves dangerously poised between the maternal world and the world of men.

They remain virgins psychologically, and their libido leads them to constantly control their own and others reactions, because they don't want to lose themselves in the contact with masculine energy, which they experience as overpowering and dangerous. In these cases, the fear of responsibility, risk, and commitment in the first person hold the feminine personality back on this side of the threshold, beyond which extends the terrible and fascinating territory of the animus. These women are often sensitive and intelligent, but they become cruel because of an excess of self-defense. They fall in love with married men, for example, or with men who aren't available, in such a way that it is the situation itself which requires precautions against the risk of complete abandonment. Or they enjoy making men go crazy, being very careful not to allow themselves to be infected by passion: seductive and elusive like nymphs, they constitute an attractive danger for possible projections of the anima on the man's part.

From the point of view of the masculine principle, these women don't really dare compare themselves with others, and they tend to withdraw every time life calls them to measure themselves with a plan, an idea, the commitment to some value; and one could say that never has modesty, in the end, resulted more false.

The dreams of these women are systematically inhabited by thieves, rapists, assassins, terrorists, Nazis, and all kinds of delinquents. There seems to be an apparently invincible archetypal fear that these women run from. If these are men, if this is the animus, how does one find a way to keep them at bay, or escape? Carmen, Salomé, Turandot, in different ways, have interpreted this archetype of the nymph of the collective imagination: they play with men until they ask for his head or his reason, until, in certain cases, they lose themselves.

I have observed how this neurotic form expresses in women who couldn't love their fathers: in fact, without having experienced that love, which is so intense and moving, for the first man of their lives, it is with great difficulty that they can abandon themselves in the arms of another.

At times it happens that a father wasn't able to love his daughter and yet she intensely loved him. This partial relationship seems, however, sufficient to allow for contact with the animus and with the ability to love a man. A father—as the words of the hymn affirm—knows how to recognize the moment in which he has to stand aside and allow another man to burst into his daughter's heart, but perhaps a daughter can seriously experience this upsetting event only if she knows, loves, and remembers her father, or if she has embraced the pain of an unsuccessful relationship.

Blocks Facing Autonomy

The last possibility, finally, is that when a woman has separated herself from the maternal world, she falls under the dominion of the animus and isn't able to get out of it; in this case Persephone remains in the underworld forever.

This situation presents, from a clinical point of view, very spiny problems because when the ego falls to the mercy of the animus, it runs the risk (also fatal as we saw in the myth of Ariadne) of abdicating control of the personality, placing itself in a subordinate position to the masculine principle, which thus becomes an autonomous complex. In this case the fusion, loosened from maternal influence, turns to the masculine world and impedes the *coniunctio oppositorum* which would allow for the transformation of the feminine animus and ego. The first is attested to by the position of Hades at the beginning of the myth, conserving ample spaces of shadow; and the second, to this animus that delegates its own identity, crystallized in a dependent relationship.

A woman who finds herself in this psychological situation can experience her social responsibilities very intensely; for example, the determination and spirit of initiative in following her projects, aggressiveness in facing choices and conflicts, tenacity in giving shape to creative tension and so on, but she will experience all of these situations in an anxious and overbearing way, attributing egoic, abstract, often schematic and sectarian characteristics to her own ego.

Often these women are intelligent and courageous, but they are women who have betrayed their feminine identity, becoming queens of a world that isn't theirs, which, in exchange, requires serious psychic mutilation.

We have seen how important it is to become Persephone, but how it is just as essential to periodically return to unity with Demeter. The women I am writing about, conquered by the fascination with the masculine unconscious, have lost their way to return and, with it, the possibility to discover themselves to be receptive. In these cases, dreams can appear in which the image of the ego is a man, as in the following example:

THE WOMAN WHO LEFT: *I am in a hospital, and I am a man who is crying desperately because my woman has abandoned me. She's gone and I don't know why. Then I take her clothes and I put them under the bed, and finally I dress and make myself up like a woman.*

In this dream, the ego is a man after a preceding process of identi-fication with the animus. The feminine ego has gone away, she's not there anymore, luckily, however the man cries desperately for the absence of his companion, and those tears signal a possible begin-ning for a transformation. Then the protagonist of the dream dress-es and makes himself up like a woman, *he constructs* an image, a feminine *persona*, but this certainly isn't enough to restore meaning and value to being a woman. The lost companion must return and take back the clothes hidden under the bed. The dreamer knows this, and, she also cries when I reveal the content of her dream to her.

THE FILTHY OLD MAN AND THE LITTLE GIRL: *I am an old man, but not a nice, good old man, rather a mean, sort of ugly one, from whom I (I am also simultaneously myself, as if I were both) have to rescue a little girl. I despair because I don't know what has happened to the little girl the old man took away. Now I find myself pursuing them in a confused and dark atmosphere, full of tunnels and caves, perhaps an underground labyrinth; they are always a few meters ahead of me, and I am not able to catch up with them. At a certain point, I see myself while I transform, I see in the old man myself who transforms, and I slowly realize that I am becoming a woman, as if I reclaimed my own skin and I recomposed, from that duality, my original identity. Then I find myself outside, in the sun, holding the little girl by the hand, near a spring. The old man isn't there anymore.*

This dream, which was the first dream a patient of mine brought for analysis, would also prove to be a perspective dream, but from those first days it was clear to both of us that this animus (in this case negative) which had taken her over and held her future (the little girl) prisoner would have to be defeated to restore power to her ego. Other and very different masculine images would thus be able to appear to propose a less dramatic and more creative alternation in my patient's life.

In the most serious cases, the dispossession of the ego can push a woman to madness and death.

The case of Camille Claudel is, from this point of view, extraordinarily illuminating. Camille Claudel was an upper-middle class French girl, born at the end of the last century. She and her brother Paul were united, besides by incestuous desires, by a deep creative vein which pushed him to write and her to sculpt. A creative inclination induces a human being to enter into contact with his or her own unconscious and thus also with the unconscious sexual counterpart: the active presence of the animus seems to be really indispensable for a creative woman.

But it was the turn of the century, when it wasn't decorous for a girl from a good family to go around at night looking for good clay, or to spend the day sculpting marble, uncaring of her appearance, much less of finding a husband.

One day Camille met Auguste Rodin, at that time affirmed and famous. Rodin recognized the young woman's talent, and he let her work in his studio. Slowly, between the two a great passion is born, but Rodin is married and wants to stay that way. At this point Camille has only one possibility, extremely risky, before her. She knows she can't go back, and she doesn't want to renounce her art, and her animus, which has supported her up until then with tenacity and courage, allowing her to assert herself in a world impenetrable to women. On the other hand, she belongs to Rodin, who keeps her chained to him with his refusal to accept their love all the way. Thus Camille realizes her own defeat: her reputation is compromised, her family is hostile to her (even her brother, who in the meantime has become a famous writer), she hasn't gotten married, she isn't a mother, and her love has been rejected by Rodin, always more bothered and distant.

The ego, formed on the sediment of experience, is tightly interwoven with the culture in which one develops, and thus Camille Claudel's ego can't win because it doesn't correspond to the dominant social model, but it also can't win because she can't find any feminine hinterland to which to return. All the bridges are burned, and she finds herself exposed to a creative animus, socially undervalued, and a passion for a man who rejects her. It is almost inevitable to fall into the risk of *participation mystique* where the ego assumes a role completely subordinate and dependent on the masculine world, whether it is incarnated in the animus or in a man.

Thus the animus takes control of Camille's personality, and in this way, against everybody, full of courage and determination, that extraordinary artist continues to work and express as she can, closed in a solitary desperation, the meaning of her own existence. Barricaded in her studio, she sculpts and studies, she experiments with different materials and new techniques, trying to forget everything else. But forgetting herself is not easy and Camille begins to drink, behave in extravagant ways, she neglects beyond all limits her image as a woman, and she shows signs of mental derangement.

At this point, the family finally has an excuse to intervene and they commit her to an asylum, placing an end to the family shame; in that asylum Camille, who was only 30, lived for a few decades, with a lost gaze and her hands, then useless, folded up in her lap.

But it is not only at the turn of the century that the impact with the masculine principle could be dangerous, and many women, even today, realize this when it is too late.

To summarize: In the cases considered in this chapter, the *coniunctio oppositorum* has no place, or is gets consumed, but it doesn't allow for the cyclical return of the ego within the feminine circuit. For about 3,000 years, the enchanting image of Kore-Persephone has been there to remind each one of us how it is possible to abandon ourselves to passion without dying from it. We can return to the maternal world without being imprisoned by it. And in the same way, Demeter tells us how, through the path of her pain, it is possible to be the solid guarantor, the solitary keeper of the autonomy, and the wisdom of the feminine archetype.

Bibliography

Bachofen, J. J. *Myth, Religion and Mother Right*. Ralph Manheim, trans. Bollingen Series No. 84. Princeton: Princeton University Press, 1967.

Donne, John. "Batter my Heart," in *A Treasury of Great Poems: English and American*. Louis Untermeyer, ed. New York: Simon and Schuster, 1942.

Graves, Robert and Raphael Patai. *Hebrew Myths: The Book of Genesis*. New York: Doubleday, 1989.

Hesse, H. *Narcissus & Goldmund*. New York: Bantam, 1971.

Homer. *The Homeric Hymns*. Apostolos N. Athanassakis, trans. Baltimore: Johns Hopkins University Press, 1976.

———. *The Iliad*, Book XVIII, v 590–605. R. Lathimore, trans. Chicago: University of Chicago Press, 1951.

———. *The Odyssey*. Robert Fitzgerald, trans. New York: Anchor Press, 1963.

C. G. Jung. *The Collected Works*, Vol. 9. Part 1: *The Archetypes & the Collective Unconscious*. Gerhard Adler, et al, eds. R. F. Hull, trans. Bollingen Series No. 20. Princeton: Princeton University Press, 1968.

———. *The Collected Works*, Vol. 10, *Civilization in Transition*. R. F. C. Hull, trans. Gerhard Adler, et al, eds. Bollingen Series No. 20. Princeton: Princeton University Press, 1970.

K. Kerenji. *Nel Labyrinto*. Torino: Boringhieri, 1983.

Silvia Di Lorenzo. *Modern Woman & Her Shadow*. Boston: Sigo Press, 1992.

Monick, E. *Phallos: Sacred Image of the Masculine*. Toronto: Inner City Books, 1987.

Mookerjee, Ajit. *Kali: The Feminine Force*. Rochester, VT: Inner Traditions/Destiny Books, 1988.

Erich Neumann. *The Great Mother: An Analysis of the Archetype*. Ralph Manheim, trans. Bollingen Series No. 47. Princeton: Princeton University Press, 1964.

———. *The Origins & History of Consciousness*. R. F. Hull, trans. Bollingen Series No. 42. Princeton: Princeton University Press, 1954.

New English Bible. New York: Cambridge University Press, 1971.

Pausanias, I 40, 3. *Guide to Greece*, Peter Levi, trans. London & New York: Viking Penguin, 1984.

Plutarch. *Morales*. C. W. King, trans. London: George Bell & Sons, 1882.

Puirce, Jill. *The Mystic Spiral*. London: Thames and Hudson, 1974.

Ravenna, A. and T. Federici. *Commento alla Genesi di Beresit Rabba*. Milan: Utet, 1978.

Trevi, M. and A. Romano. *Saggi Sull'ombra*. Venice: Marsilio, 1975.

Valcarenghi, Marina. *Nel Nome del Padre: Appuunti Sulla Transgressione Nell Analisi e Nel Mito*. Milan: Tranchida, 1987.

Index

A

abduction, 195
  blocks facing, 249
Achilles, 159
Adam, 44
Aegeus, 100, 101, 102
Aeneas, 136, 178
Aethra, 100, 101
aggressiveness, 196
alchemy, 9
anima, 17, 26, 69, 78, 82, 117,
    192, 237-238
  Ariadne as, 163-164
  Kore's, 204
  projection, 237, 250
Anima Mundi, 162
animus, 59, 82, 117, 125, 163,
    166, 173, 187, 199, 200,
    201, 247, 248, 249
  becomes the other, 209
  feminine ego, 178

  irruption of, 186
  possessed by, 9
  projection of the masculine, 238
  regressive, 123, 166
  transformation of the
    feminine, 252
  unconscious, 170
anti-depressants, 216
Aphrodite, 50, 155, 235
  lost daughters of, 57
Apollo, 68, 136
  oracle of, 93
apple, 4
archetype
  feminine, 248
  fragmentation of, 198
archetypical whole, 132
Ariadne, 91, 97, 98, 103, 105,
    106, 109, 110, 123, 136,
    155, 161, 163, 167, 172,
    176, 177

dreams (cont.)
    burned plantation, 230
    center of love, 25
    chase, 195
    communion with the bull, 115
    copper pots, 221
    death the deceiver, 224
    desert and fear, 230
    filthy old man and the little
        girl, 253
    Hermes and the restaurant, 232
    jewels of the ascent, 27
    labyrinth and death, 145
    labyrinth of eros, 143
    Lake and death, 246
    little girl in the labyrinth, 140
    man and the ball of thread, 15
    man and the dancer, 48
    man from the mountains, 195
    Mary's desert, 24
    methane gas meter, 218
    mirror and the shadow, 246
    Mommy and the shoot-out, 246
    Pan's mother, 75
    postponed wedding, 239
    pressure 20, 219
    the quarrel, 239
    road of the meeting, 17
    secret in the cave, 74
    strange prostitute, 58
    Superman's abyss, 206
    the surprise, 240
    tenderness and the
        earthquake, 246
    the title, 240
    tortoise man, 67

    what had to happen, 59
    woman and the first thing
        to do, 58
    woman of the spring, 173
    woman of the Vikings, 10
    woman who left, 252
drive, aggressive, 39

E

ecstatic condition, 64
ego
    feminine, 74, 139-140, 202,
        209, 220, 231, 252-255
    masculine, 78
    regressive aspect of, 125
ekal tirani, 132
Eleusinian Mysteries, 183, 197,
    222
Eliade, Mircea, 45
energy, instinctual, 39
erections, 65
erma, 66, 72
eros, 111, 145
Europa, 119
Europhrosyne, 91
Eve, 49, 51

F

father, law of the, 233
fatherhood, 33
feeling, 36
    activity of, 21
    feminine, 22, 25
    masculine, 22, 26, 33, 35
    phallic, 32, 33

felix culpa, 50
fertility
    masculine, 111
    natural, 55
Francesca, 187
Franz, M. L. von, 10
Freud, 62
frigidity, 56
fruit, eats that, 235
fusionality, maternal, 242

G

Gaia, 190
garden, 203
geranos, 154, 155
Gilgamesh, 136
goddess, immortal, 228
Great Mother, 83, 95, 110, 111,
    112, 117, 129, 130, 199
    archetype of, 96
    Earth, 190
    shadow of, 214

H

Hades, 181, 183, 190, 193, 200,
    208
head, losing one's, 205
Hecate, 50, 57, 64, 213, 214
Helios, 215, 220
hepatitis, 173
Hephaestus, 51, 158
Heraclides, 129
    Hermes, 64, 67, 69
hero, solar, 164
Herodotus, 99

Hesse, Hermann, 138
Homer, 23, 158
human beast, 69

I

impotent, 14
Inanna, 136
instinct
    activity of, 39
    female sexual, 65
    feminine, 40, 42, 44, 49
    liberation of, 46
    masculine, 62, 70, 202
    must be sacrificed, 117
    phallic, 42, 64, 65, 66, 81
    receptive aspect of, 39, 42
    sexual, 44
    shadow of, 77
    uroboric bisexuality, 111
Isis, cult of, 53
Isolde, 187

J

Juliet of Verona, 187
Jung, C. G., 9, 55, 62, 63, 67, 86,
    87, 190, 237, 244, 245, 247
Jungfrudans, 154

K

Kali, 45
Keleos, 220
Kerenji, K., 130, 153, 154, 155,
    157

Photo by Paola Mattioli

MARINA VALCARENGHI is a psychoanalyst and teacher, a board member and teacher for training in psychoanalysts at LISTA (Libera Scuola di Terapia Analitica), in Italy, and a board member of the Italian journal "Quaderni di Psiche." She has written *I Manicomi Criminali* (Milan, 1975), *Child Labour in Italy* (London, 1980), *Nel Nome del Padre—Edipo e Prometeo* (Milan, 1987), *Psicoanalisi e Politica*, with Giorgio Galli (Milan, 1992), and this book, first published in Italian as *Una Passione per Due* (Milan, 1994), as well as ten children's books and numerous articles. She has a degree in law from the University of Milan (1966), worked in government offices in Rome before becoming a journalist, and then studied Jungian psychology in Milan and Zurich. She lives and works in Milan. She has one son.